The Modernist
Response to
Chinese Art

THE
Modernist
Response
TO
Chinese
Art

Pound, Moore,
Stevens

Zhaoming Qian

University of Virginia Press

CHARLOTTESVILLE AND LONDON

The University of Virginia Press
© 2003 by the Rector and Visitors of the University of Virginia
All rights reserved
Printed in the United States of America on acid-free paper

First published 2003

9 8 7 6 5 4 3 2 1

LIBRARY OF CONGRESS CATALOGING-IN-PUBLICATION DATA

Qian, Zhaoming.
   The modernist response to Chinese art : Pound, Moore,
Stevens / Zhaoming Qian.
      p.   cm.
Includes bibliographical references and index.
ISBN 0-8139-2175-9 (alk. paper) — ISBN 0-8139-2176-7 (pbk. : alk. paper)
   1. American poetry—20th century—History and criticism.   2. Art and
literature—United States—History—20th century.   3. Stevens, Wallace, 1879–
1955—Knowledge—China.   4. Moore, Marianne, 1887–1972—Knowledge—
China.   5. Stevens, Wallace, 1879–1955—Knowledge—Art.   6. Moore,
Marianne, 1887–1972—Knowledge—Art.   7. Pound, Ezra, 1885–1972—
Knowledge—China.   8. Pound, Ezra, 1885–1972—Knowledge—Art.   9. Art,
Chinese—Appreciation—United States.   10. Modernism (Literature)—United
States.   11. American poetry—Chinese influences.   12. China—In literature.
13. Art in literature.   I. Title.
   PS310.A76 Q53   2002
   811'.5209357—dc21
                                                          2002009361

To May

and

to Yuyan and Yuli

Contents

Illustrations

Abbreviations

BMA   Bryn Mawr, Pennsylvania, Bryn Mawr College, Miriam Coffin Canaday Library, Bryn Mawr College Archives

BMCA   London, British Museum, Central Archives

BMPDA   London, British Museum, Department of Prints and Drawings Archives

HL-WAS   San Marino, California, Huntington Library, Wallace Stevens Collection

LL-PM   Bloomington, Indiana University, Lilly Library, Ezra Pound Manuscripts

RML-MMC   Philadelphia, Rosenbach Museum and Library, Marianne Moore Collection

UPMA   Philadelphia, University of Pennsylvania Museum, Museum Archives

YCAL-PP   New Haven, Connecticut, Yale University, Beinecke Rare Book and Manuscript Library, Yale Collection of American Literature, Ezra Pound Papers (Mss. 43)

YCAL-RP   New Haven, Connecticut, Yale University, Beinecke Rare Book and Manuscript Library, Yale Collection of American Literature, Olga Rudge Papers (Mss. 54)

BOOKS BY MARIANNE MOORE

BMM   *Becoming Marianne Moore: The Early Poems, 1907–1924,* ed. Robin G. Schulze (Berkeley and Los Angeles: Univ. of California Press, 2002)

CPMM   *The Complete Poems of Marianne Moore* (New York: Macmillan, 1981)

MMR	*A Marianne Moore Reader* (New York: Viking, 1961)
PrMM	*The Complete Prose of Marianne Moore,* ed. Patricia C. Willis, (New York: Viking, 1986)
SLMM	*The Selected Letters of Marianne Moore,* ed. Bonnie Costello, Celeste Goodridge, and Cristanne Miller (New York: Knopf, 1997)
SPMM	*Selected Poems of Marianne Moore* (New York: Macmillan, 1935)

BOOKS BY EZRA POUND

ABCR	*ABC of Reading* (1934; reprint, New York: New Directions, 1987)
C	*The Cantos,* 14th printing (New York: New Directions, 1998)
Con	*Confucius: The Great Digest, The Unwobbling Pivot, The Analects* (1951; reprint, New York: New Directions, 1969)
L/DP	*Ezra and Dorothy Pound: Letters in Captivity, 1945–1946,* ed. Omar Pound and Robert Spoo (New York: Oxford Univ. Press, 1999)
L/DS	*Ezra Pound and Dorothy Shakespear: Their Letters 1909–1914,* ed. Omar Pound and A. Walton Litz (New York: New Directions, 1984)
P&P	*Ezra Pound's Poetry and Prose Contributions to Periodicals,* 11 vols., ed. Lea Baechler, A. Walton Litz, and James Longenbach (New York: Garland, 1991)
EP&VA	*Ezra Pound and the Visual Arts,* ed. Harriet Zinnes (New York: New Directions, 1980)
GB	*Gaudier-Brzeska: A Memoir* (1916; reprint, New York: New Directions, 1974)
GK	*Guide to Kulchur* (1938; reprint, New York: New Directions, 1970)
LE	*Literary Essays of Ezra Pound,* ed. T. S. Eliot (1954; reprint, New York: New Directions, 1968)
P	*Personae: The Shorter Poems of Ezra Pound,* ed. Lea Baechler and A. Walton Litz (New York: New Directions, 1990)
SLEP	*Selected Letters of Ezra Pound,* ed. D. D. Paige (1950; reprint, New York: New Directions, 1971)
SR	*The Spirit of Romance* (1910; reprint, New York: New Directions, 1968)

BOOKS BY WALLACE STEVENS

CPWS	*The Collected Poems of Wallace Stevens* (New York: Knopf, 1954)
L	*Letters of Wallace Stevens,* ed. Holly Stevens (New York: Knopf, 1966)
NA	*The Necessary Angel: Essays on Reality and the Imagination* (New York: Knopf, 1951)

OP   *Opus Posthumous: Poems, Plays, Prose,* ed. Milton J. Bates (New York: Knopf, 1989)

SP   Holly Stevens, *Souvenirs and Prophecies: The Young Wallace Stevens* (New York: Knopf, 1977)

Preface

From Whistler and the Japanese, or Chinese . . . the fragment of
the English-speaking world . . . learned to enjoy "arrangements"
of colours and masses. —Pound, *Visual Arts*

I was born pro-Chinese. —Moore, *Selected Letters*

For a poet to have even a second-hand contact with China is a
great matter. —Stevens, *Letters*

IT IS GENERALLY accepted that the modernist poets shared an interest in the visual arts and that this interest reaches beyond the borders
of Europe and America. Yet until now the interconnection between
modernism and Chinese art has been more frequently assumed than examined. In the booming field of interartistic studies there has been satisfactory attention only to Western art. In current debates about modernism's relation to China there has been satisfactory attention only
to interactions via the verbal medium.[1] This book attempts to correct
these omissions. It explores the impact of Chinese art on three American modernist poets, in terms of both its specific importance to their
development and its larger importance to modernism generally.

Though my claims extend from my study of 1995, *Orientalism and
Modernism: The Legacy of China in Pound and Williams,* I have tried to
go beyond its scope and approach. In *Orientalism and Modernism* I am
concerned primarily with the role Ezra Pound and William Carlos Williams's interest in Chinese culture played in their 1913–23 transition
toward modernism. In this volume, I have broadened my field to consider the Chinese influence not only on Pound —*throughout* his career—

but also on two other major modernists, Marianne Moore and Wallace Stevens.[2] Whereas in my earlier work the specific point of emphasis is the impact of Chinese poetry, here it is the challenge posed to modernism by Chinese art. Precisely what attracted the three poets at the forefront of American modernism to Chinese ink paintings, sculptures, and calligraphic objects? How could they share Chinese artists' Dao, an aesthetic held to be beyond verbal representation? Beginning with these questions, the book uncovers an intricate interchange between vision and verse and across age and culture.

Without the pioneering efforts of W. J. T. Mitchell, Wendy Steiner, and others in the study of verbal and visual representation, it would be difficult to prove art's ability to display Confucian ideals and the Dao to the American modernists. An understanding of visual culture—its power and boundary—is vital to our examination of the links, especially the Moore-China and Stevens-China links, for unlike Pound the two New York poets depend more extensively on images than texts to explore the Orient. Mitchell's discussion of painting's gift for transmitting ideas and Steiner's analysis of "pictorial narrativity" will prove helpful in removing probable skepticism.[3] Since this is intended as an empirical study of modernism and Chinese art and since many others have taken advantage of these theorists' arguments, I have tried to address them succinctly, testing their validity through my own examples.

The new century has brought with it a renewed interest in modernist studies. In *21st-Century Modernism* (2002) Marjorie Perloff aptly observes: "Now that the long twentieth century is finally behind us, perhaps we can begin to see this embryonic phase with new eyes. Far from being irrelevant and obsolete, the aesthetic of early modernism has provided the seeds of the materialist poetic which is increasingly our own."[4] While it is perfectly appropriate to continue to read modernist poetry against various Western traditions, I am reading Pound, Moore, and Stevens against a radically different, Eastern paradigm. There is no use trying to deny that except in the last chapters I make sparing use of the major critical works I have read. Without suspending previous readings I cannot concentrate on reconstructing and analyzing Pound, Moore, and Stevens's complex interactions with Chinese materials. My readings of certain poems against Confucianism, the Dao, or the Chan are not intended to replace the way we read them. Rather, they are meant to extend the way we interpret them.

The fourteen chapters that follow are divided into five related parts. The first group of two, "China in Galleries," focuses on the three poets' initial visual and intellectual encounter with China. Chapter 1 traces Pound's engagement with Chinese art in the "British Museum era" (1908–14). His friendship with Laurence Binyon, the English champion of Far Eastern art, brought him to the center of early promotion of Chinese aesthetic in London. Some of the striking images in the British Museum Exhibition of Chinese and Japanese Paintings (1910–12) surface in Pound's early poems. In the theory and practice of Chinese art, Pound found a model helpful in clarifying a series of concepts in his experiments. In his critical prose of the period, he frequently compared the Vorticist masterpieces of Gaudier-Brzeska and others to Chinese art. Chapter 2 treats Stevens's and Moore's similar enthusiasms for Chinese objects in their formative years. Both New York poets kept abreast of major Far Eastern art events on both sides of the Atlantic. In their initial attempts at representing Chinese art, Stevens tended to be impressionistic and Moore more precise.

The second section of essays, "Remaking Culture," stresses the dynamics of the visual medium through which Westerners encountered Chinese modes of thought. Chinese art was brought to Europe and America in the beginning of the twentieth century as a result of imperialist politics and theft. Paradoxically, the art objects that were uprooted and transferred to the West served as an apparatus of cultural power,[5] enticing beholders to enter and be influenced. Pound, Moore, and Stevens were among thousands of perceivers affected. Only they were gladly stimulated, because the sensibilities displayed—Confucian for Pound, Daoist for Moore, and Chan Buddhist for Stevens—simultaneously mirrored and challenged their own. Pound's lifelong interest in Confucianism, as I indicate in chapter 3, was sparked by his exchanges with pictures of Confucian ideals in the British Museum. The pictures that charmed him can be traced in his subsequent dialogues with Confucius from *Cathay* (1915) through the China Cantos (1939). Chinese aesthetic cannot be understood, I argue in chapter 4, without understanding Daoism. Just as the Ming and Qing animal pictures that appealed to Moore were inspired by Daoist notions, so were the Tang and Song landscapes that impressed Pound's eye. The Dao is respected by both Confucians and Daoists, which accounts in large part for the confusion of Pound's Orientalism: his avowed Confucianism versus his Daoism in deep impulses. The fusion of the Dao into Buddhism brought about Chan Buddhism. Chapter 5 demonstrates that Stevens's well-known Chan-like manner is linked to his familiarity with Chan art. My readings of "Thirteen Ways of Looking at a Blackbird" and "The Snow Man" against Chan aesthetic validate Stevens's stress of a greater interest in Oriental art.[6] His transformation from emphasis on "thingness" in "Thirteen Ways" to dual emphasis on "thingness"/"nothingness" in "The Snow Man" had to do with his musings around 1919 on Chan paintings and books such as Samuel Beal's *Buddhism in China.*

The third segment of essays, "Picturing the Other," derives its title from Mitchell, who makes evident in *Picture Theory,* "the fascination in the problem of ekphrasis, the verbal representation of visual representation."[7] My readings of individual poems—Stevens's "Six Significant Landscapes," Moore's "Nine Nectarines," and Pound's Canto 49—in chapters 6 through 8 aim primarily to illustrate claims outlined in part 2. But because all three illustrations are extraordinary instances of modernist ekphrasis, they also serve to augment Mitchell's model. In their ekphrastic attempts, Stevens, Moore, and Pound seek to explore not only the passage to another medium but the passage to another age and another culture as well.

With the fourth division of essays, "The Poets as Critics and Connoisseurs," we turn from the three modernists' creative response to Chinese art to their critical and collecting interests. Chapter 9 focuses centrally on Pound's career-long parleying with Fenollosa's *The Chinese Written Character,* but it also calls attention to his 1915 critique of Binyon's Orientalism, a mind "constantly trying to justify Chinese intelligence by dragging it a little nearer to some Western precedent."[8] Chapter 10 concerns Stevens's desire to keep a small collection of Far Eastern art. He took delight in genuine Chinese, Japanese, and Korean objects, and not in Western imitations of them. As his letters of August 1953 reveal, he distinguished between the Orient and Orientalism.[9] For him the former is the body of objective knowledge about the Far East, and the latter is Western artists' idealist handling of it. Chapter 11 considers Moore's dissatisfaction with Western writers' hegemonic Orientalist treatment of Chinese art and her admiration for Mai-mai Sze's *The Tao of Painting* (1956). Her exchanges with *The Tao* and its Chinese painter-author helped redefine her poetics in the late 1950s and early 1960s.

So far I have not discussed a sufficiently large number of poems in terms of the connections between China and each of the three poets. The deferment of substantial practical criticism is necessary partly because its strength depends on the building up of my previous arguments and partly because in my view it is the late works of the three individuals that best exemplify the remarkable and complex interaction between modernism and the Orient. My readings of late Moore, late Stevens, and late Pound in part 5, "Late Modernism and the Orient" (chapters 12–14), are intended to open up some of the finest and most difficult modernist lyrics while illuminating a variety of ways in which Chinese aesthetic helped reinforce modernism.

Why should I choose a five-part plan over a simple division into individual poets? Because the five-section organization offers greater freedom of moving between the figures and from issue to issue. It has enabled me to establish more parallels as well as distinctions among Pound, Moore, and Stevens. Together these parallels and distinctions convey a larger sense of how important the Orient (China in particular) was not only to the three poets but to American modernism generally. This design, I envision, will enhance the book's appeal for several special audiences. For students of Chinese art, part 1, "China in Galleries," brings much needed attention to the role of early collections of Chinese art in England and America. For readers interested in Eastern philosophy and religion, part 2, "Remaking Culture," corrects some common misconceptions about Confucianism and Daoism. For those working in interarts and intercultural comparisons, part 3, "Picturing the Other," expands the notion of ekphrasis. Finally, for students of the Orient, part 4, "The Poets as Critics and Connoisseurs," identifies in the modernist poets both linkage to and revolt against their predecessors' (or peers') hegemonic Orientalism.[10] Their illustrations intensify awareness of modernist Orientalism not as a monolithic and constant conception but as an ambivalent and shifting process.

Given the scope of my project, I have frequently trampled over the territory of others. Nevertheless, the readers I most want to reach are consistently the scholars and students devoted to poetic modernism. "What poets learn from visual artists is usually not what those artists see in one another's work," remarks Charles Altieri. Following his example, I offer speculations primarily from the modernist poet's and the literary historian's perspectives. In that way, as Altieri adds, "Even if we miss or distort what would engage painters, we might well be following precisely the tracts that fascinated those whose business is words."[11]

A word about the transliteration of Chinese names and terms: Except for established usage with personal names (for example, Confucius), I have followed the pinyin system. In my quotations from early writers, however, I have retained their Wade-Giles usage while adding in parentheses or square brackets the corresponding pinyin spelling.

I began the research for this study with a fellowship from the Beinecke Rare Book and Manuscript Library of Yale University and continued it with a research grant and a sabbatical leave from the University of New Orleans (UNO). A generous fellowship from the National Endowment for the Humanities enabled me to complete the book. Additional grants from the UNO Office of Research and College of Liberal Arts have helped defray the costs of art and permissions. For all this support I am grateful.

Portions of the book have appeared, in slightly different form, in *The Wallace Stevens Journal, Ezra Pound and Poetic Influence,* edited by Helen M. Dennis (Amsterdam: Rodopi, 2000), and *Ezra Pound and China,* edited by me (Ann Arbor: University of Michigan Press, 2003). I am grateful to the editors and publishers for their permission to reprint. I thank Patricia Willis for inviting me to give a lecture at a conference on "Modernism and the Orient" at Yale. This developed into chapter 6 of the manuscript. I thank also Viorica Patea and Maria Eugenia Diaz of the University of Salamanca, Spain, for inviting me to present what became chapter 7 of this book at a conference held there on "Transgressing Boundaries and Strategies of Renewal in American poetry." I enjoyed directing the Eighteenth International Ezra Pound Conference in Beijing, where I spoke on what emerged as chapter 8 of this study.

For their cheerful assistance I would like to thank the directors, curators, archivists, and librarians of the following institutions: Ralph Franklin, Steve Jones, and Patricia Willis at the Beinecke Rare Book and Manuscript Library of Yale University; Michael Barsanti, Evelyn Feldman and Elizabeth Fuller at the Rosenbach Museum and Library; Christine Fagan, Sara S. Hodson, and David Zeidberg at the Huntington Library; Timothy Clark, Christopher Date, Anne Farrer, Carol Michaelson, and Janet Wallace at the British Museum; Chrisso E. S. Boulis, Charles Kline, Alex Pezzati, and Jennifer Jane White at the University of Pennsylvania Museum; Laila Abdel-Malek, Christopher Atkins, Erin Bennett, and Maureen Melton at the Museum of Fine Arts, Boston. I am especially grateful to Jan Fontein, formerly of the Museum of Fine Arts, Boston, and Jessica Rawson, formerly of the British Museum, for their guidance.

Without the generous help of the surviving heirs of Ezra Pound,

Marianne Moore, and Wallace Stevens, this project could not have been completed in its current form. Mary de Rachewiltz was unusually enthusiastic about the project, sharing with me her knowledge of Pound in Rapallo (1993), New Orleans (1996), Beijing, Tai'an, and Qufu (1999). Omar Pound was remarkably helpful over the years, verifying facts about Dorothy Pound's notes and artworks while in rehabilitation after his surgery. Marianne Craig Moore answered my questions about Maimai Sze with great generosity and patience. Peter Hanchak took an early interest in my research. At his invitation, I examined Stevens's Chinese, Japanese, and Korean objects in his collection. With forty photographs supplied by the heirs and various museums and libraries, this study will enable the reader to stand and contemplate with the three modernists in the early part of the twentieth century, reconstructing their dialogues with the Chinese masters.

Among the many individuals who provided assistance are: Dore Ashton (Cooper Union for the Advancement of Science and Art), Rebecca Barker (Freer Gallery of Art), Renzhi Cai (Tulane Medical Center), Lina Chen (Wellesley College), April Caprak (Burke Library, Hamilton College), John Crockett (Unionville, Connecticut), David Gordon (Alna, Maine), Sylvia Inwood (Detroit Institute of Arts), Jeanie James (Metropolitan Museum of Art), Ryan Janda (University of Pennsylvania), Annett Juliano (Brooklyn College, CUNY), Dorsey Kleitz (Tokyo Women's Christian University), Doreen Leach (V & A Museum), Li Hongfei (*Renmin Ribao*), Li Jingping (Beijing University Press), Tom Lentz (Freer Gallery of Art), Mary Lineberger (Cleveland Museum of Art), Liu Fei (*Renmin Ribao*), Lu Minghua (Shanghai Museum), Tom Mazzullo (Emerson Gallery, Hamilton College), Akitoshi Nagahata (Nagoya University), Dennis Palmore (New Directions Publishing Corporation), Betsy Rose (National Poetry Foundation), Wesley Rusnell (Roswell Museum and Art Center), Robin Schulze (Penn State University), Abigail Smith (Harvard Art Museums), Saundra Taylor (Lilly Library, Indiana University), Lorett Treese (Miriam Coffin Canaday Library, Bryn Mawr College), Carol Turley (Special Collections, UCLA), C. C. Wang (New York City), Wang Lina (Beijing Library), Yan Jian (Shanghai Antique Store), Yuba (Idemitsu Museum of Arts), and Zhang Mi (Shanghai Museum).

I am grateful to Bonnie Costello, the late Donald Gallup, and Emily Mitchell Wallace, for guiding me to the poets' heirs. I have learned in various ways from Milton Bates, Mary Cheadle, Peter H. Lee, Earl Miner, Ira Nadel, Qiu Ke'an, and Richard Taylor.

I would like to thank my colleagues at the University of New Orleans—Rick Barton, Linda Blanton, Robert Cashner, John Cooke, John
Gery, Lawrence Jenkens, Shirley Laska, Carl Malmgren, Jane Prud-
homme, and Shengru Tu—for their cheers and friendship. I am grateful
to the late Mary FitzGerald for her strenuous support.

Most of all, I am indebted to Barry Ahearn, A. Walton Litz, Glen
MacLeod, and Peter Schmidt, whose sustained interest and faithful support inspired me to make this a strong book in every way. I greatly
appreciate the help of Ronald Bush, Linda Leavell, and Marjorie Perloff, who provided detailed readings of the entire manuscript. Daniel
Albright, George Bornstein, Wendy Flory, Haun Saussy, and Patricia
Willis read different chapters of the book. I owe particular thanks to
these colleagues as well for their suggestions for improvement.

My deep gratitude goes to my editor, Cathie Brettschneider of the
University of Virginia Press, for her especially warm and energetic
roles. It has been a pleasure to work with David Sewell, my project editor; Jill Hughes, my copyeditor; and Martha Farlow, my text designer.
Finally, I must thank my wife and daughters, who have encouraged
me to write on modernism and Chinese art, and to whom this book is
dedicated.

Grateful acknowledgment is given to New Directions Publishing Corporation and Faber & Faber Ltd. for permission to quote from the
copyrighted works by Ezra Pound. Previously unpublished writing by
Ezra Pound, copyright 2002 by Mary de Rachewiltz and Omar S.
Pound, is used by permission of New Directions Publishing Corporation. Passages from "Nine Nectarines" by Marianne Moore are used
by permission of Scribner, a division of Simon & Schuster, Inc. and
Faber & Faber Ltd. Passages from other copyrighted works by Marianne Moore are used by permission of Viking Penguin, a division of
Penguin Putnam, Inc. and Faber & Faber Ltd. For permission to use
previously unpublished material of Marianne Moore and her family,
copyright 2002, I am grateful to Marianne Craig Moore. Permission
to quote from the copyrighted works by Wallace Stevens is granted by
Alfred A. Knopf, a division of Random House, Inc. and Faber & Faber
Ltd. Thanks are due Peter Hanchak for permission to use previously
unpublished material of Wallace Stevens.

PART 1

*China in
Galleries*

ONE

Pound and Chinese
Art in the "British
Museum Era"

IT MAY AT FIRST seem odd to think of Chinese art as a stimulus to Ezra Pound's modernism. But this intercultural, interartistic relation can be traced to the very beginning of Pound's career. Indeed, his rise, like the rise of poetic modernism itself, coincided with the first phase of Europe's passion for Chinese aesthetic. If our increased awareness of Pound's preoccupation with modern art has helped in bringing his poetry into what Geoffrey Hartman terms "the fold of cultural discourse,"[1] then our recognition of his visual engagement with China will bring his poetry further into that fold.

Consider a few events in the period 1908–12. In 1908, the year following Picasso's path-breaking, antimimetic *Les Demoiselles d'Avignon* and the year of Pound's arrival in Europe, Laurence Binyon's *Painting in the Far East,* the first serious study of Far Eastern pictorial art in English,[2] appeared in print. Two years later, in 1910, Roger Fry staged the first Postimpressionist show (Manet, Cézanne, Gauguin, van Gogh, Picasso, Matisse, etc.), a key project in London, in Reed Way Dasenbrock's opinion, presumably leading to "Virginia Woolf's famous pronouncement that human nature changed in 1910."[3] In 1910, there had been another influential project, the British Museum Exhibition of Chinese and Japanese Paintings, which was extended on through 1912, the year of Fry's second Postimpressionist show (Cézanne, Picasso, Matisse, etc.). In 1912, which also saw the births of *Poetry* magazine in Chicago and Pound's Imagist club in the British Museum tearoom, Ernest Fenollosa's posthumous *Epochs of Chinese and Japanese Art* came out in London.

Having mentioned the key events of two parallel trends in the magic period of 1908–12, I must hasten to add that Pound did not come into

1. East Asian exhibits in the University of Pennsylvania Furness Building, 1898. In 1899–1900 these exhibits were moved to the Free Museum of Science and Art, where they were displayed in the gallery immediately west of its entrance. From the Collections of the University of Pennsylvania Archives. (Courtesy, University of Pennsylvania Archives, Philadelphia)

contact with Chinese art in London first. Pound had grown up in the United States in a period in which "Chinoiserie was very popular . . . among the middle classes."[4] His parents, like so many of their generation who had seen Chinese and Japanese artifacts at the Philadelphia Centennial Exhibition, had a Ming vase placed in the parlor of their house in suburban Philadelphia.[5] Pound had been born too late for the centennial fair. However, he had started college at Penn just in time for a rich collection of Chinese art—ceramics, wood-carvings, ink paintings, and calligraphic objects (fig. 1)—displayed in the newly opened Free Museum of Science and Art, now the University of Pennsylvania Museum.[6] He had also arrived in time for the more widely publicized "Buddhist Temple," "the brainchild" of Maxwell Sommerville, vice president at the museum, who between 1895 and 1903 had shipped more than six tons of material from Japan and China "for the purpose of teaching Philadelphians about Buddhist beliefs and ritual through a visual display of the widest possible range of objects."[7] As a photograph of 1903 shows, Sommerville would be robed as a Buddhist priest

2. Maxwell Sommerville (1829–1904) at the Penn "Buddhist Temple," 1903. (Courtesy, University of Pennsylvania Museum, Philadelphia; photograph by Pierce and Jones)

and guide visitors through his exhibition (fig. 2). It seems certain that young Pound had visited both galleries at the museum.[8] He could have told his close friends at Penn—Hilda Doolittle (H. D.) and Bill Williams—that his family, too, owned some art objects from the Far East. On a visit to his beloved "Aunt Frank" in New York in his last years in America, he had been shown a screen book with waterscape scenes alongside manuscript poems in Chinese and Japanese (figs. 27–33). This screen book, a relic from Japan,[9] was to become the main source of Pound's Canto 49.

It is important to review these facts that account for why Pound would appear so comfortable in his move toward the Orient in his early

London years as he was expanding into the European avant-garde in all
the arts. However, it would be wrong to conclude that Pound's notions
of China had been formed in adolescence. Pound's appreciation of Chinese culture was awakened not in America but in England in the years
1909–14, his "B. M. era" (C, 526), and his mentor in Chinese art was
the British Museum art expert Laurence Binyon.

Binyon (1869–1943) must be singled out for his pivotal role in fos-
tering an early admiration for Chinese art in England. The Oxford-
trained art expert entered the British Museum Department of Prints
and Drawings in 1895, where he had spent the first ten years studying
Dutch etching, compiling a four-volume *Catalogue of English Drawings
in the British Museum,* writing on William Blake's engravings, and then,
by 1905, gradually turning his attention to Far Eastern art.[10] It was due
to his *Painting in the Far East;* his lectures and articles on the subject
in 1909–14; and, above all, the British Museum 1910–12 Exhibition of
Chinese and Japanese Paintings, installed under his curatorial eye, that
Chinese art was for the first time held in high respect in London. True,
the late-nineteenth-century vogue for Japonisme had paved the way
for English enthusiasm for China.[11] But it was Binyon's *Painting in the
Far East* that first jolted people like Pound into a realization that "Of all
the nations of the East, the Chinese is that which through all its history
has shown the strongest aesthetic instinct, the fullest and richest imagination" (*Painting,* 5). Pound's 1914 analogy of China to "a new Greece"
could conceivably have owed something to Binyon's 1908 statement,[12]
"The Japanese look to China as we look to Italy and Greece: for them
it is the classic land, the source from which their art has drawn not
only methods, materials, and principles of design, but an endless variety
of theme and motive" (6). In the British Museum 1910–12 Exhibition
of Chinese and Japanese Paintings, mounted under Binyon's direction,
pride of place deservedly went to Chinese paintings. The English public was provided with its first opportunity to see as well as read about
over a hundred examples of the world's oldest continuous tradition of
pictorial art.[13]

Binyon's pursuits would have been out of the question had not the
British Museum acquired several distinguished groups of Chinese
paintings in 1903–10. For decades Sidney Colvin, Keeper of the Department of Prints and Drawings, had lamented the meager size and
quality of their Chinese holdings acquired via Japan, which had caused
a "crisis of representation." In the British Museum 1888 Exhibition of
Chinese and Japanese Paintings, China was represented by only thirteen

trivial items as compared with 224 Japanese works.[14] Colvin had tried to encourage acquisition in the Chinese direction. Not until the beginning of the twentieth century, when China's resistance to overseas commodification of its art collapsed, had the British Museum been able to enrich its Chinese collection with a growing number of paintings.

Of these the most impressive was a handscroll titled *Admonitions of the Instructress to Court Ladies* (figs. 3, 10–13), which had remained in the Qing imperial collection of art until 1900, when the Allied troops of Britain, France, and six other powers looted Beijing and destroyed a large portion of the palace art. In March 1903 this painting, formerly accessible only to members of the Qing court and to aristocrats, was brought to the British Museum by Captain C. Johnson of 9 Egerton Terrace SW, London, and purchased upon recommendation of Colvin for the ridiculous amount of 1,250 pounds.[15] The *Admonitions* seems to match the "Elgin Marbles" in the British Museum. Whereas Lord Elgin at least paid a sum of money to cover up his pillage during the Turkish invasion of Greece, Captain Johnson did not even try to camouflage his robbery during the Allied occupation of Beijing. The painting was believed to have been produced in the fourth century A.D. by Gu Kaizhi (ca. 345–406), and still is attributed to this ancestor personage of a whole tradition of figure painting. In a memo to the British Museum

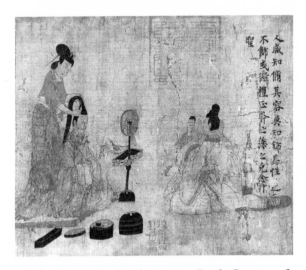

3. After Gu Kaizhi (ca. 345–406), 7th century, "Toilet," a scene from *Admonitions of the Instructress to Court Ladies.* © The British Museum. (Courtesy, British Museum, London)

board of trustees, Colvin claims, "Professor Giles and others after the most minute examination have satisfied themselves that there can be here no question of copy or forgery, and that the specimen is a historical rarity of the first rank."[16] Nonetheless, it has proved to be a Tang dynasty (618–907) copy of Gu Kaizhi's masterpiece.[17] Still, the British Museum could congratulate itself on having acquired for its collection one of the world's earliest and most magnificent antiquities.

If the purchase of the *Admonitions* was made possible by imperialist politics and theft, so was the British Museum acquisition of the Stein collection, composed of *Paradise of Śākyamuni* and nearly three hundred other Buddhist paintings from Dunhuang. These objects had been part of the Buddhist artworks of the fifth to the eleventh centuries A.D. kept in the cave shrines of Qianfodong ("Caves of the Thousand Buddhas") near Dunhuang in northwest China. In about 1900, the year of the Allied occupation of Beijing, a Daoist priest named Wang Yuanlu first discovered Buddhist objects in one of the caves walled up at the beginning of the eleventh century.[18] After the news of his discovery spread to Europe, the Budapest-born British archaeologist Sir Marc Aurel Stein (1862–1943) launched three expeditions to the sites on the ancient "Silk Route," and it was in 1907 during his second expedition (1906–9) that he arrived at Dunhuang and entered a major walled-up cave—Cave 17, or the Library Chamber. There he found ancient Buddhist paintings and texts and removed hundreds of them from their ceremonial niches.[19] The British Museum had paid two-fifths of the expenses for this expedition, and so it had received a corresponding share of the "treasure-trove."[20] Where there is theft there is emulation. After Britain had gathered the lion's share, French, Russian, and Japanese missions followed on Stein's heels and seized their portions of the Dunhuang frescoes, paintings, and manuscripts.[21]

Lastly, a 1910 addition to the British Museum store of Chinese material was one of nearly 150 paintings ranging in dates from the ninth to the nineteenth centuries formed by Frau Olga-Julia Wegener from Berlin during four years' residence in post–Allied-occupation Beijing. This collection was the backbone of the British Museum 1910–12 exhibition. When part of it was shown in Paris in 1911, it inspired Guillaume Apollinaire to write a review, in which he remarks: "Chinese art—powerful, noble, and sweeping—might well inherit the admiration that has hitherto been reserved for the Japanese, who, aping the great art of China, have produced only a dwarf."[22] Like the *Admonitions,* the Wegener collection was an object of envy to French and German art institutions. In his review, Apollinaire addresses this sentiment as an expression of the European art-world politics: "When Mm. de Wegener's collection was shown in London, it was a great success, and the British Museum spent several hundred thousand francs to acquire some of these ancient paintings. It caused quite a scandal in Berlin! People heaped violent reproaches on the German museums for having allowed a first-rate German collection to escape from them while they were spending thousands on a *Flora* falsely attributed to Leonardo da Vinci."[23]

The glorious moments for the British Museum Department of Prints and Drawings culminated in 1909. In that year two of its world-class collections arrived—the Stein collection, for uncrating and cataloging, and the Wegener collection, for preliminary viewing and negotiating a price. No doubt Binyon was increasingly absorbed by tasks such as these, for in the beginning of that year he was promoted to Assistant Keeper of the Department in charge of Oriental affairs. Coincidentally, it was at that moment that Pound first met Binyon, and the two quickly developed a friendship that was to last for a lifetime.

Pound is most likely to have heard of Binyon's reputation in the winter of 1908–9, when he spent a great deal of his time in the British Museum. *Painting in the Far East* had been out for just a few months. Pound could have flipped through this profusely illustrated book in the museum bookstore or in the reading room. However, it was probably because Binyon was a poet that London publisher Elkin Mathews had offered to introduce him to Pound. By early 1909, aside from his art books, Binyon had published more than half a dozen volumes of verse, including *Penthesilea* (1905), whose character, an Amazon queen, would, forty-odd years later, appear in Canto 80: "Mr Binyon's young prodigies / pronounced the word: Penthesilea" (*C*, 526).

The Binyon Pound first met in early February 1909 was, nevertheless, one who had just heard Dr. Stein's account of his explorations in northwest China and had probably discussed with him and other parties the terms under which the Buddhist art was to be transferred from their first stop in London, the National History Museum, to the British Museum.[24] And, more important, he was preparing to give a course of lectures on Oriental art and thought. It was to be announced in the London *Times* the following Thursday, 11 February 1909: "Mr. Laurence Binyon will give a course of four lectures on Art and Thought in East and West, in the small theatre of the Albert Hall, Kensington, at 5:30 on Wednesday afternoons, March 10, 17, 24, and 31." Binyon was to give

Pound a ticket for these slide lectures. On March 15, Pound would tell his mother that he had been to a lecture on Oriental art, which he found "intensely interesting." And a few days later, he would mention to his father his "hearing [another] Binyon lecture."[25]

This was the Binyon Mathews presented to Pound on Friday, 5 February 1909 in a restaurant near the British Museum. Sure enough, the older man would be glad to talk about poetry, but for the moment his most affectionate topics would be the *Admonitions,* Stein's discovery of Buddhist art in "Chinese Turkestan," its arrival in London, and his plan for an exhibition of Chinese and Japanese paintings—an explosion in art—in 1910. Pound would be delighted to hear inside stories about a possible "Oriental Renaissance."

The two men, one twenty-three years old and the other almost forty, were soon lunching together. Pound would call Binyon "BinBin," "one of the best loved men in London." In "him & in his work" he savored "a sort of pervading slow charm."[26] Presumably it was not "Bin-Bin" the poet with echoes of Wordsworth and Matthew Arnold but "BinBin" the champion of Oriental art who had attracted Ezra to his circle of friends, who regularly met in the Vienna Café on New Oxford Street. A statement Binyon repeated in those gatherings—"Slowness is beauty"—kept coming back to Pound at Pisa, where he seized glimpses of "a white ox," "dark sheep," and "[a] lizard" (*C,* 448), even though he recalled not believing it then.[27] The phrase eventually found its place in Canto 87: "BinBin 'is beauty'. / 'Slowness is beauty'" (*C,* 592).

During that period Binyon was also seeing Mary McNeil Fenollosa, who was in and out of his department, familiarly known as the Print Room, seeking assistance in locating art objects her late husband Ernest Fenollosa (1853–1908) had planned to use as illustrations for *Epochs* (1912).[28] Binyon was to introduce Pound to her in 1913, whose gift—the Fenollosa Notebooks—would start the young poet from America on his path to the Orient.[29] But in 1909 Binyon had somewhat prepared Pound for his *Cathay* enterprise by inviting him to his lectures on "Art and Thought in East and West." No less than those given by Fenollosa in America,[30] Binyon's lectures of 1909 were designed in such a way as to open the eyes of many to a splendid culture in the East.

It is a fair guess that Binyon's lectures would have drawn material from *Painting in the Far East,* and that some of his new insights would go into *The Flight of the Dragon* (1911), a book Pound would review in 1915. However, we must not conclude that these lectures were the substance in brief of either of the two books.[31] Binyon gave a number of lectures illustrated by examples from the British Museum collection during that period, each with a spattering of fresh material. In January 1912, for example, he gave one such talk at the London Institution in Finsbury Circus. According to the London *Times,* in that lecture Binyon threw on the screen images from the *Admonitions,* Dunhuang Buddhist art, and Song landscapes while he surveyed the manifestation of diverse Chinese modes of thought, focusing finally on Daoism, whose concepts he compared to those of Wordsworth.[32]

While the precise contents of the lectures Pound heard in March 1909 remain unknown, it seems certain that in those extended attempts Binyon had examined a larger number of paintings in relation to Eastern ideals. Presumably he had capitalized on those occasions to bring insights to a remote culture and philosophy. Throughout the lectures, Pound's eye would be continuously engaged as Binyon projected on the screen image after image and explored distinctive Chinese views of art, nature, and society. Although Pound had been exposed to Chinese art in America, not until March 1909 did he have his first opportunity to hear an art expert systematically consider Oriental art and aesthetic. After the lectures Pound would go to the British Museum and inspect for himself some of the rare artworks Binyon had described. And above all, he had the privilege to discuss all aspects of Oriental culture with Binyon during lunch hours.

This opportunity, extending throughout the "B. M. era," to learn from England's most eminent connoisseur of Oriental art, and to study the British Museum collection of Chinese and Japanese paintings proved immeasurably favorable when Pound set out to rework Fenollosa's versions of Chinese poetry. In discussing Pound's London years, literary historians tend to underestimate the role played by Binyon. Of course, W. B. Yeats and Ford Madox Ford were more important, as Pound used to recall seeing "Ford in the afternoons and Yeats in the evenings."[33] But during that idyllic period, Pound was also meeting Binyon and his circle during lunchtime. To his last days, according to Olga Rudge, Pound dreamed of Binyon and his twin daughters: "They were born when E. [Ezra] just got to London."[34] Pound's lifelong enthusiasm for Oriental culture was nursed in 1909–14, and his friendship with Binyon constituted an indispensable part of his balanced education in his London years.

From late 1909 until mid-1910 Binyon was increasingly consumed by the organization of the 1910–12 exhibition, which served dramatically to escalate England's interest in Chinese taste. Binyon designed the layout of the show, wrote all the captions, and supervised its installation. He also prepared a catalogue with elaborate notes for the visiting public—*Guide to an Exhibition of Chinese and Japanese Paintings*. Pound had lunched with Binyon during the whole period and learned all about the *Admonitions* and other glories of Chinese art in the British Museum without having to wait until the exhibition finally opened on Monday, 20 June 1910.

Held in the large Print and Drawing Gallery in the White Wing of the museum, now subdivided into Rooms 43, 44, and 45, the exhibition attracted large crowds and led to an avalanche of articles on Far Eastern art in periodicals such as the *Burlington Magazine* and newspapers such as the *Times*. Ironically, it was the landscapes and the flower-and-bird pictures rather than the *Admonitions* or the Buddhist art from Dunhuang that made the strongest impressions on spectators. One reviewer claims that "no classical European master ever expressed the structure of mountain and rock as it is expressed here."[35]

Pound, who sailed for the United States on 18 June 1910, missed the exhibition's opening, but he returned in mid-February 1911, well over a year before the show was finally removed.[36] By early 1911 so many reviews and articles had been published on the exhibition that few Londoners with any interest in China could have remained oblivious to its attraction. Pound almost certainly saw the show. He was articulate in his appreciation of Chinese art. The opening stanza of his 1913 poem "A Song of the Degrees" might be regarded as a tribute to the Chinese sense of color: "Rest me with Chinese colours, / For I think the glass is evil" (*P*, 95). And in "Three Cantos," Pound even emulates in words the "blue-and-green style" of several Chinese landscapes on view: "Daub out in blue of scarabs, and with that greeny turquoise? / Or with China . . ." (233).

As chapter 2 will show, the many Chinese dragons presented in the exhibition were a special attraction. These images are recognized by the Chinese as the descendants of the mighty *long*, which is rendered into English as "dragons." Pound pays homage to the creature in his 1913 poem "Further Instructions." What he had in mind while giving the lines "I will get you a green coat out of China / With dragons worked upon it" (*P*, 95) was surely not the image he had drawn at age fifteen, but one like the sketch his fiancée, Dorothy Shakespear, had copied off a Chinese master.[37]

In a 1977 essay, Woon-ping Chin Holaday notices some affinity between Pound's Guanyin (Kuanon in Japanese) in Canto 74 and the exhibition's nos. 39 and 44. Guanyin as Savior from Perils is portrayed variously in the show. Pound's first Guanyin in "Three Cantos" appears to match no. 25, *Standing Guanyin.*[38]

> Fine screens depicted, sea waves curled high,
> Small boats with gods upon them,
> Bright flame above the river! Kwannon
> Footing a boat that's but one lotus petal,
> With some proud four spread-genius
> Leading along, one hand upraised for gladness,
> Saying, "Tis she, his friend, the mighty goddess!   (*P,* 233)

True, in *Standing Guanyin* one sees no flame above waves or "Small boats with gods upon them." Such details may be found in other pictures. Of no. 44, *The Unsurpassable Guanyin,* Binyon notes that "by earnest prayer to Kwanyin, [one] may see the flames turned into living water" (*Guide,* 23). No. 80, *The Earthly Paradise,* on the other hand, presents gods in a small boat. In inventing his Guanyin in "Three Cantos," it seems, Pound has blended details from a number of pictures.

It was not the exhibition's particular colors or images but rather the distinctive aesthetic ideas behind the works that had exerted a more penetrating impact on Pound. In the years 1911–12, Pound was experimenting with a series of new concepts of form and design in poetry. Considering various affinities between Chinese aesthetic laws and those new poetic ideas, one becomes less doubtful about the contribution of Chinese art to Pound's Imagist poetics.

In discussing Pound's best-known Imagist poem, "In a Station of the Metro," critics tend to attribute its beauty exclusively to the influence of the Japanese haiku. The poem's unique form and motif may be drawn at once from the haiku and Chinese painting. An example of what use Pound might make of the latter is *A Lady Meditating by a Lake* (fig. 4). A careful look reveals that the picture too relies on juxtaposition to express emotion. One may ask why the meditating lady's face is portrayed with the fewest strokes, whereas the blossoming trees in the background are delineated with detail. The answer lies in the fact that Chinese artists attach great importance to suggestion. The blossoming trees on the same "flattened" plane of attention are used to equate the lady's state of mind. Pound might have learned a lesson from paintings such as this. Of his Metro experience he says that he suddenly found "an equation . . . not in speech, but in little splotches of colour" (*GB,* 87). He calls this "super-position," that is, "one idea set on top of another"

(89). If haiku poems contain "poetic patterns" that function for Pound as "super-position," so do paintings such as *A Lady Meditating by a Lake*. It is in the latter, however, that one really catches sight of "splotches of colour" that equate emotion.

The Metro poem seems alluding to "a painting that would speak only by arrangements in colour" (*GB*, 87). The second line appears an effort to emulate a Chinese blossom sketched in monochrome. Moore's favorite Chinese picture, *A Breath of Spring* (fig. 38), will bear witness that "Petals on a wet, black bough" (*P*, 111) can be diverse tones in little black dots covered along one flowing calligraphic tone of black. The whole thing set against a blank space evokes subtle emotions.

Pound owed his appreciation of Chinese ideas about space, composition, and tonality partly to Binyon and partly to James Whistler, whose art suggests the Orient. Whistler had always been Pound's favorite artist. At Penn he had recommended Whistler's "Ten O'clock Lecture" to H. D. (Hilda Doolittle). And shortly after his arrival in London, he had examined his works and the works of J. M. W. Turner in the British Museum. His enthusiasm is recorded in a letter to his mother: "Whistler and Turner, to whom it is theoretically necessary to be 'educated up.' When you first see their pictures you say 'wot't-'ell' but when you leave the pictures you see beauty in mists, shadows, a hundred places where you never dreamed of seeing it before. The answer to their work is in nature" (*EP&VA*, 287).

Since Pound had a taste for Whistler and Turner, especially for their "beauty in mists, shadows," naturally he would be drawn to Chinese landscapes "preeminent . . . in suggesting infinite horizons, the look of mountains beyond mountains melting away into remote sky" (Binyon, *Flight*, 60–61). Such an example was "Snowy Evening" from a version of the *Eight Views* (fig. 5). Like the Whistler of *Nocturne in Blue and Gold*, the artist of "Snowy Evening" painted his boats with a few strokes — a technique that parallels Pound's Imagist tenet: "To use absolutely no word that does not contribute to the presentation" (*LE*, 3). Another feature of "Snowy Evening" would have appealed to Pound—its positioning of the boats and distant mountains in the upper third of the scroll, leaving a broad space below gray and empty. This design, comparable to Whistler's *Nocturne in Blue and Gold*, corresponded well with Pound's Imagist, and later Vorticist, belief in "convey[ing] an emotion by means of an arrangement of shapes, or planes, or colours" (*GB*, 81). "From Whistler and the Japanese, or Chinese," Pound would later re-

4. After Qiu Ying (ca. 1510–ca. 1552), *A Lady Meditating by a Lake.* © The British Museum. (Courtesy, British Museum, London)

5. Yunqiao Zhuren (17th century), "Snowy Evening," a scene from the *Eight Views.* © The British Museum. (Courtesy, British Museum, London)

mark, "the fragment of the English-speaking world . . . learned to enjoy 'arrangements' of colours and masses" (*EP&VA,* 192).

"Snowy Evening" and other Chinese landscapes might also have taught Pound's future wife, Dorothy Shakespear, a lesson around 1912 when she began drifting away from the Victorian watercolor tradition she had adhered to in earlier years. Her oil painting *Landscape: Devil's Cheese Ring* (fig. 6), executed no later than 1915, bears a resemblance to "Snowy Evening." Both pictures place distant hills in the top right-hand section and trees in the lower left-hand section, and both leave a diagonal space between their objects. Admittedly, *Devil's Cheese Ring* has absorbed Cubist elements, but it also shows a Chinese compositional design and a Chinese sense of naturalness.

Devil's Cheese Ring seems Dorothy's response to Pound's "Δώρια" arguably written for her:

Be in me as the eternal moods
    of the bleak wind, and not
As transient things are —
    gaiety of flowers.
Have me in the strong loneliness
    of sunless cliffs
And of grey waters.   (*P,* 64)

Curiously, both works resemble "Snowy Evening" in motif ("bleak wind," "sunless cliffs," and "grey waters") as well as compositional pattern. Pound could have in mind "Snowy Evening," *Devil's Cheese Ring, Nocturne in Blue and Gold,* and "Δώρια" all together when he made the statement: "By the 'image' I mean such an equation; not an equation of mathematics, not something about *a, b,* and *c,* having something to do with form, but about *sea, cliffs, night,* having something to do with mood" (*GB,* 92).

Dorothy Shakespear surely shared her parents', and later her husband's, enthusiasm for Chinese culture. As a 1901 notebook of hers shows, at age fifteen she was already learning the Chinese language.[39] Around 1920, when Pound began promoting Fenollosa's essay on "The Chinese Written Character" and developing his "ideogrammic method" for *The Cantos,* he would find his wife's knowledge of Chinese enormously handy. She subsequently drew a large number of the characters for Pound's modernist epic.[40]

Regardless of whether or not Ezra and Dorothy actually visited the 1910–12 exhibition together, it appears to have held a firm grip on both

6. Dorothy Shakespear Pound (1886–1973), *Landscape: Devil's Cheese Ring.* Gift of Omar S. Pound. (Courtesy, Fred L. Emerson Gallery, Hamilton College, Clinton, New York)

of them. It whetted their appetite for Chinese and Japanese art, and once it was removed they started to study reserve material in the Print Room. Pound first entered his name into the Print Room visitors book on 27 September 1912.[41] On another visit, 3 January 1913, he ran into Binyon just back from a trip to the United States, where he had seen art collections such as Charles Freer's in Detroit. On that day Pound had gone through a portfolio of Japanese prints, and in a letter written the following evening he told Dorothy that he felt "ages older & wiser" contemplating "mediaeval japanese prints." Of Binyon he commented, "Bin-Bin *adest* lamenting that England will never have a collection comparable to the 'Fuller' lot in the U.S." (*L/DS,* 177).[42]

Dorothy began showing up in the Print Room in mid-February 1913. Her initial visit was made on Tuesday, 18 February. In a letter of 22 February, she announced to Pound, "I have obtained an admission to the Print Room—& have seen a portfolio of [Kitagawa] Utamaro. I wonder which you liked so much?" (*L/DS,* 190). Within the next five weeks she returned to the Print Room at least seven more times—on 22, 24, 27 February and 1, 21, 22, and 23 March.[43] It seems most likely that she was working on some reserve material (Chinese or Japanese), for several times she went back early the next morning (among the earliest who signed in) to continue her work. There is reason to suspect that throughout the winter of 1912–13 Dorothy was making sketches of Chinese paintings. The proof for this is Pound's statement in a letter to his father, dated 3 December 1912: "This being Tuesday. And D' goes on painting chinese pictures."[44] There are a number of examples of Chinese style in Omar Pound's collection of Dorothy's pictures. Some of these—*A Chinese Dragon* and *An Imperial Palace Tower*—are probably from that period.[45]

The Print Room was closed in September 1913 for rearrangement and rehousing in a new section of the building—an extension along the north side of the museum on Montague Place, where it still resides. Pound expressed the shared disappointment and frustration in a letter to Dorothy, 23 September 1913: "That print-room is closed INDEFINITELY—while they move into the new wing of the museo—which means, I should think, six months—There's small use of your imagining you'll be let into *that* plaisance" (*L/DS,* 259). The extension—King Edward VII Galleries—was not completed until May 1914. By that summer war broke out and the "B. M. era" was brought to an end. Yet Pound need not have felt upset in late 1913, for he met Mrs. Fenollosa between September and October, and before the year was out he received Fenollosa's notes and manuscripts. Thus began for Pound four decades of studying Chinese poetry and the written character, which would augment his already strong passion for Eastern modes of thought.

Thanks to a happy combination of events, notably the arrival of the Fenollosa notebooks and the growing availability of Chinese objects in London galleries and markets,[46] Pound responded most productively to Chinese art in his Vorticist years. In the first place, he was able to make use of the knowledge he had acquired from Binyon and the British Museum Chinese collection in his *Cathay* enterprise. More important, he was deliberately broadening the basic Imagist/Vorticist tenets by absorbing Chinese aestheticism. As a result, he became even more firmly convinced of an Oriental Renaissance. "I should like to see China replace Greece as the body of antiquity," he writes in a letter to John Quinn dated 3 September 1916 (*EP&VA,* 241). Meanwhile, in a series of essays on Vorticism he keeps attaching more importance to the stimulus of Chinese art than do the Vorticist artists themselves.

Thus for Pound, Wyndham Lewis's Vorticist painting owed at least some of its taut linear energy and innate sense of abstract pattern to Chinese precedents. "But if any man is to bring into Western art the power of Chinese painting it will be Lewis," he asserted (*EP&VA*, 230). Here he is alluding to Chinese art's reliance on lines and to its most respectful "First Canon," also known as "rhythmic vitality." In a 1915 review of Binyon's *The Flight of the Dragon*, Pound would urge attention to a lucid summary of this principle radically at odds with mimesis: "FOR INDEED IT IS NOT ESSENTIAL THAT THE SUBJECT-MATTER SHOULD REPRESENT OR BE LIKE ANYTHING IN NATURE; ONLY IT MUST BE ALIVE WITH A RHYTHMIC VITALITY OF ITS OWN" (*P&P*, 2:99). Like Pound, Lewis was a regular patron of the Vienna Café. It was scarcely unexpected for Pound to think that the Vorticist leader might have derived some of his "volcanic force" from the Chinese emphasis on "rhythmic vitality," an aesthetic brought to light by their mutual friend, Binyon.

Pound also used Edward Wadsworth's woodcuts as an example of the contribution he believed Chinese art had made to the advent of Vorticism. Referring to his friend's "arrangements in pure form" called *Khaki,* which has not survived,[47] Pound asserted that it "does not 'look like' anything, save perhaps a Chinese or Japanese painting with the representative patches removed. The feeling I get from this picture is very much the feeling I get from certain Eastern paintings, and I think the feeling that went into it is probably very much the same as that which moved certain Chinese painters" (*EP&VA*, 192–93). We are unaware of Wadsworth's interest in Oriental art, but in the years 1913–15 he produced a group of woodcuts in a startlingly consistent style. As the famous example *New Delight* demonstrates, several of their characteristics—a combination of two matching colors, generous use of empty space, diagonal emphasis, and an atmosphere of harmony—can be traced to Oriental influence.[48]

Henri Gaudier-Brzeska was the only Vorticist artist who avowedly shared with Pound an enthusiasm for Chinese art. In an article for *Blast* 1 (June 1914) reprinted in Pound's *A Memoir* (*GB*, 20–24), the young sculptor links Vortex and China in a juxtaposition that suggests the genesis of Vorticism in Chinese civilization: "The black-haired men who wandered through the pass of Khotan into the valley of the YELLOW RIVER lived peacefully tilling their lands, and they grew prosperous. . . . The Shang and Chow [Zhou] dynasties produced the convex bronze vases" (*GB*, 22–23).

Apparently Gaudier had been reading Fenollosa, who speaks in *Epochs* of the "black-haired Chinese" (1:12) who "settled along the Ho-

angho [the Yellow River]" and who were "only a peaceful and prosperous, order-loving tribe" (1:9). It was perhaps Pound who introduced
Gaudier to *Epochs* and it was perhaps Pound also who stimulated him
to study the Chinese character.[49] "[A]fter he had spent, what could not
have been more than a few days studying the subject at the museum,"
states Pound in *A Memoir*, "he could understand the primitive Chinese
ideographs (not the later more sophisticated forms), and he was very
much disgusted with the lexicographers who 'hadn't sense enough that
that was a horse,' or a cow or a tree or whatever it might be, 'what the
. . . else could it be! The . . . fools!'" (*GB*, 46). Gaudier seemed impressed by the potential energy of calligraphic strokes. His sketches of
a cock and of Pound indicate that he kept the stylized strokes of the
primitive Chinese characters securely in the back of his mind. Pound's
fascination with these "calligraphic drawings" is evidenced by his in-
clusion of them in his *Memoir* (plates IX and X). For him these pictures
may have afforded a possibility of moving freely between poetry and
painting, a path toward his "ideogrammic method."

By 1914 Pound and Gaudier were both attracted to ritual bronzes
of the Shang and Zhou societies (the second to first millennia B.C.) in
London museums. In the 1910s Western awareness of bronze art in ancient China was still in its infancy. In discussing this subject, Gaudier
was therefore unavoidably hampered by not knowing the utilitarian or

7. Six-dynasties bronze drum, with four frog-shaped handles on top, ca. 5th
century A.D. © The British Museum. (Courtesy, British Museum, London)

ritual values of the objects.[50] Thus by "convex bronze vases" (*GB*, 23), he most probably refers to *hu*, a pear-shaped wine vessel developed in the Western Zhou for ancestor worship. In writing "the centuple spherical frog presided over the inverted truncated cone that is the bronze war drum" (*GB*, 23), he possibly had in mind the British Museum bronze drum with four frog-shaped handles on top (fig. 7).[51]

Except for a few oversights, Gaudier's comments exhibit considerable sensitivity. He was ahead of his time in pointing out the "[m]aturity" and "fecundity" of ancient Chinese bronzes (*GB*, 23), for subsequent archaeological findings would show that during the Shang-Zhou periods bronze art not only developed in sophistication of design but also proliferated from central China to border regions. Gaudier and Pound might both have been influenced by Fenollosa, who says of Chinese bronzes: Their "shapes . . . have now become specially plastic and beautiful; severe and strong in design, with simple firm outline, and of a dignity and variety which make even Greek vases look somewhat thin" (*Epochs*, 1:11). Different from Fenollosa, the two Vorticist colleagues see in Chinese ritual bronzes a form of the primitive Vortex.

Furthermore, Pound perceived a "comfortable feeling" in Zhou animal-shaped vessels brought out by rotundity. In his review of the London Goupil Exhibition, he compares Gaudier's *Boy with a Coney* (*GB*, plate XXIII) to a Zhou bronze animal, noting that it at least suggests "the bronze animals of that period" (*EP&VA*, 183). His analogy is a subtle compliment, as Picasso's epoch-making *Les Demoiselles d'Avignon* similarly bears a signature of primitivism. To this Gaudier responds: "It is better than they. They had, it is true, a maturity brought by continuous rotundities—my statuette has more monumental concentration—a result of the use of flat and round surfaces" (*GB*, 32). As a British Museum bronze finial will testify, a human figure with creatures is a common motif in Shang-Zhou bronze design and their style well matches Gaudier's statuette.[52]

Just how much or how little Gaudier was influenced by Chinese primitive art is difficult to say. But Pound's delight in Shang-Zhou bronzes was real and palpable as it is registered in "Three Cantos": "Exult with Shang in squatness? The sea-monster / Bulges the squarish bronzes" (*P*, 233).

Chinese Art

Arrives in

America: Stevens

and Moore

DURING THE YEARS 1909–14 American enthusiasm for Chinese art also escalated. In Boston this was due, in part, to the effort of Okakura Kakuzō (1862–1913).[1] As Ernest Fenollosa's successor at the Museum of Fine Arts, Boston (MFA), he had an ambition to create "the finest collection of oriental art under one roof in the world."[2] Since the Oriental Wing established by Fenollosa in 1890–95 consisted chiefly of Japanese objects,[3] he took the initiative to give top priority to the acquisition of Chinese material. His pursuit was assisted by Hayasaki Kōkichi (1874–1956), a veteran art trader who acted as the MFA's buyer in China.[4] This happened to be the period during which China's last imperial dynasty, the Qing (1644–1911), was collapsing, and tons of art treasures were slipping through the hands of its power elite. As a result, Hayasaki was able to secure for the Museum of Fine Arts such rarities as the handscroll *Clear Weather in the Valley,* traditionally attributed to Dong Yuan, and the album leaf *Bare Willows and Distant Mountains,* by Ma Yuan (fig. 41).[5] By 1912 Laurence Binyon of the British Museum could no longer overlook American collections of Far Eastern art, hence his study trip to the U.S. in November of that year.[6]

With the Museum of Fine Arts leading the way, entrepreneur Charles Lang Freer (1856–1919), who had spent considerable personal wealth on Whistler and Japanese prints, went all out to buy Chinese bronzes, porcelains, and ink paintings. His unmatched combination of connoisseurship and money enabled him quickly to assemble a private collection of Chinese art including masterpieces such as *The Nymph of the Luo River,* attributed to Gu Kaizhi, and *Clearing Autumn Skies over Mountains and Valleys,* attributed to Guo Xi (ca. 1023-ca. 1085).[7] In late November 1912 Binyon traveled to Detroit to inspect the Freer Collection. As Pound reported, upon return he wailed that "England will never have a collection comparable to the 'Fuller' lot [the Freer Collection] in the U.S." (*L/DS,* 177). "He ought to know," commented Pound.[8]

During his 1910 brief return to America, Pound made a whirlwind tour of the Metropolitan Museum of Art and presumably saw nothing particularly impressive in its newly formed Department of Far Eastern Art.[9] He would not have known, however, that a year earlier, in March 1909, when he was attending Binyon's lectures in London, the New York public had an opportunity to view an exhibition of Chinese paintings. The collection was brought to the U.S. by Isaac Taylor Headland (1859–1942), a professor at Beijing University, who witnessed the decline of the Qing house during its last decade. In April 1909 this exhibition, first installed in the Century Club in New York City, was sent to be shown in the galleries of the Pratt Institute in Brooklyn. In a catalogue Headland offers a brief discussion of the Chinese method and ideal. "The expression through art of a mood or an emotion," he remarks, is "the goal of the Chinese painter." A Chinese landscape tends to have a perspective "taken from a hilltop instead of from the level," he elucidates, and as a result, often its subjects "are three-fourths or four-fifths land and the remainder sky." This theory, Headland says, is "as accurate as our own although based upon different conventions."[10]

Such an introduction proved useful. Without it the American public would find it hard to appreciate, say, a Song landscape attributed to Mi Fu, whose dark trees and misty mountain peaks are intended to be viewed as the expression of an artist in solemn contemplation.[11] Still, the way Chinese artists apply their color and light must have struck the American viewers as being very unusual. In describing the hand-scroll *The Pleasure-grounds of Qin Shihuang,* a reviewer for *The New York Times* observes that it is "difficult to say which is most to be admired, the delicate color in pale reds and greens and blues on a warm brownish ground, or the flexible drawing placing each figure with its full individuality in its relation to all the other figures."[12] He designates a similar sentiment about "[t]he green and gold of the mellow color" in *Springtime,* a sixteenth-century landscape.[13] For this critic, however, the most precious object of the exhibition was *Mongols Hunting,* by the fourteenth-century painter Zhao Mengfu. Curiously, as he explains, it was not the lively activity of the hunting scene, but rather "the reserved color scheme, with its faint pinks and greens" in the background that prompted him to hail this piece as a work of "the greatest refinement."[14] He also calls attention to a number of fine tapestry pictures, whose "perfections of surface and color" he suggests will "put Western tapestries, however high in grade, well into the background."[15]

Wallace Stevens, then a lawyer residing in New York, was among the hundred or so visitors to the show on the evening of 18 March 1909. In a letter of that night to his fiancée, Elsie Moll, he speaks favorably of the tapestry pictures, "some antiquated musical instruments," and "two cabinets of carved jade" (L, 137). Nonetheless, what impressed him most that evening was Headland's collection of pictures "all from the Chinese, painted centuries ago" (137). Chinese colors, one recalls, overwhelmed Pound in London around 1910. Remarkably, they seized Stevens's imagination at about the same historical moment. While Pound expressed his fascination through invocation: "Rest me with Chinese colours" (P, 95), Stevens responded by verbalizing striking combinations of Chinese colors, which he sent off to Elsie "to make a private exhibition":

"pale orange, green and crimson, and white,
and gold, and brown;"

and

"deep lapis-lazuli and orange, and opaque
green, fawn-color, black, and gold;"

and

"lapis blue and vermilion, white, and gold
and green."   (L, 137)

An examination of the first two lists, which later became Stevens's manuscript poem "Colors" (OP, 3–4), reveals that they match *The Pleasure-grounds of Qin Shihuang* and *Springtime* in the exhibition. Like Pound's Metro poem, Stevens's "Colors" suggests a modernist way of responding to Chinese art. From the outset, it seems, both poets recognized Chinese painting as a model of nonmimetic art with emphasis on emotional coloring. Of the two works, Stevens's appears to be the more abstract. Where Pound treats both the object and its coloring in his Metro poem, Stevens presents nothing but coloring in "Colors." Stevens's impressionistic use of color is visible in other poems of the period, notably "Shower": "Pink and purple / In water-mist" (SP, 231), and the third section of "Carnet de Voyage":

. . . .
Blood-red and hue
Of shadowy blue,
And amber sheen,
And water-green,
And yellow flash,
And diamond ash.   (*OP*, 6)

These exercises, according to George Lensing, "predate the Imagist experiments in color."[16] They contributed to Stevens's early style. As Robert Buttel notes, "'Colors' prepared Stevens for the accomplished control of color and light in 'Sunday Morning,' particularly in the first section."[17]

Stevens apparently required very little in the way of an education to respond warmly and productively to Chinese art. This was in part because ever since his Cambridge years Oriental art had been one of his preoccupations. For Stevens, as for his Harvard schoolmates Arthur Davison Ficke and Witter Bynner, Oriental art had generally meant Japanese art. This was not surprising, for the Oriental Wing that opened their eyes to the Far East consisted chiefly of Japanese objects. In early March 1909 (no more than a couple of weeks before he saw Headland's collection of Chinese art), Stevens dined with Bynner at the Players Club in New York. One of the topics of their conversation was Japanese prints. That evening Stevens also requested Bynner to stop by Bunkio Matsuki's—"one of the best Japanese stores in [Boston]"—to get some Japanese prints for Elsie.[18] The prints never arrived. So Stevens had to send Elsie Chinese pictures in words. To make her appreciate his effort, he remarked in his letter: "I do not know if you feel as I do about a place so remote and unknown as China—the irreality of it. So much so, that the little realities of it seem wonderful and beyond belief" (*L*, 137).

Bynner was also a poet. Like Stevens, he came to appreciate Chinese aesthetic through Japanese art. In 1917 he sailed to Japan and China with Arthur Ficke. Different from Ficke, who cared only for Japanese prints,[19] Bynner brought back from that trip four Chinese scroll paintings. One of these, *Two Fishermen*, stimulated him to write an essay titled "The Chinese Brush."[20] Another, *A Deer under a Tree*, is believed to have been in a photograph. "My records indicate," Bynner remarked in a letter of 1940 to Pound, "that a photograph of a portrait of my more patient phiz went to you long ago accompanying a Chinese deer: one of my paintings brought back in 1917."[21] In 1920 Bynner took a second trip to China and did not return until the following year. This time he shipped back to America about two hundred scroll paintings and over a hundred jade girdle clasps. In November 1923, after a cruise to California by way of Havana and the Panama Canal, Mr. and Mrs. Stevens stopped by Santa Fe to visit Bynner.[22] They most probably saw some of Bynner's Chinese treasures in his pink abode.[23] Over a year earlier, Stevens had also purchased a few pretty things from China through Harriet Monroe's sister.[24] It is a fair guess that when the two friends met in Santa Fe, they traded stories about China and their newly acquired Chinese objects.

Stevens's Chinese, Japanese, and Korean art holdings cannot be compared with Bynner's collection of Chinese art, which was bequeathed in 1952 to the Roswell Museum and Art Center in Roswell, New Mexico. Once hailed as "the hope of the future for American poetry,"[25] Bynner is now remembered chiefly for his translations from the Chinese: *The Jade Mountain: A Chinese Anthology: Being Three Hundred Poems of the T'ang Dynasty 618–906* (with Kiang Kang-hu) (1929) and *The Way of Life According to Laotzu* (1944). Ironically, Stevens, earlier the less fortunate poet, a man who appeared to have been influenced by Bynner's Orientalism, was the first to discover China as a robust creative source.

Just as the British Museum collection of Far Eastern art alone could not have awakened Pound's enthusiasm for China, so Headland's exhibition was unlikely to have guided Stevens's interest to Chinese culture all by itself. As his letter of 18 March 1909 reveals, during that eventful week Stevens had been "reading about the Chinese feeling about landscape" in New York's Astor Library (*L,* 137). Less than a decade earlier, Fenollosa, also a Harvard graduate, did considerable research in that library.[26] On 14 May 1909, Stevens copied what he considered to be essential of his Astor Library notes into his journal. These included passages from Okakura's *The Ideals of the East* (1903) and Binyon's *Painting in the Far East* (1908).

It was perhaps Okakura's *The Ideals of the East* that first introduced Stevens to Chan Buddhism. From *The Ideals of the East* he might have acquired an understanding of Neo-Confucianism, "an amalgamation of Taoist, Buddhist, and Confucian thought, acting chiefly . . . through the Taoist mind"; and of Chan, "introduced into China" through India but thoroughly transformed by absorbing "Laoist [Daoist] ideas."[27] That Stevens had carefully read Okakura, adviser to the MFA Department of Chinese and Japanese Art, is evidenced by his sensible statement,

"Kakuzo Okakura is a cultivated, but not an original thinker" (*SP*, 221).
He seemed to think more highly of Binyon, the British champion of
Far Eastern art, in whom he found "a kind of sedateness . . . less than
tranquillity" (222), and from whose *Painting in the Far East* he was able
to learn a great deal more about Chinese landscape painting.

Like Pound, Stevens was charmed by Binyon's "slow beauty," for in
mid-March 1909 he was also perusing his books of verse—*Lyric Poems,
Porphyrion,* and so on—in the Astor Library. He even put some of the
British poet-art critic's lines into his journal. On 9 May 1909, Binyon's
poems preserved in the journal again caught his eye, and he copied out
two of them for Elsie, remarking that they were "both by Lawrence [*sic*]
Binyon—a very clever chap, who is attached to the British Museum, in
London" (*L*, 143).

Interestingly, Pound and Stevens, who both came under the impact
of *Painting in the Far East* in 1909, were enchanted by different things.
Where Pound's taste was for the art and poetry of the Tang, Stevens
preferred "the refinement of Sung society" to "the glory of the Täng
emperors" (*SP*, 221). Into his journal Stevens entered mostly things of
the Song, including this list of subjects about nature and landscape:

> The Evening Bell from a Distant Temple
> Sunset Glow over a Fishing Village
> Fine Weather after Storm at a Lonely Mountain Town
> Homeward-bound Boats off a Distant Coast
> The Autumn Moon over Lake Tung-t'ing
> Wild Geese on a Sandy Plain
> Night Rain in Hsiao-Hsiang
> [Evening Snow]   (*SP*, 222)[28]

About this list Stevens commented, "it is so comprehensive. Any twilight picture is included" (*L*, 138). This list, the "Eight Views of the Xiao
and Xiang Rivers," a traditional series of subjects passed down from
the Song period, is copied from Binyon's *Painting in the Far East* (133).
The idea that Chinese artists competed in presenting shifting perspectives may have, with other things, incited Stevens to try out multiple
points of view in poetry. "Six Significant Landscapes" and "Thirteen
Ways of Looking at a Blackbird" seem remarkable fruit of this experiment. Pound probably viewed both Chinese and Japanese versions of
the "Eight Views" in the British Museum around 1910. However, he
did not involve the scenes until two decades later, when he produced
his own version of the "Eight Views" in Canto 49.

And of a little landscape poem by the Song poet-essayist Wang An-shi (1021–86), which he copied out for Elsie on 18 March 1909 he re-marked,[29] "I don't know of anything more beautiful than that any-where, or more Chinese." He was quite bewitched by its imagery: "I am going to poke around more or less in the dust of Asia for a week or two and have no idea what I shall disturb and bring to light. — Curious thing, how little we know about Asia, and all that. It makes me wild to learn it all in a night" (L, 138).

Stevens's discovery of China as a challenge to his imagination drew him to more galleries that exhibited Chinese art. In September 1909, he and Elsie got married and went to Boston for honeymooning. There is reason to suspect that he took his bride on a tour of his favorite Museum of Fine Arts and introduced her to the great Japanese collec-tions. There to greet them would be Chinese Buddhist paintings pur-chased through Fenollosa, Chinese Buddhist paintings in the Bigelow Collection, as well as freshly acquired landscapes by Ma Yuan and his followers.[30]

With the Qing dynasty at an end, Hayasaki was far from the only dealer capitalizing on its panic-stricken aristocrats and smuggling whole assemblages of rare porcelains, bronzes, and ink paintings into America. In 1909–13, one could witness sales of Chinese imperial col-lections of art — collections that had resisted public consumption and commodification — in the New York marketplace.[31] Stevens went to one such auction in the American Art Galleries on New Year's Day, 1911. "The sole object of interest for me in such things," he remarked to his wife in a letter, "is their beauty" (L, 169). His more detailed descrip-tion of the things that arrested his eye confirms his unabated admira-tion for Chinese colors: "Cucumber-green, camellia-leaf-green, apple-green etc. moonlight, blue, etc. ox-blood, chicken-blood, cherry, peach-blow etc. etc. Oh! and mirror-black: that is so black and with such a glaze that you can see yourself in it. — And now that I am home again, and writing, in semi-obscurity, lights lit, boats whistling, in the peculiar muteness and silence of fog — I wish, intensely, that I had some of those vivid colors here" (L, 169).

No less than his 1909 "Colors," this passage evinces Stevens's remark-able talent for abstraction. In representing Chinese paintings, porce-lains, and ivories alike, he has overlooked all painted and carved objects and recaptured only the essential — their emotional coloring. Critics such as Glen MacLeod have aptly suggested that Stevens's transition toward modernism began with the great Armory Show of 1913 in New

York City.[32] The March 1909 and January 1911 color representations testify, however, that Stevens's early contact with Chinese art had, along with his exposure to projects such as Alfred Stieglitz's *Camera Work* (1903–17),[33] prepared him for this process.

Furthermore, it is clear from a comment made on 20 August 1911 to his wife—"I always have the wise sayings of [Ming?] Tzŭ and K'Ung Fu-Tzŭ to think of" (*L*, 171)—that in the summer of 1911 Stevens was reading Confucius and Mencius. Unlike Pound, whose lifelong fascination with Confucius began about the same moment, Stevens never really fell under the spell of Confucianism. In August 1911, it seems, he was searching for some aesthetic alternative from the East, some motivating force that underlay Chinese art. To his gratification, on 19 August 1911, while going through the newspapers, he came across a translation of excerpts from "The Noble Features of the Forest and the Stream" (*Linquan gaozhi*), a collection of writings on Chinese painting by Guo Xi.[34]

The name Guo Xi (Kuo Hsi) might have appeared familiar to Stevens.[35] Indeed, he probably recalled mention of him in *Painting in the Far East* as "one of the greatest of all Chinese landscape painters" (128). Of this master living almost a thousand years before, Binyon notes that he published discourses on landscape, in which he "insists on [the 'far-off effect'] as necessary to unit." "The painter must have varied experience, must build on incessant observation, he says, but above all things he must seize essentials and discard the trivial." Due to his influence, according to Binyon, the "Sung landscape is built up of tones rather than of lines. . . . The artists worked almost entirely in monochrome; and they chose for subject all that is most elemental and august in nature" (128–29).

Of this work, unmistakably Guo Xi's "The Noble Features of the Forest and the Stream," Fenollosa remarks in *Epochs* that "with the exception of some relatively dry portions, it is one of the greatest essays of the world." To this he adds, "It proves to us what an integral part landscape had come to play in Chinese culture and imagination; and it shows us just why Zen symbolism of nature gave such a splendid insight into characteristic forms" (*Epochs*, 2:11). A year before anyone was able to take advantage of *Epochs*, which presented extracts from Guo Xi along with the above comment, Stevens had already mused on a different version of this work in a newspaper. Sure enough, he was fascinated by Guo Xi's insights, which strangely reflected his own. In his letter of 20 August 1911 to Elsie, he called the piece "a very interesting document," and to show his new discovery he enclosed the clipping of the newspaper's editorial note.[36]

If Binyon's summary of Guo Xi's treatise somehow failed to impress Stevens, the August 1911 newspaper translation of it apparently succeeded in doing so. As the editorial note stressed, the Song master "expressed once [and] for all the guiding sentiment of Chinese landscape painting." The aim of the landscape painter, according to Guo Xi, is to enable those who wish to "enjoy a life amidst the luxuries of nature" but "are debarred from indulging in such pleasures" to "behold the grandeur of nature without stepping out of their houses."[37] The passage seemed to be addressed to Stevens, who had for years tried in vain, as James Longenbach notes, to find "aesthetic satisfaction" within "professional security,"[38] and who had longed to be able to bring to life the spirit of nature in his own art.

It is easy to imagine Stevens's joy over meeting his own mind in an ancient treatise. He may well have wondered why an eleventh-century Chinese artist should articulate his inclinations so well. This poses a query that has to be looked into in subsequent chapters along with related matters such as why Chinese art should flourish in modernism. Suffice it to say here that Stevens was not the only modernist who confronted this enigma. W. B. Yeats defines the perception in a different context—when he praises the Bengali poet Rabindranath Tagore: "A whole people, a whole civilization, immeasurably strange to us, seems to have been taken up into this imagination; and yet we are not moved because of its strangeness, but because we have met our own image."[39]

One of the arguments emphasized throughout this study is that a single modernist poet's appreciation of Chinese art is best understood in the broader context of modernist appreciation of Chinese aesthetic as a whole. Pound and Stevens, with their fruitful reactions to Chinese art around 1910, offer two illustrations. Marianne Moore's case will reinforce this point. In late March 1909, when Stevens was under the impact of *Painting in the Far East,* "pok[ing] around more or less in the dust of Asia" (*L,* 138) in New York and Pound was musing on Binyon's lectures on "Art and Thought in East and West" in London, their fellow modernist Moore, then a senior at Bryn Mawr College, was attracted to the Oriental art exhibits of the University of Pennsylvania Museum.

On 27 March Moore went on a tour of the University of Pennsylvania (Penn) Museum with Professor George A. Barton and his Oriental history class. Though she was a biology major, Moore took Professor Barton's class in Oriental history as a free elective in the fall of 1908. The Bryn Mawr 1908–9 class lists indicate that her group of twelve students met at 11 A.M. in Room C, Taylor Hall, Monday through Friday.[40] The course offered is described in the catalogue as treating "in broad outlines the history and civilization of the classical orient: . . . Egyptians, Babylonians, Assyrians, Phoenicians, Hebrews, Hittites, Sabaeans, and Persians."[41] Dr. Barton's lectures are said to have been "illustrated by archaeological specimens and by photographs."[42] In the spring semester of 1909 Professor Barton took his Oriental history class to the Penn Museum for a tour of its extraordinary archaeological collections. By then Penn was claimed to have "taken its place among the world's leading centers of Semitic scholarship, a place it still retains."[43] Barton certainly had taken good advantage of its resources by way of using photographs and slides. Over a decade later, in 1922, he would become a distinguished member of the Penn faculty.[44] According to the Bryn Mawr records, Moore was not enrolled in Dr. Barton's class in the spring of 1909.[45] Nevertheless, her strong interest in the subject must have prompted her to ask special permission to go with the group. As her letter home, dated 28 March 1909, reveals, Moore not only joined Professor Barton's class that day but also enjoyed the tour more than any other student. "It was the most stimulating adventure I've had for a long time," she writes. "Many of the class strayed away and yawned and whispered 'Oh! Were you ever so bored.' I found everything, however, to occupy me."[46]

The tour was of course intended as a special learning experience—a walk through the ancient history of the "classical orient" illustrated by archaeological specimens. However, in those early years (1900–1915) a walk through the Penn Museum's Egyptian, Babylonian, and Assyrian collections would unavoidably bring attention to its Chinese artifacts. Six years later, in 1915, when the Harrison Rotunda (now familiarly known as the Chinese Rotunda) was erected, its large circular gallery would be given to the Chinese collection. And seventeen years later, in 1926, when the Coxe Wing was added to the museum building, Egypt would likewise get the magnificent Penn home it deserved. However, in late March 1909 when everything in the museum was still crowded in a relatively small area, it was most unlikely that Moore had spent half a day viewing the Near East collections without having noticed some gorgeous Chinese objects.

Since the sole purpose of the tour was to explore the museum's ancient Near East collections, it is not surprising that in her letter home Moore keeps admiring things Egyptian, Babylonian, and Assyrian.

After providing a detailed description of Egyptian carvings, she never-theless refers to some enamels, "painted perhaps of lotuses" in "ideal unrealizable variety": "Blues and greens, oranges, gold, crimson, queer lavenders, all sorts of colors, and not fumbled—Most of the strings were carefully assorted all of one color; the stones cut the same way or the strings twisted the same way. I lost my head completely."[47]

The opening of the passage is strikingly reminiscent of "Colors," a 1909 verbalization of Chinese painting. While there is no way of proving that Moore had certain Chinese objects in mind, her delin-eation of the enamels unmistakably reveals a sensibility analogous to Stevens's. It is this sensitivity to unusual combinations of colors and light that would later stimulate Moore to respond more creatively to Chinese art. Indeed, it was with this sensitivity that she produced some of her most painterly lines in "Nine Nectarines": "Fuzzless through slender crescent leaves / of green or blue or / both, in the Chinese style" (CPMM, 29).

On that day Moore was also enchanted by some amber-colored gems and lapis lazuli talismans. In her letter home she reports: "The jewels took my eye especially—yellow gold the color of a book edge—fine filigree work and gold mops and bumps, smoothed off and set in de-signs and inlaid lapis lazuli (in the shape of a lion rampant)."[48] An object on view surfaces in "A Talisman," a poem of 1912, in which an ornament is metamorphosed into a seagull: "Of lapis lazuli; / A scarab of the sea, / With wings spread."[49] Museum catalogues verify that Moore's descrip-tions manifestly represent certain specimens from Maxwell Sommer-ville's glyptic collection.[50] As Professor of Glyptology, Sommerville was better known for his collection of more than four thousand gems, amu-lets, and talismans from all over the world than for his "Buddhist Tem-ple." The two collections he curated had been overhauled and placed back on exhibition by early March 1909.[51] It was highly possible for Moore to have visited the whole museum in 1909, since it consisted of only a U-shaped building with two floors of galleries. Indeed, Barton might have encouraged his class to take a look at the refurbished glyp-tic collection. Once in the gallery for Sommerville's gems, they would have moved on to his Buddhist images.

It was no small privilege for Moore to receive an introduction to "Oriental History" under an instructor who was well on his way to a permanent place as one of the most prolific of American scholars in As-syrian and Hebrew studies.[52] By early 1909 Barton had published no less than half a dozen scholarly works.[53] He could have begun expanding his research beyond the "classical orient," the fruit of which manifested itself in *The Religions of the World* (1917).

The Religions of the World's small compass of some four hundred pages does not permit detailed treatment, but chapter 11, "The Religions of China," unfolds a sensible picture of the development of Chinese outlooks. On two key issues Barton shows his shrewd vision. In the first place, he rightly considers the Western assumption of a connection between the Chinese and the Sumerians of Babylonia or the Elamites "far from convincing." For him it is much more "probable that the Chinese developed out of the Mongolian stock in the region where they still live."[54] By contrast, in *Epochs* Fenollosa makes no effort to refute the so-called Western origin of the Chinese "in the direction of the Caspian" (1:8), and his ambiguity might have misled Gaudier and Pound into saying, "The black-haired men . . . wandered through the pass of Khotan into the valley of the YELLOW RIVER" (*GB,* 22). Another illustration of Barton's sensibility is his view that "Confucianism, Taoism, and Buddhism are not mutually exclusive religions, and in China millions think it better to gain what benefits they may from being on good terms with all three."[55] Not many scholars of Barton's day share this insight.

A look at the volume's bibliography confirms Barton's familiarity with works on Chinese civilization prior to 1909: James Legge, *The Religions of China* (1881); E. Wilson, *Chinese Literature* (1900); R. K. Douglas, *Confucianism and Taoism* (1900); H. A. Giles, *A History of Chinese Literature* (1901) and *China and the Chinese* (1902); J. J. M. De Groot, *The Religious Systems of China,* 6 vols. (1892–1910); T. Kudo, *The Ethics of Confucius* (1904); and E. H. Parker, *China and Religion* (1905). The range of his inquiry, coupled with the dates of most of the works listed, seems to suggest that as early as 1909 Barton was already devoting part of his time to the study of Chinese religions.[56] If that was the case, Moore may well have been prompted on that day to compare Far Eastern and Near Eastern art objects and even make a whirlwind tour of Sommerville's collections remaining open for the last weeks.

Two other circumstances of the period corroborate the presumption that Moore's initial brush with Chinese art coincided with Stevens's. The first had to do with the daughters of Dr. George Norcross, the minister in her hometown of Carlisle, Pennsylvania. Elizabeth, the oldest daughter, was engaged to an attorney in Portland. Prior to her wedding in December 1908, she kept sending her sisters, Mary and Louise, pretty things through the Chinese Trading Company, which the Moores would view first and admire. In January 1908, as Mary Norcross reported to Marianne at Bryn Mawr, Elizabeth had sent home three camphor-wood chests "made in nests so that one fits inside the next larger and so on." At Mary's request, Elizabeth had also included a teakwood tray with "carving on the two sides" for her to save as a birthday present for Mrs. Moore.[57] Once this beautiful artwork arrived in the Moore apartment, it became a treasured token. To this day, it remains in perfect condition in the Moore Room at the Rosenbach Museum and Library in Philadelphia (fig. 8). The simple fact that for over six decades—from the Carlisle years through the Greenwich Village, Brooklyn, and Manhattan periods—this Chinese tray never parted company with Moore is valid proof of her passion for Chinese art.

Another factor that should provide clues to Marianne Moore's long concealed early contact with Chinese art was her summer 1911 visit to the British Museum. While in London Marianne and her mother stayed at 22 Upper Bedford Place in Bloomsbury. In late July they spent several days touring the British Museum galleries. In the summer of 1911, one recalls, the British Museum Exhibition of Chinese and Japanese Paintings reached its heyday. Each weekend hundreds of people went to the museum especially for that show. It is quite impossible that the event did not make any impression on the Moores.

One way to track down the Moores' possible visit to the exhibition is to check the visitors' books of the Print Room, which Ezra Pound and Dorothy Shakespear frequented a little later in 1912–13. Located in the White Wing, in what is now the Late-Medieval Room (Room 42), and adjacent to the large Eastern gallery for the exhibition, now divided into Rooms 43–45, the Print Room of 1884–1914 served both as the office of the Department of Prints and Drawings and as its reference area.[58] On receipt of a ticket of permission to the Print Room a visitor was required to first sign the visitors' book and then specify in writing which prints or drawings she or he wished to consult. As a rule, Binyon and other staff of the department would rotate serving as the duty officer of the day. The Print Room Visitors Book, vol. 21, designates that thirty-one visitors signed in on Thursday, 27 July, Marianne Moore and her mother among them. Marianne, who signed both her name and her mother's, gave their address as "Carlisle, Pennsylvania, USA" (fig. 9).

While the request form the Moores handed in has not survived and so there is no way of knowing what reserve material they examined, it is certain that they walked past the Exhibition of Chinese and Japa-

8. Marianne Moore's Chinese carved wooden tray. (Courtesy, Rosenbach Museum and Library, Philadelphia)

9. Marianne Moore, signature in the Print Room visitors book (tenth signature). © The British Museum. (Courtesy, British Museum, London)

nese Paintings twice on that particular day—on their way to the Print Room and on their way out of it. They might have been to the Print Room on a previous day to request a ticket of permission. Should that be the case, they ought to have walked past the exhibition four times.

It is unthinkable that Marianne and her mother would have walked past a widely publicized, enormous exhibition twice (or four times) without having glanced at a few of its most imposing pictures. They certainly lingered for a moment either before entering the Print Room or while retreating from it. They would have been attracted to the show especially because many of its pictures catered to their idiosyncratic tastes. The exhibition was extraordinarily strong in flower-and-bird pictures, to which Binyon had provided very enticing labels: *Magnolia, Peonies, and Pirus Japonica; Lotuses and White Egret; Wild Geese, Lotuses and Rushes; Fowls, Bamboos and Flowering Trees; Willow and Stream, with Sheld-Duck, Mynah and Woodpecker; Pheasant and Plum Tree by a Mountain Stream; Narcissus Flowering by a Rock; Paradise-Flycatchers and Flowers; Roses and Jasmine; Chrysanthemums; Cormorants;* and so on (*Guide*, 21–30). Of these pictures a reviewer remarks, "The great Chinese masters had the secret of representing flowers, no less than animals, as if they had a human significance and dignity."[59] Needless to say, as a group they would appeal to Marianne and her mother.

For many visitors the greater charms of the exhibition were, nonetheless, its pictures of animals, the real as well as the imagined. *A Boy-Rishi Riding on a Goat, Tethered Horses, The Hundred Stags,* and *Tiger* (*Guide*, 20–25) should be among those likely to have drawn the Moores. What would have been of most interest to Marianne would probably be pictures of Chinese mythical creatures. The reviewer who admired Chinese pictures of flowers and birds lavished even higher praise on Chinese pictures of imagined animals: "The Chinese have a curious power of making imaginary animals look as true to life as real ones."[60] To verify this statement visitors only had to see the scrolls *Procession with a Ch'ilin [Qilin] at a Temple in a Mountain Gorge* and *A Ch'ilin [Qilin] Bringing Flowers to a Lady* (*Guide*, 26, 28). Marianne would have paused to read about the creature's mythological lore should she have stopped in front of one of them. The *qilin* or kylin unicorn, a note by Binyon indicates, "is a fabulous animal, emblematic of good," whose "coming portends happiness" (28).

It may appear a bit odd though that Moore does not explicitly refer to Far Eastern art in the British Museum in her letters home from London. To answer this question, it is useful first to repeat what Linda

Leavell has said about Moore: She was "an intensely private person, 'armored' to some extent even among those persons closest to her."[61] Secondly, Moore described her tours around the British Museum only in one surviving letter,[62] and it is quite impossible for her to include everything that had impressed her in that single letter. Years later, she wrote "An Egyptian Pulled Glass Bottle in the Shape of a Fish" based on an object that she might have seen in the British Museum but that she never mentions in any of her letters. Lastly, Chinese and Japanese names are difficult for a Westerner to remember. Apollinaire, for one, acknowledges this predicament in his review of a similar show in Paris.[63] Moore would have had trouble giving the name of the *qilin* back in 1911 even if she was impressed by images of the creature in the British Museum.

Two decades later, in her 1931 "Nine Nectarines," Moore would pay tribute to "the nectarine-loving kylin / of pony appearance—the long- / tailed or the tailless" (*CPMM*, 30). While composing the lines "It was a Chinese / who imagined this masterpiece" (30), I do not think she had in mind the artist who designed the *qilin* for the porcelain. Rather, she was admiring the Chinese who invented the *qilin* that had since inspired varied imitations, including those on the porcelain as well as those she probably recalled seeing elsewhere.

The many dragons in the British Museum 1910–12 exhibition, as noted above, made a strong impression on beholders. They would have captured the eye of Moore. A signal example of this was the hanging scroll *Three Men Watching the Birth of a Dragon,* accompanied by a note to this effect: "The Dragon, conceived of as the genius of mist and water, producing storms and rain, came to be associated in the Taoist imagination with the power of the fluid and free spirit. . . . The scene illustrates the legend, told of more than one Chinese master, of a dragon painted with such force and truth that it sprang into actual life" (Binyon, *Guide,* 26–27). Nonetheless, to most visitors what would have appeared more imposing was perhaps the long handscroll *Arhat and Apsara,* or *Sixteen Luohans Crossing the Sea* (22), in which one of the Buddhist saints is shown riding a dragon and another a *qilin.* Both mythical animals portrayed exhibit the same kind of naturalness and vigor as in beautifully painted real animals. Just as she made a physical drawing of "an Assyrian leopard with pig eyes,"[64] Moore could have made mental sketches of a dragon and a *qilin* unicorn. The dragon later became a popular subject for Moore. In "The Plumet Basilisk," a poem of 1932, she would describe dragons as painted "As by a Chinese brush" and with "eight green / bands" (*CPMM,* 22); and in "O to Be a Dragon," a poem of 1959, she would express a wish to be a dragon. Her personal copies of books about the dragon—*Dragons* and *Animals in Paintings from Asia*—are further evidence of her interest in the mythical animal.[65] Although Moore probably did not start studying the Chinese dragon until 1923, her first image of this creature may well have been in the British Museum.

Moore's early brush with Chinese art prepared her to engage with it more fervently and more fruitfully in the crucial decade of 1915–24. Her arrival on the New York literary scene coincided with the peak of a vogue for European avant-garde art and the peak of a vogue for Chinese art. Glen MacLeod in *Wallace Stevens and Modern Art* and Linda Leavell in *Marianne Moore and the Visual Arts* have respectively treated the role Stevens's and Moore's interest in modern art played in their experimental poetry. As both poets are shown to have developed a habit of attending museums and reading art reviews, it was possible for them to have kept abreast not only of the latest European painting and sculpture but also of the newly arrived Chinese art.

In 1916–18, the most experimental period for both Stevens and Moore, the American craze for China was in full swing. Among the widely publicized Chinese art shows of 1916 was one largely drawn from the collections of J. P. Morgan, the Duveen brothers in London, the Worch Company of Paris, and the New York dealer C. T. Loo, installed in the newly erected Harrison Rotunda of the University of Pennsylvania Museum. A broad range of porcelains, jade vessels, sculpture, and ink paintings was represented, including two stone reliefs said to be among the six commissioned during the lifetime of the emperor who founded the Tang dynasty.[66] Significantly, this exhibition was recorded in a photograph by the noted artist Charles Sheeler, who two years later would document the modern art in the Walter Arensberg apartment in a set of photographs.[67]

A second extensive exhibition of Chinese art was organized in March 1916 by S. C. Bosch Reitz, curator of Far Eastern art, for the Metropolitan Museum of Art (Met). Drawn from the collections of Charles Freer of Detroit, Howard Mansfield of New York,[68] and others, the exhibition prompted detailed comment in an article—"Keramic Wares of the Sung Dynasty" by Rose Sickler Williams—prefacing Bosch Reitz's *Catalogue of an Exhibition of Early Chinese Pottery and Sculpture*. The supportive review states, "[N]othing is more cheering in the study of art than these opportunities to reject early preference and to find new loves companioning the old."[69] And it concludes by predicting "in the near future a public hot on the trail of Sung and Tang."[70]

Yet another exhibition of art was being shown in New York at the Bourgeois Gallery in March 1916, which included Chinese, Japanese, and Persian paintings as well as Han and Song Chinese pottery and sculpture. Its prize was a large scroll painting signed by the great Song master Li Tang, described in *The New York Times* as showing a sage and his disciples on a mountainside in a landscape diversified by trees, streams, and waterfalls.[71]

American passion for Chinese art continued to soar in 1918, when about a dozen Chinese art shows were staged in the New York area alone. March of that year witnessed three of them: the Chinese art objects brought to America by a certain Kain Tong-Wong at the Anderson Gallery, the Chinese paintings from the collection of V. G. Simkhovitch at the Century Association, and the Ton-Ying collection of Chinese art at the Anderson Gallery.[72] These were followed by two exhibitions at the Metropolitan Museum of Art—old Chinese paintings in April and Chinese ceramics in August—and one at the Brooklyn Museum of Art—Chinese wall vases in August.[73] In November was the exhibition of Chinese portraits and potteries at the Montross Gallery, and in December the exhibition of Chinese paintings from the collection of E. Josenhans of Paris at the American Art Galleries.[74]

The booming exhibitions of Chinese art in this period sparked a considerable number of reviews and illustrated articles in newspapers. Their coverage was frequently coupled with the coverage of modern art in town. By juxtaposing the two trends, critics intended to allude to Chinese art as one of the influences on the growth of avant-garde art on both sides of the Atlantic.[75] This comparison could not have escaped the attentive eye of Stevens or Moore. If they had to miss most of the shows, they were at least aware of their proliferation. In fact, Stevens probably saw the Bourgeois Gallery show in March 1916, for the hilltop view of its centerpiece anticipated the setting of his play of that year, *Three Travelers Watch a Sunrise.* He is more likely to have attended the Exhibition of Early Chinese Pottery and Sculpture at the Metropolitan Museum. An object on view—a pear-shaped vase with three figures painted on it—seems to have offered a motif for *Three Travelers,* in which the three Chinese are said to be "three figures / Painted on porcelain" (*OP,* 153), and another object—a Song dynasty bowl—might have occasioned his manuscript poem "Bowl":[76] "For what emperor / Was this bowl of Earth designed? / Here are more things / Than on any bowl of the Sungs" (*OP,* 24).

By exploring Chinese art, Stevens of course benefited more than just borrowing a few motifs. After all, he was primarily interested in comparing Chinese ancients to European and American modernists — their shared vision of change, multiple perspectives, and inclination to transform "painting into a kind of writing."[77] In *Three Travelers* Stevens has the first Chinese say, "There are as many points of view / From which to regard her / As there are sides to a round bottle" (*OP*, 156). The notion expressed is traceable to the vase with three figures in the Metropolitan Museum as well as to Binyon — his description of the *Eight Views* (*Painting,* 133) and summary of Guo Xi's dictum: "Those who study flower-painting take a single stalk and put it into a deep hole, and then examine it from above, thus seeing it from all points of view" (*Flight,* 48–49).[78] Indeed, it should also recall, as Earl Miner notes, Hiroshige's *Eight Views of Omi* and Hokusai's *Thirty-six Views of Fuji.*[79]

Similarly, as Jeanne Heuving has shown, around 1917 Moore was undergoing a transformation in her poetics.[80] Her adoption of multiple perspectives in the period was at least partly due to her increased interchanges with Chinese art. She might have attended the Metropolitan Museum exhibition of 1916. A trace of this is in her poem of the year, "Critics and Connoisseurs," in which she uses "Certain Ming / products" as a perceived detail to illustrate what she means by "conscious fastidiousness." For her these products are "well enough in their way," but not as good as spontaneous efforts such as a child's "attempt to make an imperfectly bal- / lasted animal stand up" or "to make a pup / eat his meat from the plate" (*CPMM,* 38). Moore's selection of the example is remarkably fitting, for *The New York Times* review of the exhibition also suggests that "the elaborated Ming product" was distinguished from early Chinese wares by its exquisiteness and lack of spontaneity. Gaudier and Pound's assertion that after the Han and Tang, the Chinese "found the Ming and found artistic ruin and sterility" (*GB,* 23) is an overstatement. It is more sensible to acknowledge the Ming products' fine workmanship while criticizing their overdone fastidiousness, as Moore does in her 1916 poem.

A photograph from a de Zayas Gallery catalogue of Chinese jades, bronzes, stones, and pottery in the Moore library seems to suggest that Moore went to de Zayas Gallery for that show in March 1920. De Zayas Gallery was known for its modern art. In December of that year it displayed Matisse's *The Blue Nude,* which inspired William Carlos Williams to write his famous review "A Matisse."[81] Thus it is clear that the two currents — avant-garde art and Chinese art — were in those days running side by side. They were often promoted and enjoyed by artists and poets at odds with foregoing norms.

As characteristic of the trend, *The New York Times* art review of 11 March 1923 likened the Postimpressionists displayed at the Durand-Ruel Galleries to the Chinese masters shown at the Metropolitan Museum, calling the former "The Independents" and the latter "Other Independents." Of the latter show it was said that great care was exercised in arranging the collection to give the greatest advantage for study and comparison; the Song landscapes filled different alcoves, figure paintings were kept together, and flower and animal pieces were given special corners.[82] Moore toured the Met's exhibition of Chinese paintings at least twice. Her friend Monroe Wheeler was with her during her first visit. Both of them were enchanted by the way the Chinese portrayed animals. Gazing at a falcon, Moore reports, the future director of exhibitions and publications at the Museum of Modern Art exclaimed: "It's like hammered silver" (*SLMM*, 194).

By the early 1920s Moore had studied Chinese objects on display and in print with such care that she seemed capable of not only making distinctions between products of different periods but identifying particular Chinese colors from those of other cultures.[83] As mentioned previously, in March 1909 she had "lost [her] head completely," beholding the outlandish colors of ancient Egyptian or Babylonian objects at the Penn Museum: "Blues and greens, oranges, gold, crimson, queer lavenders."[84] A few years later, between 1915 and 1924, she was admiring Chinese colors with greater zest. Yes, Pound and Stevens both have responded ardently to Chinese colors. But Moore has done so more expertly; her early poetry and prose distinguish between gradations of Chinese pigments. By remarking on the "imperial floor-coverings of coach- / wheel yellow" in "Critics and Connoisseurs" (*CPMM*, 38), she has vividly presented a particular Chinese yellow, the yellow of the Ming imperial robes and drapes. And by referring to "the Chinese vermilion of / the poincianas" in "People's Surroundings" (56), a poem of 1922, she has identified a popular Chinese red—the bridal red or the brilliant red of Chinese lanterns and walls. Furthermore, Moore is capable of seeing Chinese colors as expressive of aesthetic concepts. In her 1923 review of H. D.'s *Hymen*, she admires Chinese yellows in the same breath with H. D.'s sense of color associated with ideas. "In this instinctive ritual of beauty," she remarks, "one is reminded of the supernatural yellows of China—of an aesthetic consciousness which values simultaneously, ivory and the chiseled ivory of speech" (*PrMM*, 81).

In contrast to Pound, who admired Shang-Zhou bronzes and Tang landscape paintings, and Stevens, who preferred "the refinement of Sung [Song] society," Moore showed a passion for the artifacts of late imperial China—the Yuan, Ming, and Qing products—throughout her long career. This preference was perhaps due to her early involvement with the Arts and Crafts movement in America.[85] In her early poetry Moore does occasionally make general comments on Chinese national character. Her 1920 poem "England," for example, lists the "sublimated wisdom of China" along with "Egyptian discernment" as some of the qualities of "noted superiority" (*CPMM*, 47). Moreover, in her 1921 "The Labor of Hercules," she speaks of the notion that "the Oriental is not immoral" as one of a series of fixed values "one keeps on knowing" (53). Apart from these few exceptions, her initial interest in China seemed to center on decorative art she had viewed in museums and galleries. In "Picking and Choosing" (1920), for instance, she praises the English stage designer and critic Gordon Craig for being outspoken in naming particularities like "Chinese cherry" as what he delights in (45). In describing a wealthy estate in "People's Surroundings" (1922), she names "Chinese carved glass" along with "old Persian velvet" in her listing of things elegant in its garden (55). Last but not least, in "Bowls" (1923), she expresses as much delight in the sight of lawn bowling as in the sight of "Chinese lacquer-carving" (59). Apparently for her both the game and the art demand meticulous skill and attention.

Just as she has a habit of reflecting on "exotic animals and other 'things' about which the reader is not likely to have preconceptions,"[86] she tends to turn to the more obscure for quotations, often without bothering to indicate their actual sources. One example of this is her quotation from a certain "Tu Muh" in "Well Moused, Lion," a review of Stevens's *Harmonium*. With an unerring eye, in that review she has identified the Chinese influences in Stevens's first book. "In his positiveness, aplomb, and verbal security," she observes, Stevens "has the mind and the method of China" (*PrMM*, 95).[87] However, a quotation in that review remains without a definite source: "One feels, however, an achieved remoteness as in Tu Muh's lyric criticism: 'Powerful is the painting . . . and high is it hung on the spotless wall in the lofty hall of your mansion.'" (91). Nothing to the effect of her quotation can be found in the published works of the Tang poet Du Mu (803–52) (*Fanchuan wenji* in twenty volumes). A letter Moore wrote on 5 May 1923 reveals that the passage was taken from a manuscript poem she saw at the Metropolitan Museum (*SLMM*, 197). As a loan piece to the Met with no record, this could have been the hand of a fifteenth-to-sixteenth-century art critic whose name was also pronounced Du Mu. In *An Introduction to the Study of Chinese Painting,* Arthur Waley cites the art critic Du Mu (1459–1525) as recounting how the Yuan painter Wang Meng (1308–85) "covered one of his walls with silk and began painting a huge picture of Mount T'ai, adding a touch whenever he felt in the right humour." When the painting was finished, there was a heavy snowstorm. So powerful was the effect that Wang Meng decided to change the view into a snow scene. He "fastened his brush to a small bow and twanged to a shower of white dots on to the silk—in fact, created a miniature snowstorm."[88]

Chinese art arrived in England and America at roughly the same moment, a moment when international modernism was gathering force and innovative poets such as Pound, Moore, and Stevens had a great yearning for absorbing aesthetic "otherness" from the East. In what manner, then, did Chinese art communicate Confucian ideals, the Dao, and Chan? How did it serve the modernist poets as an initiator, an eye-opener to new ways of defining their poetics? The three chapters in part 2 will explore these questions.

PART 2

Remaking

Culture

THREE

Pound and
Pictures of
Confucian
Ideals

POUND'S EARLIEST reference to Confucius, to the best of my knowledge, occurs in his letter of 2 October 1913 to Dorothy Shakespear: "I'm
stocked up with K'ung fu Tsze [Confucius], and Men Tsze [Mencius],
etc." (L/DS, 264). His letter to his father, dated 22 September 1915, suggests that from 1913 through 1915 he relied chiefly on M. G. Pauthier's
Les quatre livres (The Four Books) to study Confucianism: "I wonder if
there is a decent translation of Confucius. I've Pauthier's french version. NOT the odes, but the 'Four Books.'"[1] In any event, Pound's encounter with Pauthier's Confucius predates Allen Upward's and Fenollosa's.[2] This chronology by no means invalidates dating his earliest
exchanges with Confucianism from 1909 to 1912. About that time he
was initiated into Confucian ideals via the British Museum collection
of Chinese paintings and via Binyon's illustrated publications, slide lectures, and conversations.

It is useful to emphasize here the argumentative value of the visual.
W. J. T. Mitchell reminds us in Picture Theory that "people have always
known, at least since Moses denounced the Golden Calf, that images
were dangerous, that they can captivate the onlooker and steal the soul."
Yet today not a few of us are skeptical about art's ability to narrate and
convince. The skepticism, according to Mitchell, stems from "a confusion between differences of medium and differences in meaning." We
suppose that the visual arts lend spatial and static features to verbal communication, that arguments and ideas are the proper domain of language. As Mitchell rightly points out, "neither of these 'gifts' is really
the exclusive property of their donors: paintings can tell stories, make
arguments, and signify abstract ideas; words can describe or embody
static, spatial states of affairs."[3]

To appreciate the persuasive gift of Chinese art transferred to the West, we need think only of the *Admonitions of the Instructress to Court Ladies,* a monument that confronted Pound and other visitors to the British Museum 1910–12 Exhibition of Chinese and Japanese Paintings. An early copy of a long handscroll by the fourth-century painter Gu Kaizhi, it depicts Han palace activities by juxtaposing nine individual episodes from a tract by the third-century poet Zhang Hua.[4] All the subjects treated are said to be drawn from the Han palace tutor Ban Zhao.[5] At the right side of each panel is inscribed in Chinese characters a quotation from Zhang Hua. Unfortunately, the quotation for the first surviving panel has been torn away with three lost panels. Although in this painting, as in numerous other Chinese paintings, text and picture are presented side by side, it is generally the latter that first arrests the beholder's eye. This occurs even to Chinese viewers, because to them as to those outside Chinese culture it is the visual images that make strikingly visible the palace tutor's anecdotes for promoting Confucian ideals.

Consider, for example, the opening panel, "Lady Feng and the Bear" (fig. 10).[6] The image presented makes obvious how Lady Feng throws herself in the path and shields the wild beast from the emperor. The structure of the composition—with the alarmed emperor and two pan-

10. After Gu Kaizhi (ca. 345–406), 7th century, "Lady Feng and the Bear," a scene from *Admonitions of the Instructress to Court Ladies.* © The British Museum. (Courtesy, British Museum, London)

icked ladies on the right, Lady Feng and two soldiers in the left center, and the raging animal at the lower left—brings into the open the context, circumstance, and atmosphere of the classic episode. It invites our eyes to glance from the right to the left and finally to focus on the fierce encounter. Here we are pinched into Lady Feng's gaze, gesture, and bold stance, which combine admirably to spell out her extraordinary courage. Her heroic act becomes all the more striking when compared to the attitudes of other figures in the scene—the emperor's fright, the other ladies' panic, and one of the soldiers' horrified look. Words cannot express all this in simultaneity.

From their attires, headdresses, and distinct outward demeanor we can tell that the male figure on the right is a lord, whereas all other figures are his subordinates—the armed men are his guards and the women dressed in rich clothing with fashionable coiffures are his wives or concubines. Without the aid of words, however, we cannot make out the lord's exact status. Nor are we certain that the monstrous creature is a bear. These details are nevertheless not important. The aim of art, according to Gu Kaizhi, is to "transmit the spirit" (*chuan shen*). So long as the inner spirit of the subject is communicated, matters such as its likeness to nature can be overlooked.[7] In this particular illustration the psyche praised is Lady Feng's loyalty/heroism. This theme is explicit enough, although its underlying value will perplex many Western viewers. For them, the lord should come forward to protect Lady Feng rather than the other way round. Walter Benjamin would use the expression "shock" to describe the bewilderment.[8] Martin Heidegger would call it a "thrust," and Gianni Vattimo would term it "disorientation."[9] From these theorists' standpoint, a viewer's perplexity signifies his or her opening up to a new code of value. It signals, in this case, initiation into a Confucian standard in its authentic social-cultural context.

In a similar manner, the next panel brings into light the psychological and humanistic circumstance in which "Lady Ban [Ban Jieyu] Refuses to Ride" (fig. 11). It makes present, before our eyes, nuances of duty and sensibility crucial to recognition of social value and personality in ancient China. For Gu Kaizhi a painting must capture the inner essence of its subjects by bringing into the open the interaction between figures.[10] Significantly, in this scene the imaginary conversation between the emperor and Lady Ban—his invitation and her refusal—is implied by animated facial expressions and gesticulations. Even though we cannot hear their remarks, we miss little of what they express by the

11. After Gu Kaizhi (ca. 345–406), 7th century, "Lady Ban Refuses to Ride," a scene from *Admonitions of the Instructress to Court Ladies.* © The British Museum. (Courtesy, British Museum, London)

meeting of their eyes. The emperor, whose torso is unrevealed, seems to be imploring Lady Ban to join him in the procession, an honor otherwise monopolized by the lady already seated by his side. Lady Ban, on the other hand, appears to be stating with perfect justice that it is her obligation to stay behind. The emperor's disappointment is suggested by a frown, whereas the seated lady's complacency is hinted at by a grin. The juxtaposition of the emperor and his ladies at cross-purposes highlights a moral issue confronting a ruler: whether it is appropriate to be with favorite ladies on public duty.

From the way Lady Ban's profile is rendered, a figure almost identical with Lady Feng in the previous panel, we can safely assume that she is meant to be regarded as another role model for court ladies. Her refusal, therefore, must be taken as a bold and righteous act. As for why her refusal is morally correct, Lady Ban seems to be offering an explanation, which the picture does not elaborate. Here we see the need for curatorial notes, what J. Hillis Miller calls "necessary 'signposts.'" Indeed, as Miller observes, "picture cannot be understood without accompanying words."[11] His assertion explains why an unidentified calligrapher has inscribed each panel with a corresponding quotation from Zhang Hua. In the Lady Ban scene the inscription reads *Banjie you ci ge huan tong nian fu qi bu huai fang yan lu yuan,* or in Binyon's words, Lady Ban "[refuses] the Emperor's invitation to ride with him in his palanquin. 'In days of old,' she is reported to have answered, 'only ministers rode beside their monarch'" (*Painting,* 40).[12] So it is a sense of decorum and duty that has prompted Lady Ban to turn down an offer other ladies would be only too glad to accept. Once this meaning gets across, the viewer is introduced into another Confucian tenet: An individual's duty is to the public interest of the empire rather than the private interest of the emperor.

In the other panels we get glimpses of routine activities in the Han inner court, the so-called imperial daily life scenes. We may see court ladies carrying out their toilet (fig. 3), or the lord and his consort having a conversation in a bedchamber (fig. 12), or the lord and his consort spending time with princes and princesses (fig. 13).[13] It is not unusual that a viewer fails to identify the group as an imperial family circle. His or her inability to do so nonetheless serves the pictures' purposes all the better, for the imperial household portrayed is intended to be recognized, first and foremost, as a family in harmony—husband and wife sincere to each other (*cheng*), parents loving their children (*ci*), women mindful of their conduct (*li*), and youngsters acting in accord with nature (*ziran*). Like the pictorial narratives in the first two panels, these

12. After Gu Kaizhi (ca. 345–406), 7th century, "Bedchamber Conversation," a scene from *Admonitions of the Instructress to Court Ladies.* © The British Museum. (Courtesy, British Museum, London)

13. After Gu Kaizhi (ca. 345–406), 7th century, "Family Group," a scene from *Admonitions of the Instructress to Court Ladies*. © The British Museum. (Courtesy, British Museum, London)

scenes make an argument; they do not specify the identities of their figures but rather testify to the virtue of devotion to establishing order within the family and maintaining good husband-wife, parent-child, lord-servant relationships.

In discussing the relation between picture (illustration) and text (illustrated), Miller argues that the two media each "may bring out disturbing elements the other hides" (*Illustration*, 130). The *Admonitions* scroll seems illustrative of this point in the way one medium brings out what the other medium hides. The "Toilet Scene" referred to above clarifies only the cultural setting for the quotation, "All can adorn their faces, none can adorn her heart" (Binyon, *Guide*, 14). What it hides is the implication of the imagery that is made explicit by the latter half of the quotation. For non-Chinese beholders, nonetheless, what texts conceal and pictures make present, the so-called authentic visual representations of ancient Chinese rites and exploits, are especially valuable. Without their aid people in the West can hardly be initiated into Chinese modes of thought. Furthermore, unusual visual details tend to sustain in memory for years or even decades. Those who have seen the British Museum *Admonitions* may forget the labels attached to its panels but remember striking images that illustrated how the ancient

Chinese maintained "order" in their family. The memory will serve as an appropriate context for appreciating Confucius in verbal texts, say a dicta from the *Daxue* (*The Great Digest*), which reads in Pound's translation, "wanting good government in their state, they first establish order in their own families; wanting order in the home, they first disciplined themselves; desiring self-discipline, they rectified their hearts" (*Con*, 31).

Having seen the power of the visual in transmitting ideas in a remote culture, we might return to the question of Pound's creative response to Chinese art in the "British Museum era." The "British Museum era" was an era of art exhibitions, slide lectures, and illustrated catalogues. Pound was able to take advantage of all these modes of communication in his study of Chinese art. He was privileged to view the *Admonitions* and other distinguished Chinese paintings in the British Museum as frequently as he wished. Gazing at such works, he most certainly experienced the "shock" leading to "disorientation" described above. Pound's visual encounter with China predates his encounter with China through the Fenollosa papers. This implies that Pound was visually and conceptually prepared in his 1914–15 reworking of Fenollosa's Chinese poems. He could apply his visual discoveries about China to his *Cathay* translations where appropriate. While it is hard to speculate where Pound experienced "shock," it is possible to trace the profit he gained from his visual perception of China in his Fenollosa venture.

Pound in fact set out to pursue Chinese poetry right after his meeting with Mrs. Fenollosa in London in late September 1913. His visual encounter with China had prepared him for both his dialogues with Mrs. Fenollosa and his Chinese adaptations.[14] Of the four Chinese poems he produced shortly after his meeting with Mrs. Fenollosa, three, namely "After Ch'u Yuan," "Liu Ch'e," and "Fan-Piece, For Her Imperial Lord," are adapted from H. A. Giles. It is no accident that from about 150 versions of Chinese poems available in Giles's *A History of Chinese Literature* (1901) Pound picked only three, of which two are Han court lyrics, whose subjects he could relate to the *Admonitions*.

Pound might turn to both Giles's translation and the *Admonitions* for images for "Liu Ch'e," a poem in which a Han emperor (Emperor Wu) speaks sorrowfully of his deceased harem favorite. Compared with Giles's poem, the *Admonitions* presents far more convincing details of interactions between Han emperors and court ladies. In following the painter's fine brush, one can feel the rhythm of the light silk flowing from court women's long dresses. With these pictures in mind it was

not so difficult for Pound to recapture the emperor's sense of loss in
the opening lines of "Liu Ch'e": "The rustling of the silk is discon-
tinued, / Dusk drifts over the court-yard" (*P*, 110). The "Bedchamber
Scene," moreover, provides a clue to the Confucian vision of the elegy;
what the emperor really misses is a sincere "husband-wife" relationship. Pound has probably taken his cue from that scene to change Giles's
"For she, my pride, my lovely one, is lost" to his "And she the rejoicer
of the heart is beneath them" (*P*, 111).[15] His choice of the word "heart"
catches a Confucian code ringing also in "The Toilet Scene." Binyon's
label for it says it all: "All can adorn their faces, none can adorn her
heart" (*Guide*, 14).

In adapting Giles's version of a Han poem to "Fan-Piece, For Her
Imperial Lord," Pound has better reason to recall the *Admonitions* for
visual cues. The speaker of this poem is Lady Ban, a figure in history
and a subject of the *Admonitions*.[16] Where the poem in which she speaks
relies on a metaphor to hint at the emperor's fickleness in affection, the
painting presents him with a new favorite. He gazes at Lady Ban, who
gazes back at him. The interchanging gazes can be rendered into statements signifying contrasting states of mind and codes of values: the
emperor's indulgence in feminine charm against Lady Ban's preoccupation with public duty and a true relationship. This visible contrast is
helpful in clarifying the ambivalence in Lady Ban's poem. Pound surely
can borrow the power of art's superimposing one psychological state
upon another to create his verbal version of a woman's unspeakable an-
guish and anger. Indeed, his last line superimposing a fan of white silk's
fate on a woman's fate recaptures Lady Ban's reproach: "You also are
laid aside" (*P*, 111).[17]

There is no question that Pound benefits more by his visual exchanges with China in his 1914–15 *Cathay* enterprise. In *Ezra Pound's
Cathay*, Wai-lim Yip contends that "even within the limits of free improvisation and paraphrase . . . [Pound] sometimes tends to come closer
in sensibility to the original than a literal translation might."[18] My own
comparison of *Cathay* poems with the corresponding Chinese texts and
Fenollosa's notes also indicates that Pound is sometimes "able to go beneath Fenollosa's fragmented gloss to 'a radiant node or cluster' in the
original poetry."[19] Without Chinese to draw on how is Pound able to
resurrect meaning from Fenollosa's crippled notes? The short answer
is that Pound sometimes has Chinese pictures in mind to help detect
false representation. In questions of past Chinese life and sensitivity a
learned scholar is not necessarily a better guide than a past Chinese art-

work. Pound has proved himself astute by following in several instances his common sense, enlightened by past Chinese pictures, rather than relying upon the scholarship of Fenollosa's instructors.

A telling illustration of how Pound benefits from Chinese art is in "Taking Leave of a Friend," a version of an eight-line poem by the Tang poet Li Bo (701–62). Mori and Ariga gloss the Chinese expression *hui shou* in line 7 as "Shaking hands" or "Brandishing [hands]."[20] Pound rejects both apparently because he finds neither culturally suitable in the context. For users of modern Chinese, *hui shou* simply means "wave hand(s)." How does Pound know that Mori and Ariga's gloss that includes that meaning does not fit the eighth-century Chinese context? What makes him think that "bow[ing] over their clasped hands" (*P*, 141) should represent the proper farewell etiquette in Tang China? A plausible explanation is that he has been in the presence of a visual representation of a farewell (or greeting) scene in Confucian China.

While a modern Chinese dictionary will verify that the literal meaning of *hui shou* is "wave hand(s)," an illustration for "Taking Leave of a Friend" in a 1992 edition of *Three Hundred Poems of the Tang* (*Tang shi san bai shou*, 141) shows that Pound is not alone in rendering Li Bo's *hui shou* as "bow over their clasped hands."[21] What has prompted the Chinese illustrator to discard the dictionary meaning for *hui shou*? Presumably, he also finds waving hands inappropriate. The Confucian conception of *li*, or decorum, would not permit such a gesture for farewell. But does the illustrator have documentation for his rendering? One may find various forms of Confucian etiquette described in texts of the Tang period. Nevertheless, he has most probably just followed some old masters. One of the masterpieces portraying *hui shou* is Shen Zhou's *Farewell at a Spring River*. Another is Zhu Bang's *The Forbidden City*. The latter, a hanging scroll in the British Museum since 1881,[22] could have given Pound the cue that "bow over their clasped hands" is the proper reading of Li Bo's *hui shou*. It is proper because it brings to light its cultural meaning that is concealed in a past text.

We might at this point turn to the portrayal of women in the *Admonitions* and other paintings in the British Museum 1910–12 exhibition. Female figures in these masterworks seem to illustrate what women should be like in a Confucian patriarchal society; they appear attentive to their looks, careful about their demeanor, and obliging to their male superiors. Martin Powers makes a valid point when he notes that art in Han China and thereafter tends to promote Confucian standards and project its political message.[23]

This is not to say, however, that this art has completely suppressed female expression. Many of the common women's issues—their desire, hope, anxiety, disappointment, melancholy, grief, anger, despair, and protest—are in fact addressed in a conservative or "orthodox" manner in a genre that may be termed "the solitary woman." The British Museum 1910–12 exhibition presents several instances, most notably *A Lady Meditating by a Lake* (fig. 4) and *A Portrait of a Lady*. In chapter 1 we remarked of *A Lady Meditating by a Lake*'s use of juxtaposition. For most beholders what is more disorienting is a paradox built on this painting's superimposing material wealth on spiritual emptiness. The richly clad woman's eternal gaze can be interpreted as suggesting loneliness and frustration. This theme is echoed in *A Portrait of a Lady,* whose beautifully dressed young woman shares with the meditating lady an idle gaze.[24]

It may be noted that "the solitary woman" is also a distinguished genre in Chinese poetry. Not surprisingly, it is represented in *Cathay* by a group of remarkable examples. A comparison between paintings of the kind and "The Beautiful Toilet," "The Jewel Stairs' Grievance," and "The River-Merchant's Wife: A Letter" reveals that Pound might be responding in part to art in rewriting these poems. By this I am not simply suggesting that Pound may borrow images from the paintings. More importantly, I think the paintings can serve as a secondary source clarifying settings, situations, and states of mind essential to his comprehension of the poems.

Let us first consider the poem Pound calls "The Beautiful Toilet." The original piece, the second of a group of nineteen Han lyrics, has no title. According to Hugh Kenner, Fenollosa's gloss for the fifth line has supplied the two words for Pound's heading.[25] Although this is true, pictures such as "The Toilet Scene" from the *Admonitions* and *A Lady Meditating by a Lake* could also be its inspiration. Indeed, it is in the paintings rather than in Fenollosa's "merest glosses" that one perceives the vision for naming the poem "The Beautiful Toilet."[26]

Comparing the glosses to the original poem,[27] we observe that Fenollosa has blurred the heroine's view in the first six lines—the contrast between the gorgeous life outside (*he bian cao* and *yuan zhong liu*) and her lonely consciousness inside (*lou shang nu* and *dang chuang pu*). In Pound's hands, this opposition is recaptured. He has added the words "And within" to the third line to the effect of highlighting a sharp turn from the outside to the inside. Fenollosa's gloss for the last line, on the other hand, hardly communicates the poem's complaint about the woman's entrapment in her marriage (*kong chuang nan du shou*). In his last line, Pound converts Fenollosa's gloss into a reproach of "leav[ing] her too much alone" (*P*, 132), reproducing something close enough to the original effect. Pound's poetic instinct alone could not work the miracle. A glance at *A Lady Meditating by a Lake* confirms its power of illuminating the poem's circumstance and mood. The contrast between what is without and what is within is emphasized there, and the lone woman's gaze signifies her yearning for earthly happiness and dissatisfaction with a life in a "neglected" home.

If "The Beautiful Toilet" parallels a painting with an accompanying caption (in its last four lines), "The Jewel Stairs' Grievance" resembles a painting without a caption. In rendering that piece by Li Bo, Pound may be responding more directly to art. In his 1918 essay on "Chinese Poetry," he asserts that "certain Chinese poets have been content to set forth their matter without moralizing and without comment" (*P&P*, 3:84). The poem he cites for illustration is precisely "The Jewel Stairs' Grievance." Despite what he claims, he appends a note to that poem, stating that "Gauze stockings, therefore a court lady . . . she has come early, for the dew has not merely whitened the stairs, but has soaked her stockings" (*P*, 136). By concluding that "The poem is especially prized because she utters no direct reproach," however, he hits a point that well defines the genre to which the poem belongs.

"The solitary woman" is essentially a genre of female complaint. Its dynamics depend on its capacity for bringing about an awareness of injustices done to women without having to denounce the Confucian culture that makes such injustices possible. The energy of this tradition lies in its refusal to portray ideal man-woman relationships and its insistence on exposing diverse ills in such ties. As a consequence, we rely to some degree on this discourse to learn about women's sufferings and complaints in Confucian China. In works such as the *Admonitions,* "Fan-Piece," "The Beautiful Toilet," and "The Jewel Stairs' Grievance," we are brought face to face with the immorality of the Confucian paternalistic system, in Rey Chow's description, a system "resting on the sexual stability, chastity, and fidelity of women while men were openly promiscuous or polygamous."[28]

While this genre has a critical edge, its strength is marred by features such as restraint, reticence, self-effacement, and submissiveness. To put it crudely, this tradition works within the masculine bias and the larger Confucian culture. For one thing, the lone woman is shown as inferior to the male other she addresses. One perceives a man's "authority" even in his physical absence. For another, she is not searching for liberation. Typically, she is hoping against hope. In art this attribute is epitomized by an eternal gaze, whereas in poetry it is symbolized by a long wait. Having observed the genre's double quality, I still have not sufficiently designated its complexity. Remarkably, Pound seems aware of some psychic energy in the lone woman's muteness. In "The Jewel Stairs' Grievance" he recaptures both the reticence and its biting force by presenting the lady "let[ting] down the crystal curtain / And watch[ing] the moon through the clear autumn" (P, 136). His note brings to light his sympathy for the lyric's critical sense.

Pound's rendering of "The River-Merchant's Wife" offers further proof of his interest in and knowledge of the genre of "the solitary woman." Since elsewhere I have demonstrated Pound's success in speaking in the voice of a Tang-dynasty teenage wife,[29] here I need focus only on art's possible role as his secondary source. Ronald Bush in "Pound and Li Po" compares Pound's version carefully to Fenollosa's notes. While some of the alterations Bush notices prove to represent Pound's resurrection force, two stand out as instances of his inventiveness. Where Li Bo or Fenollosa's wife says something like "in the fifth month . . . to where monkeys whine" and "now the eighth month,"[30] Pound has her declare, "And you have been gone five months. / The monkeys make sorrowful noise overhead" (P, 134). Bush is legitimate in noting that "Pound's wife reveals reservations about whether her domestic happiness will ever be restored, and she telescopes the river narrows with the dark passages of her heart."[31] Moreover, in the last lines, Pound suppresses the wife's assertion, "not caring that the way be far,"[32] and has her state that "And I will come out to meet you / As far as Cho-fu-Sa." In doing so, Bush observes, he has the wife "aver that if her husband lets her know beforehand, she will come out to meet him . . . so far and no farther."[33]

Li Bo's monologue on which "The River-Merchant's Wife" is based is not a perfect example of "the solitary woman," however. Bush's comparison reveals that Pound's invention has both reinforced and subverted traits of the tradition, thus making a refined type of it. How is that possible? After all, Li Bo's poem contains attributes of the genre. A look at a passage that Pound renders fairly well is sufficient:

> The leaves fall early this autumn, in wind.
> The paired butterflies are already yellow with August
> Over the grass in the West garden;
> They hurt me. I grow older.   (P, 134)

Details such as fallen leaves, thick grass, and a garden are reminiscent of *A Lady Meditating by a Lake* (fig. 4) and comparable Chinese paintings. In pictorial representations of the "solitary woman," such details are used to suggest resentment and despair. The resemblance of Li Bo's garden scene to these pictures might encourage Pound to make the above changes in an effort to increase the teenage wife's desperation.

So far we still have not isolated—even with the revelation of visions from the British Museum into *Cathay*—a single instance in which art plays a role in Pound's calculated attempt at Confucian ethics. To proceed to that point, we must dwell first on Canto 13. At age sixty, Pound was able to recall in Canto 74 "Kuanon of all delights" (*C*, 448), an image from the British Museum 1910–12 exhibition. It follows that over two decades earlier—at age thirty-eight, when he was working on Canto 13, the Confucian Canto—he should have a sharper vision of whatever Confucian ideals in art had appealed to him about 1910. Naturally, relevant pictures in his mind would come to life to juxtapose with whatever words they matched while he worked his way through Pauthier's *Les quatre livres,* and drafted line by line his Confucius for *The Cantos.*

The Pound of Canto 13 is very much like the earlier Pound of *Cathay.* His infatuation with China is infatuation with both Chinese art and Chinese poetry. In inventing his Confucius in Canto 13,[34] therefore, he cannot but open and close in a fashion that recalls at once Chinese painting and *Cathay:*

> Kung walked
> > by the dynastic temple
> and into the cedar grove,
> > and then out by the lower river,
>
> . . . .
>
> The blossoms of the apricot
> > blow from the east to the west,
> And I have tried to keep them from falling."   (*C*, 58, 60)

As Carroll Terrell testifies, neither of the two painterly passages is based on *Les quatre livres.*[35]

Apart from these fragments, Pound's Confucius is traceable to Pauthier and to three of the "Four Books"—the *Lunyu,* the *Daxue,* and the *Zhongyong,* what Pound would call *The Analects, The Great Digest,* and *The Unwobbling Pivot.* The *Lunyu,* the most extensively used source, alone has twenty chapters.[36] By compressing so much into a single canto, Pound has unavoidably weeded out a great deal. Does Pound have any guidelines to go by in his selection procedure? Mary Paterson Cheadle believes that Pound's choice of a long passage from the *Lunyu*, Confucius's conversation with four disciples, is made under the impact of his own distrust of "Christian constraints on individual privacy and liberty."[37] This is possible. Pound's belief in the importance of individuality can indeed prompt him to make his Confucius appear "more generous, even more democratic."[38] Cheadle must have noticed that where Pauthier's Confucius replies, "Chacun d'eux a exprimé son opinion; et voilà tout,"[39] Pound's says: "They have all answered correctly, / "That is to say, each in his nature"(*C*, 58). So the much-admired stress on "each in his nature" is Poundian.

Cheadle acknowledges, nevertheless, that the above rationale cannot justify Pound's choice of a more important passage,[40] a key Confucian tenet stated in the opening section of the *Daxue*. In Canto 13 Pound rewrites it thus:

> If a man have not order within him
> He can not spread order about him;
> And if a man have not order within him
> His family will not act with due order;
> And if the prince have not order within him
> He can not put order in his dominions.   (*C*, 59)

Admittedly, what we hear is a Poundian voice, but the spirit is that of Confucius, for the concern for "order" is Confucian. This concern, central to Confucianism, has been institutionalized in Chinese philosophy, education, popular culture, literature, and art. Could it be that words crystallizing the Confucian concern bring back to Pound's mind pictures that represent the same and that together they make the Confucian concern shine? This could certainly be the case. The Confucian emphasis on "order" within a man, within his family, and within his state *is* represented in Pauthier's text as well as in pictures that have impressed on Pound's eye. Words can bring preexisting pictures back to life to illuminate an abstract idea. Pauthier does provide the word *ordre*, which best describes the spirit of Pound's pictures. In the 1917 "Three Cantos," Pound made an attempt at the Confucian preoccupation by stating that "Confucius later taught the world good manners, / Started with himself, built out perfection" (*P*, 233). That version presents the dictum all right but misses the key word. Evidently it is Pauthier's Confucius who has given Pound the word that brings into the open the essence of the *Daxue's* first tenet.

Pound's delight in the discovery is manifest in his use of the word "order" six times in a passage whose source introduces the word *ordre* but twice. Following the passage is the word repeated for a seventh time: "And Kung gave the words 'order' / and 'brotherly deference'" (*C,* 59).[41] What's more, in a previous section, Pound has had three of Confucius's disciples use that word without the authority of Pauthier.[42] "Order" is a Confucian word. In section 1 of the *Daxue,* the relevant passage contains four verbs connoting the sense of "order" (*zhi, qi, xiu,* and *zheng*) each repeated once.[43] The word play is lost in translation. By "overusing" it Pound has surprisingly recaptured something close enough to the original spirit.

Confucian maxims in translation tend to be disturbingly elusive. Working his way through Pauthier's Confucius, Pound is bound to represent only what he can appreciate. There are, of course, a number of factors contributing to his selection decisions. Of these, the Chinese pictures stand out in his memory. It is inappropriate to overemphasize their impact, and it is also inappropriate to underestimate it.

In 1934, exactly a decade after the making of Canto 13, and six years after the appearance of *Ta Hio,* a version of the *Daxue* drawn from Pauthier,[44] Pound said—in answer to Eliot's question, "What does Mr. Pound believe?"—that "I believe the *Ta Hio.*" A central tenet of the *Daxue,* the Confucian emphasis on individuality and social responsibility, on "order" starting from oneself and one's own family, is alluded to in "Three Cantos." This same emphasis is evident in a number of Chinese paintings accessible to Pound in 1909–13. So, by 1937, when Pound called the *Ta Hio* "the most valuable work I have done in three decades" (*P&P:*7, 239), he had known a key *Daxue* tenet for nearly thirty years. And by 1945, when Pound finished another version of the *Daxue, The Great Digest,*[45] he had encountered that idea for almost four decades. Pound's interest in Confucianism was for a long time centered on the *Daxue.* Intriguingly, this interest was first sparked by a group of Chinese paintings.

Besides his repeated attempts at the *Daxue,* Pound has produced versions of the *Zhongyoung* and the *Lunyu* from the "Four Books," which he names *The Unwobbling Pivot* and *The Analects.* The "Four Books" represent the Confucius of the great Neo-Confucian Zhu Xi (1130–1200). So, Pound's Confucianism is essentially Neo-Confucianism. In the 1930s Pound encountered another Confucius, one of J-A-M de

Moyriac de Mailla's *Histoire générale de la Chine* drawn from a Manchu version of the "Comprehensive Mirror," which served as the source of his 1939 China Cantos (Cantos 53–61).[46] Even in his parleying with the Confucius of the *Histoire,* his Chinese pictures loom large. This is particularly true in Canto 54 (the Han section). Rendering a minister's admonition to the Han dynasty founder, Pound cannot resist introducing images from the British Museum into his poetry. He has the minister call the emperor "A hot lord and unlettered," who overlooked integrity "when he had first seen palace women, their / splendour" (*C,* 276). De Mailla's minister only says, "Séduit par les plaisirs, voulez-vous qu'on vous regarde comme un second Li-Koué?" or "Since you are seduced by pleasures, do you want to be considered a second Li-koue?"[47]

Pound seems to be responding in part to art when dealing with the tale of Lady Feng. De Mailla's version of the story is available in John Nolde's *Blossoms from the East: The China Cantos of Ezra Pound.*[48] In rewriting it Pound appears uninterested in much of its verbal detail.[49] What we see in Canto 54 is a representation of the climactic moment reminiscent of the *Admonitions:*

> And Fong-chi led the bear back to its cage
>   which tale is as follows:
> Fong-chi and Fou-chi had titles but only as Queens of
>   HAN YUEN
> and in the imperial garden a bear forced the bars of his cage
> and of the court ladies only Fong faced him
>   who seeing this went back quietly to his cage.   (*C,* 280)

In retelling the story de Mailla consistently refers to the wives as "*les femmes.*" Pound's phrase, "court ladies," recalls the English title for Gu Kaizhi's masterpiece. Further, it should be noticed that Pound's presentation blots out a subtle aspect elucidated by de Mailla. Instead of confronting the bear as the painting has shown, his Lady Feng waits for the emperor and stands between him and the bear: "la seule Fong-chi, eut le courage, de l'attendre, et de se mettre entre l'empereur et l'animal."[50]

We might at this point turn to Miller, who writes: "Illustrations are always falsifying abstractions from the ungraspable idea they never adequately bring into the open. What they bring to light they also hide" (*Illustration,* 150). His comment is eminently useful in deemphasizing and decentralizing pictures' illuminating effect. In Pound's case, his pictures in memory both orient and subvert, both elucidate and hide, both represent and misrepresent. Just as the Lady Feng scene at once aids and interferes with his reading of a verbal account of her story, other panels from the *Admonitions* illuminate for him one aspect of the *Daxue* while obliterating other aspects. Small wonder that until the mid-1930s Pound remains oblivious to the Confucian concern for verbal precision underscored in the text he celebrates for its stress on "order." It is in Pound's 1945 *The Great Digest* that the slighted Confucian preoccupation in the *Daxue* finally receives due respect: "and wanting to rectify their hearts, they sought precise verbal definitions of their inarticulate thoughts [the tones given off by the heart]; wishing to attain precise verbal definitions, they set to extend their knowledge to the utmost. This completion of knowledge is rooted in sorting things into organic categories" (*Con,* 31).[51]

The Confucian concern for verbal precision is to mark Pound's Confucianism in the Late Cantos. To that subject we shall return in the final chapter. On the assumption that Confucianism cannot be understood without an understanding of its complicated and ambiguous relation to Daoism, I now turn to Pound, Moore, and the eternal Dao.

FOUR

The Eternal Dao:

Pound and

Moore

MY DISCUSSION of Pound's exchange with Confucianism in the previous chapter maps the patterns developed in the ways modernist poets embraced other Chinese modes of thought. For various reasons Confucianism has been accepted as synonymous with Chinese culture. This equation is somewhat misleading because it eclipses the fact that two other philosophies—Daoism and Chan Buddhism—have played a no less decisive role in shaping the Chinese outlook. This chapter uses Pound and Moore as examples to illustrate the modernist sympathy for Daoist aesthetic and attempts to clarify some common misconceptions regarding Daoism and Confucianism. Chapter 5 explores similar patterns in Stevens's response to Chan Buddhism to a degree prepared by Daoist philosophy.

In *Marianne Moore and China,* Cynthia Stamy justly calls attention to Moore's familiarity with both Confucian and Daoist classics—her close readings of Arthur Waley's version of *The Analects of Confucius* (1938), Pound's version of *Confucius: The Great Digest, The Unwobbling Pivot* (1951), and Bynner's version of *The Way of Life According to Laotzu* (1944).[1] What Stamy has not shown, and I shall stress here, is that Daoism had a great deal more attraction for Moore. Daoist aesthetic had no less fascination for Pound. This assertion does not contradict my foregoing claim concerning Pound's appreciation of Confucian ideals in art. In the first place, his use of the *Admonitions* does not imply that his passion for Chinese art is confined to the moral-symbolic type. In the second place, Daoist aesthetic saturates even works of art with strong Confucian ideas. Gu Kaizhi's disregard of appearance in favor of inner spirit is based on the Daoist principle of the *Yin* and *Yang,* or voids and solids.[2] The effect produced in his masterpiece is apt to strike Pound and his peers as antimimetic, and from that surface their interest might shift to the Confucian ethic.

Daoism that has made a captivating and complete Chinese art possible at all is traditionally held to be founded by Laozi (sixth century B.C.) and Zhuangzi (ca. 369-ca. 286 B.C.). The Chinese conception of the Dao, or the Way, however, originated millennia before Laozi's time, which overlapped Confucius's time (551–479 B.C.).[3] It is no coincidence, therefore, that the term "Dao" should appear in both Laozi's *Daode jing* (*Tao Te Ching*) and Confucius's *Lunyu* (*The Analects*).[4] If the Confucians have consistently urged attention to the Dao within the individual, the family, and the state, the Daoists stress the Dao of inner life that corresponds to the Dao of Heaven and Earth. While the Confucians seek to define and account for the Dao, the Daoists steadfastly refuse to do so, as Laozi has taught, "The Dao that can be talked about is not the true Dao."[5] For them, as Wu Tung notes, the Dao is "manifest in the changing forms and eternal laws of Nature . . . in the *qi,* or spirit-energy, of a rock, the evanescent mists and clouds of mountain peaks, or the roaring thunder of a waterfall—the animating breath of life itself."[6]

In the practice of art in China we are apt to find a conspicuous desire to embody this spirit-energy, a desire to attain the Dao. For Chinese artists in the Daoist vein, creating a picture is a way of escaping from their own preoccupations into the Daoist ideals.[7] Consequently, the finest of their works—often landscapes or pictures of flowers and birds—have a power of drawing the beholders out of themselves into the spirit-energy of Heaven and Earth, a power of getting the unsayable message of the Dao said.

To see all this, we must examine some Chinese artworks. Let us begin by surveying "Wild Geese Descending to Sandbar" (fig. 14), Ming artist Yunqiao Zhuren's copy of a scene from the *Eight Views.*[8] As we gaze at this allurement in the British Museum 1910-12 exhibition, we are overwhelmed by serenity and harmony. Human beings are part of nature and get along most comfortably by uniting with their surroundings. What could be a more wholesome embodiment of this fundamental Daoist precept than this picture? At first sight, we may not notice the two human figures. They look perfectly content to be no loftier than the geese, the reeds, and so forth, and perfectly content to contemplate rather than master.

If we continue to gaze, we may enter into this picture, beginning to feel—even hear—the wind: The throbbing of the wild geese, the

平沙落雁
西風渺渺里
雁一聲聲
度秋山
浴室山秋
瀟湘霜葉
涨雲雅客人

14. Yunqiao Zhuren (17th century), "Wild Geese Descending to Sandbar," a scene from the *Eight Views of the Xiao and Xiang Rivers*. © The British Museum. (Courtesy, British Museum, London)

quivering of the reeds, and the swirling of the water seem to correspond to one another. We may begin to perceive the spirit-energy passing from the wild geese, the reeds, and the water to the gazers in the picture and then to us. In quiet gazing, we may identify ourselves with the painted figures, apprehending that things have been like this for millennia.

Each moment we tend to respond to the picture differently. In one instant, we see hundreds of things in the shadows; and in another instant, all the things change to nothing. For one moment, everything is moving; and another moment, the whole complex becomes still again. In one second, we perceive geese flying and reeds swaying; and in another second all turn into ink splashes. Thus we are opening ourselves to what the Daoists mean when they speak paradoxically of being within nonbeing, action within inaction, and likeness within unlikeness.

Many, perhaps, have already noticed a poem inscribed in the upper right. It may be rendered as follows:

> The west wind brings wild geese from afar
> To this section of the Lake Dongting;
> They descend to the feathery, golden sandbar
> While the Xiao and Xiang rush against frost.

Like the picture, the poem diverts attention away from human concerns to permanence/change of the universe.

Just as ancient Greeks and Renaissance Italians viewed painting and poetry as sister arts, so the Chinese call them "twin sisters."[9] "A picture is a soundless poem, and a poem is a speaking picture," a Chinese saying goes.[10] Of China's foremost painter-poet Wang Wei (699–759), it is said that there are paintings in his poems and that there are poems in his paintings.[11] The British Museum preserves an early-fourteenth-century copy of his lost masterwork *Wangchuan Villa* (fig. 15), which was displayed in 1910–12.[12]

Measuring eleven inches in height and over seventeen feet in length, this long handscroll ideally fulfills the purpose of Daoist art. As we un-

15. Zhao Mengfu (1254–1322) after Wang Wei (699–759), a section from *Wangchuan Villa,* 1309. © The British Museum. (Courtesy, British Museum, London)

roll the painting from right to left,[13] scene after scene of Wang Wei's country home looms into our view. At first glance, we are likely to see only leafy trees, winding streams, and misted mountains. Not until we have gazed close enough do we observe bridges, stone fences, and pavilions half concealed among shrubs and rocks. Human endeavors and the natural landscape fuse so completely here that few will think of them as apart. Who could own this place? What is out there in the mountains? Are there birds singing in the woods, or fish darting around in the streams? Viewing this picture, Pound would think of Whistler and Turner. With "beauty in mists, shadows" over an indefinitely vast area, it has an instinct for suggesting many a different meaning beyond human language.

Yet attempts have been made to represent the Wangchuan Villa in words. In two poetic sequences, "Wangchuan Villa" and "Farm Field Pleasure," Wang Wei embodies a total of twenty-seven scenes.[14] While his visual representation of the villa is lost, his poems that represent the same have come down to us. Fenollosa offers two specimens—no. 17 of "Wangchuan Villa" ("Bamboo Lodge") and no. 6 of "Farm Field Pleasure"—in a notebook left to Pound.[15] Pound has duly made a draft for the former:

> Sitting in mystic bamboo grove, back unseen
> Press stops of long whistle
> Deep forest unpierced by man
> Moon and I face each other.[16]

He has also brought out a version of the latter in the *Little Review*:

> Dawn on the Mountain
> Peach flowers turn the dew crimson,
> Green willows melt in the mist,
> The servant will not sweep up the fallen petals,
>   And the nightingales
> Persist in their singing. (*P&P*, 3:217)[17]

Wang Wei's poetry, like his painting, is notoriously elusive. Pound asserts in a 1919 essay that the Tang poet's work is "untranslatable" (*LE*, 343). Despite his dissatisfaction, what he has rendered affords us a glimpse of the formal elements of Wang Wei's poetry—its shifting perspectives, its use of space, and its balance of light and shadow—replicated from his painting. Indeed, it is in his works and the works of his descendants that we perceive the full growth of an art underwritten by the Daoist assumptions of a fundamental correlation between humanity and nature, transcendence of self and language, and transcendence of physical likeness.

With its preference for "observing things in terms of things," its commitment to "forgetting self,"[18] and its mode of presentation that favors spirit over physical likeness, intuition over logic, Daoist aesthetic cannot be fully appreciated by Western readers. Nevertheless, it strikes a sympathetic chord with modernism. In their attempts to remake the past traditions, poets such as Pound, Williams, Moore, and Stevens are striving precisely for a poetry of objectivity, impersonality, and nonmimetic suggestivity. The affinities in taste and sensitivity account for why Chinese art and aesthetic should fare so well in modernism.

As a modernist, Pound was among the earliest to perceive an odd kinship in Chinese art. Upon his first arrival in Europe, he began to develop an anti-Romantic and antirepresentational poetry. In establishing his methods, he initially turned to the ancient Greeks and the medieval Troubadours for inspiration. For example, in *The Spirit of Romance* (1910), he praises the Greek and Provençal poets for their passionate identification with nature (*SR*, 92) and for their nonmimetic suggestivity (33). Notably these attributes are also found in Daoist art. According to Hugh Kenner, Pound's poetry written before his visual encounter with China already discloses an innate Daoist vision.[19] The sensibility of "Hilda's Book," whose speaker pictures himself to be a tree (*P*, 3), evidently grows out of Pound's study of classical and medieval European lyrics. Nonetheless, it appears strangely in accord with that of the "Wild Geese," "Farm Field Pleasure," and other Chinese examples.

Although Pound's pre-Imagist work exhibits an allegiance to objectivism and suggestivity, it is not until such poems as "In the Station of the Metro," "Δώρια," and "Liu Ch'e" that he makes "direct treatment of the 'thing'" and impersonality a primary fabrication in his poetics. Pound's refashioned style in the Imagist period seems directly linked to his engagement with Chinese aesthetic. As in the Metro poem one discerns verbal strategies corresponding to the nonrepresentationalism of Daoist art, so Pound going through H. D.'s "Hermes of the Ways" and other lyrics in the British Museum tearoom may well be conscious of some parallels between the Imagist principles and the principles underlying the Chinese exhibits he admired. In fact, hardly had Pound set down these tenets when he was testing verbal features comparable to the visual ones in oriental painting. In "Δώρια" and other *Ripostes* poems, one witnesses linguistic uses of space and "tonality," uses

unseen in his pre–Imagist poetry. Further, in "Psychology and Troubadours," an essay of 1912 that later became part of *The Spirit of Romance,*
Pound urges attention not only to "Our kinship to the ox" (*SR,* 92),
but to "the little cosmos" corresponding to "the greater," the "sun" and
"moon" in humanity (94). While his equation of "the little cosmos"
with "the greater" is traceable to ancient Greek psychology, it also parallels the Daoist fusion of humanity with nature and its reference to
the *Yin* and *Yang* or the "moon" element and the "sun" element in every
object, every creature, and every human being.

Unlike Pound, Moore has no significant literary models to speak
of.[20] Rather, it is her biology lab work at Bryn Mawr that foreshadows
the start of her career as an objectivist. One of her earliest poems, "A
Jelly-Fish" (*BMM,* 342), is based on five lines composed to accompany
an image she drew for her junior-year course in comparative anatomy:

> Visible, invisible,
> [the] facets of a star
> an amber colored scar
> the facets of an amethyst,
> Inhabit it there are.[21]

Oddly enough, these five lines, like her 1909 "A Jelly-Fish," are found
to echo Daoist poetry in impulse. Having inspected a simple creature
like a jellyfish, a Chinese poet would similarly be burning with a desire
to make present its precise detail. And in doing so he or she would
likewise attempt to catch something elusive, something like "visible,
invisible." Although Moore was astute enough in 1926 to justify the
"new" poetry since 1912 "as a more robust form of . . . Chinese poetry"
(*PrMM,* 120), for a long time she remained unconscious of the Daoist
parallels in "A Jelly-Fish." It was Mai-mai Sze's *The Tao of Painting* (1956)
that opened her eyes to such elements. The revelation, as we shall see
in chapter 12, stimulated her to resurrect that piece for *O to Be a Dragon*
(1959).

Daoist aesthetic's fascination for modernist poets arises from its faculty at once to reflect and to challenge their own sensibilities. Pound
would say, to the Tang and Song masterpieces "it is theoretically necessary to be 'educated up'" (*EP&VA,* 287). No one in the West "could
'make much' of [a short Chinese lyric] at one reading" (*P&P,* 3:85).
Similarly, Moore is fond of going to Chinese art exhibitions primarily
because they promise to educate her eyes. As her correspondence reveals, she takes delight not only in examining the exhibits but also in

recounting her prized items (*SLMM*, 194–97). Clearly, both poets discern something "disorienting" in Chinese art, something that would lead to ways of redefining their poetics. It is in its ability to "disorient" or to enlighten that we see the greater value of Daoist aesthetic to modernism.

To the modernist eye what is most "disorienting" in Chinese art is perhaps its almost mystic reverence for nature. We have seen how Turner and Whistler in their seascapes and Wang Wei in his artistic recreation of his country villa all endeavor to bring into the open the vital relation between the human and natural worlds. Nevertheless, a crucial difference is betrayed in the fact that for Wang Wei and other Chinese poets men and women are no more important than trees and rocks, whereas their Western counterparts are apt to place more importance on humans. Of Turner's sea pieces Binyon remarks, "The real emphasis is on the daring and skill of man, who ventures forth against the power of the senseless waves" (*Flight*, 32–33).

In the Chinese art shows held in London and New York museums, Western viewers were introduced to a tradition dedicated to painting shrubs and cliffs, animals and insects—in short, the so-called second-rate segments of nature—"as seriously as Rembrandt painted the portrait of a man." Of the scroll painting *Geese* displayed in the British Museum 1910–12 exhibition, a critic writes, "The subject seems nothing to us, but [the painter] proves that it meant all the world to him."[22] No less remarkable was the Metropolitan Museum 1923 exhibition in "teach[ing] . . . the lesson of the greatest art." "Landscape, portraiture, and flower painting are alike important to the Chinese painter," a reviewer thus characterizes Chinese art and artists.[23]

The flower and animal pictures in these exhibitions were objects of obvious attraction for Moore. It is hardly possible to overestimate the stimulus given Moore by Chinese flower-animal aesthetic. Without record of what she actually saw in the British Museum in 1911, we can do no more than speculate that she preserved a hazy memory of its most engaging pictures. As to her visits to the Metropolitan Museum 1923 exhibition, we have access to her descriptions of what she prized most: "a dragon in the clouds, concealed but for a few claws"; "a series of white horses with scarlet pompoms and smoky manes and tails"; two herd boys "mounted on water oxen" in "one of supremely delicate brush work called *Herd Boys Returning Home*"; and *Enjoying the Breeze in a Fishing-Boat* (*SLMM*, 197). A decade later, some of her sketches surface in her poems. The dragon appears in "The Plumet Basilisk," and

Herd Boys Returning Home seems to have contributed details to "The Buffalo," details such as "snake tail in a half-twist / on the flank" and "bare-leggèd herd-boys" (*CPMM*, 28), which are unseen in the poem's identified source, a photograph from *The New York Times*.[24]

By studying Chinese animal pictures, Moore of course benefits more than just recapturing some images in her own poetry. The true value for Moore of the Chinese tradition of treating animals is that it braces up her objection to the Western bias of the animal genre, a bias characterized by Andrew Lakritz as "wearing gloves."[25] According to Linda Leavell, Moore's "earlier animals had been either metaphors for named individuals ('To a Prize Bird,' 'To the Peacock of France') or for unnamed persons or types ('Critics and Connoisseurs,' 'The Monkeys'). The late animals ('Peter,' 'The Jerboa') drop their human tenors, or seem to do so, altogether."[26] It is no coincidence that "Peter," a poem of 1924, marks Moore's transition toward portraying an animal for its own sake.[27] In March and April 1923 she visited and revisited the Metropolitan Museum exhibition of Chinese art, whose dragons, horses, buffaloes, and insects gave her a lesson on how seriously an artist might go about portraying nonhumans. Later that year, she discovered in Stevens's *Harmonium* an American example of assuming "the mind and the method of China" (*PrMM*, 95). Her praise of her friend's poetry in January 1924 should indicate her desire for taking on the same mind and method.

It was her commitment to *The Dial* that interrupted her experiments that started with "Peter." Soon after she was released from that duty, she was able to bring out a series of animal poems that are now considered her best in the discourse. In them one can hardly fail to be struck by a sort of seriousness, esteem, and integrity that recall the Chinese animal pictures she had admired. Thus, in "The Jerboa," the jumping rat of the title is envisioned as living joyously like the "spirited horses," "untouched" by human greed and pride. In "The Plumet Basilisk," the Central American lizard is shown to be as powerful as the "dragon" to adapt itself to the changing environments of jungle and sea. Further, in "The Frigate Pelican," the Caribbean bird is praised for a natural ability, like that of the Chinese "buffaloes" or "insects," to be content with its own life, paying no heed to human values.

Where Moore honors and benefits from real and imagined creatures painted upon Chinese silk or porcelain, Pound applauds Tang and Song landscapes that convey the same "thrusting" message. In his 1918 essay on "Chinese Poetry," it may be noted, he celebrates Chinese landscape poetry and painting in the same breath. "Especially in their poems of nature and scenery," he observes, the Chinese "seem to excel western writers, both when they speak of their sympathy with the emotions of nature and when they describe natural things" (P&P, 3:110). As he goes on to praise Li Bo, who "speak[s] of mountainous crags with the trees clinging head downward, or of a mountain pool where the flying birds are reflected," he attributes the vitality of such descriptions to "the marvellous Chinese painting."

Pound owes his ability to connect Chinese landscape poetry with Chinese landscape painting perhaps chiefly to Fenollosa's lectures on "Landscape Poetry and Painting in Medieval China." The Beinecke Library of Yale University keeps Fenollosa's typescript and drafts of one of the lectures with Pound's markings in black, blue, and red as well as an additional copy in Dorothy's hand.[28] Leafing the notes, Pound cannot fail to be impressed by Fenollosa's attribution of Chinese "idealistic interpretation of nature" to "a discovery of parallel structures and of parallel character in the human soul and in landscape itself." He might similarly be affected by a passage on the next page: In China "the love for mountains and trees and rushing water . . . for all that is wild and free and extra-social, becomes a deliberate and rational passion, based upon a profound study of structure."

Nevertheless, what really matters for Pound is to see how Daoist exponents elucidate in simple language a correlative harmony between humanity and landscape. Where Fenollosa interprets the idea of non-discrimination, Giles repeats in A History of Chinese Literature Zhuangzi's own episode: "Once upon a time, I, Chuang Tzŭ, dreamt I was a butterfly fluttering hither and thither, to all intents and purposes a butterfly. I was conscious only of following my fancies as a butterfly, and was unconscious of my individuality as a man. Suddenly, I awaked, and there I lay, myself again. Now I do not know whether I was then a man dreaming I was a butterfly, or whether I am now a butterfly dreaming I am a man."[29]

Zhuangzi's anecdote affords Pound a way to test the Chinese freedom of shifting between different worlds, a challenge he desires most for his epic ambition. Shortly after Giles, Pound digs up in Fenollosa's notebooks a verse version of the anecdote by Li Bo.[30] Naturally he cannot resist reworking it, hence "Ancient Wisdom, Rather Cosmic" for Blast 2:

So-shu dreamed,
And having dreamed that he was a bird, a bee, and a butterfly,
He was uncertain why he should try to feel like anything else,

Hence his contentment.   (P, 123)

Needless to say, it is Pound rather than Li Bo who has made Zhuangzi (So-shu in Japanese) dream of being "a bird, a bee" aside from being a butterfly. Paradoxically, by misrepresenting Li Bo and multiplying his juxtaposition, Pound succeeds (to a degree) in bringing to light the Daoist sensibility to ambiguity and transformation. His concluding line, also invented, signals his opening up to an attitude invaluable to his poetics but by no means easy to appropriate.

The Chinese instinct for expressing meaning impersonally brings us to a second motive that justifies the modernists' zeal for Daoist aesthetic. It is commonly known that the doctrine of impersonality is at the core of the poetics of Pound and Eliot. Pound formulates his impersonal theory explicitly in "The Serious Artist" (1913): "The serious artist may like to stand on the stage, he may, apart from his art, be any kind of imbecile you like, but the two things are not connected, at least they are not concentric" (LE, 47). Eliot echoes this sense in "Tradition and the Individual Talent" (1919): "The progress of an artist is a continual self-sacrifice, a continual extinction of personality."[31] Nevertheless, it must be pointed out that in their early essays both Pound and Eliot employ two vocabularies. While at times they advocate depersonalization, at other times they stress personal expression. Sanford Schwartz aptly states that the antithetical vocabularies are intended "to bridge the distinction between subjective and objective domains."[32] When we think of Pound's and Eliot's major poems, we apprehend, however, that impersonality is a mask they wear occasionally. After comparing poems of Pound, Eliot, Williams, and Moore, Jeanne Heuving concludes that none of the male modernists named consistently writes a poetry of impersonality. The Pound of "Mauberley" and The Cantos and the Eliot of "Prufrock" and The Waste Land are primarily concerned with "establishing their authority and identity through mirroring others."[33]

By contrast, Chinese artists disciplined by Daoist notions would not allow personal identity to be revealed. In the course of painting a picture, states Binyon, the Chinese artist "was brought into direct relation with the creative power indwelling in the world, and this power, using him as a medium or instrument, breathed actual life into the strokes of his brush" (Flight, 17). His remark holds also for the Chinese poet.

As Pauline Yu notes, the Chinese poet is privileged to use a language that permits the omission of subject, gender, and number.[34] This implies that "forgetting self" in Chinese is not as trying as in Western languages. Thanks to Fenollosa, Pound becomes dimly aware of the means offered the poet by classical Chinese. In the "Exile's Letter," as I have shown elsewhere, Pound faces Li Bo's challenge and recaptures a privileged moment of depersonalization by using a series of participles.[35] Pound has no doubt benefited from his *Cathay* enterprise. The impersonal style he picks up from Li Bo sporadically turns up in *The Cantos*. When it does so in Cantos 4, 16, 49, 74, and so on, we experience some of the most compelling moments of his modernist epic.

Moore, on the other hand, never has a chance to see cribs like Fenollosa's that reveal how the Chinese speak impersonally in poetry. Nonetheless, she has attended many Chinese art shows where she has the freedom of examining for herself how Chinese painters turn themselves into "instruments" of actual life. In a dragon picture, for instance, the painter obscures all his or her concerns to be the "ruler of Rivers, Lakes, and Seas, / invisible or visible" (*CPMM*, 20). In *Herd Boys Returning Home* the artist becomes at once the buffaloes and the herd boys. Furthermore, *Enjoying the Breeze in a Fishing-Boat* signals a central "otherness" from which to move into additional "othernesses." Gazing at that picture, the beholder will identify herself first with the figure in the fishing boat and then gradually enter into the cool breeze, the clear water, and the distant hills.

Curiously, the various techniques employed in these paintings parallel Moore's aesthetic of multiple perspectives and depersonalization perfected in the 1930s. In a discussion of the aesthetic, Cristanne Miller urges attention to Leavell's claim that Moore has been influenced more by avant-garde artists than by writers.[36] While I agree that Moore's multiple point of view resembles early Cubism's multiple point of view,[37] I would argue, in addition, that Chinese painting braces up modern art in shaping what Miller describes as Moore's "non-'authorial,' abstract, shifting representation of identity or self."[38] This issue will be raised again in chapter 12. For the moment, may it suffice to state that Moore's parallels to the Chinese have not escaped her peers' notice. As early as 1937, John Gould Fletcher praised Moore for "display[ing] an objective approach akin to the Chinese."[39]

The Chinese preference for suggestion over assertion, intuition over logic leads to a third major reason for the modernists' fascination with Daoist aesthetic. We have observed how Mi Fu's painting of misty mountains communicates a spirit that transcends language. Mi's land-scape perfects the style of the "Southern School" of painting in China, which advocates going beyond physical likeness.[40] Such works can draw the viewer into the Daoist world of imagination, where he rejects the humdrum in favor of the extraordinary. Wang Wei, the founder of the school, sometimes places flowers of different seasons side by side, and once he even paints a banana tree in snow![41]

That observation captures a hallmark of Moore's poetics—her in-fatuation with juxtaposing opposed features to stir up a meaning we partly understand. To what extent might this attachment be linked to her interest in Chinese art? It is hard to estimate. But the fact that in 1924 Moore connects Stevens's imagination to "an achieved remote-ness" in Chinese painting (*PrMM*, 91) is significant. A letter of 5 May 1923 reveals that she has in mind Du Mu's poem on Wang Wei. "He took ten days to paint a river and five days a rock," writes Du Mu in a manuscript poem displayed in the Metropolitan Museum. "A master-piece cannot be produced in haste or by pressure. It was after bestowing such pains as these that Wang Tsai allowed his work to remain. Power-ful is the painting . . . and high is it hung on the spotless wall in the lofty hall of your mansion" (*SLMM*, 197).[42]

Moore's term "achieved remoteness" recaptures both aspects of Du Mu's criticism—his concern for a "remote" effect and his distrust of careless work. In the early 1920s, Moore was already gathering materi-als for poems such as "The Jerboa" and "The Buffalo."[43] Du Mu's state-ment—"A masterpiece cannot be produced in haste or by pressure"—seems to have reached her opportunely. Thereafter, she invested many more years of hard work in these poems, and the result was an art of "an achieved remoteness." Scholars admire her shifting perspective re-inforced in part by her interest in avant-garde painting. Nonetheless, in her suggestivity, elusiveness, and freedom of mingling plants and creatures from diverse regions, she betrays the spirit and techniques of Wang Wei. We grow more suspicious of this when we observe juxtapo-sitions of East and West in lines such as "In Costa Rica the true Chinese lizard face / is found" (*CPMM*, 20).

Pound's early interest in Turner and Whistler prefigures what are to be his favorite Chinese pictures. In "The Serious Artist" he pays trib-ute to Chinese painters without giving their names. In an attempt to label a few masterpieces, he states, "I mean something or other vaguely associated in my mind with work labelled Dürer, and Rembrandt, and

Velasquez, etc., and with the painters whom I scarcely know, possibly of T'ang and Sung" (*LE*, 56). Here Pound is remarkably honest about his half-knowledge, but by naming the Tang and Song he has virtually identified what Chinese works he prizes.

If Pound has been slippery in defining what quality in Chinese painting appeals to him most, he proves unequivocal in isolating that quality in the Chinese poetic tradition. In "Chinese Poetry," he asserts that "The first great distinction between Chinese taste and our own is that the Chinese *like* poetry that they have to think about, and even poetry that they have to puzzle over." To our poet that sensitivity "has occasionally broken out in Europe, notably in twelfth-century Provence and thirteenth-century Tuscany" (*P&P*, 3:85). One of Pound's ambitions has been to revive that lost taste. Through reworking Fenollosa's versions of Li Bo, he discovers a model for fulfilling that ideal. In "The Jewel-Stairs' Grievance," for instance, he notices that "everything is there, not merely by 'suggestion' but by a sort of mathematical process of reduction."

It is in Wang Wei, nonetheless, that Pound encounters the most complex model for a nonmimetic, suggestive poetry. At first reading he associates his work with French symbolism, calling him "eighth century Jules Laforgue Chinois" (*SLEP*, 93). Before long he is busy translating his lyrics. Endless toil confirms that no matter how hard he tries, he cannot succeed in preserving the best of the Tang poet in translation.[44] Pound's failure to represent Wang Wei as whole is ironically fruitful, however. The experiment affords him an approach at a moment when he is refashioning his Ur-Cantos. Wang Wei never worries about the resemblance of his representation to the referent. Why should he? Evoking an intangible spirit is, after all, far more important. In a 1919 essay, Pound therefore aligns Wang Wei with Remy de Gourmont: "[Gourmont's] spirit was the spirit of Omakitsu [Wang Wei]; his *pays natal* was near to the peach-blossom-fountain of the untranslatable poem" (*LE*, 343). Clearly, Wang Wei has enabled Pound to gain insight into the value of Gourmont's stress on a single, unifying sensibility. In Ur-Canto 4 he uses a single sensibility to tie together his "rag-bag" of subject matter. Christine Froula identifies that sensibility in a passage she calls the "Seven enigmatic lines":[45] "Smoke hangs on the stream, / The peach-trees shed bright leaves in the water . . ." (*C*, 16). As I have shown in my last critical book, not only is the passage a collage of fragmented versions of Wang Wei from Fenollosa's Chinese poetry notes, but the whole underlying spirit is also like his. More significantly, the sensibility recalling Wang Wei and his Daoism recurs in *The Cantos,* serving to bind together what may otherwise appear incoherent.[46]

My last argument depends on Hugh Kenner. In *The Pound Era* he provides a striking and clever, if ultimately limited, inquiry into Pound's evolving Daoism: "The Pound of 'The Flame'. . . like the earlier Pound of 'Hilda's Book' . . . and the later Pound of Canto 47 . . . and the 60-year-old Pound who wrote in Pisa that 'the sage delighteth in water'. . . was Taoist in his deepest impulses."[47] Taking his cue from Kenner, Reed Way Dasenbrock further describes the Middle Cantos as Confucian and *The Pisan Cantos* as Daoist.[48] Is Pound more Daoist than Confucian in his deepest impulses? If so, how do we account for his Confucianism? Or is Pound at times predominantly Confucian and at other times predominantly Daoist? If so, what will be *the* unifying sensibility that threads through *The Cantos*? Kenner and Dasenbrock have raised some questions we cannot evade.

The problem some critics have with the relation of Daoism to Confucianism apparently stems from their preconception about the conflict or antagonism between the two philosophies. Confucianism and Daoism *are* fundamentally different, but they differ only to balance each other. When Chinese civilization first emerged there was but one philosophy, that of the Dao. Its split into two schools of thought in the sixth century B.C. arose from a need to make a culture function better. In stressing the mutually complementary nature of the two outlooks, Li Zehou reminds us of an often neglected fact: "Confucius's respect for the individuality of the members of a clan . . . led directly to Zhuangzi's idea of independent individuals who abandon the world and isolate themselves from secular concerns."[49]

It is true that dissimilarities between the two philosophies gave rise to countless religious and political struggles in Chinese history. However, after each struggle the two schools always came to terms. Thus, the Han decree of "making Confucianism the orthodox philosophy" (*du-zun rushu*) in the second to first centuries B.C. resulted in the influx of Buddhism from India and the thriving of Daoism for many centuries to come. Similarly, the persecutions of Buddhists in the late ninth century only brought about a prolonged mingling of the three philosophies in Song China. In illustrating this point, Wen Fong calls attention to *Scholars of the Liuli Hall,* a late-thirteenth-century copy of a tenth-century painting, which "reflects the emergence of a new literary society in the late T'ang and early Sung periods, in which Confucianists, Taoists, and

Buddhists mingled freely, creating a harmonized synthesis of the three philosophies."[50] Pound's Confucianism, it is important to note, is derived from the "Four Books," a legacy of the Song compiled under the auspices of Zhu Xi, whose mode of thought (Neo-Confucianism), as Kenner remarks, "had assimilated much coloration from 15 centuries of Taoism."[51]

How might we characterize past Chinese poets and artists in terms of their attitude toward Confucianism and Daoism, then? They tend to pursue both in their work. In the *Admonitions,* Gu Kaizhi treats a Confucian theme by adhering to the Daoist principle of "transmitting spirit beyond physical likeness"; so does Li Bo in "Taking Leave of a Friend" and other poems. As many Chinese poets and artists served as government officials, it was characteristic of them to lead a double life, alternating between the two philosophies. Their dilemma is portrayed by Li Bo in the poem Pound calls "Exile's Letter"—when the speaker and his friend (both scholar-officials) advance, they have to think of commitment to their duties; when they are in retreat, they mix with "Intelligent men" including Daoist priests, playing music and singing and dancing to their hearts' content. For many scholar-officials the shift occurred constantly. Wang Wei, for instance, was perfectly Confucian in office. Once back home in his private estate, he withdrew totally into the Daoist-Chan Buddhist world. There he was utterly at ease, composing music, painting pictures, and chanting poems. It was at such times that he reachieved the Dao or Chan.

Just as Chinese poets and artists can alternate between Confucianism and Daoism, so Pound, influenced by them, can take advantage of both philosophies. In *The Cantos,* Pound does return again and again to a Confucian theme. Nonetheless, the aesthetic sensibility that threads through the poem is in accord with Daoist ideals. Early on, Pound himself made it clear that he had a desire to build his epic around an Eastern spirit. "[W]hen he sent the three Ur-Cantos to Miss Monroe," Kenner reports, "he had said that his long poem's theme was ('roughly') *Takasago's* theme."[52] The *Noh* image of the twin pines subsequently finds its way into Canto 4, where it evokes the same spirit as lies behind the "Seven enigmatic lines." The Daoist consciousness of Canto 4 keeps recurring throughout *The Cantos.* Canto 13, the Confucian Canto, bewilders us by presenting a Confucius superposed on a Daoist landscape, praising his disciples in Laozi's terms: "each in his nature" (*C,* 58). The speaker of Canto 47, who hears "the roots speaking together" (238), is distinctly Daoist. So is the speaker of Canto 49, who meditates over "heavy rain in the twilight," "Autumn moon," and "the monk's bell" (244). The China Cantos are Confucian in subject matter, but in creativity they are no less Daoist. The portrayal of Lady Feng in Canto 54 recaptures Gu Kaizhi's spirit beyond likeness, not to mention lines such as "some fishin' some huntin' some things cannot be / changed" (275), resounding the eternal Dao. When Pound is himself again in *The Pisan Cantos,* his Daoism appears all the more piercing: "The wind is part of the process / The rain is part of the process" (455). And not surprisingly, it rings once more at the epic's open end: "Do not move / Let the wind speak / that is paradise" (822).

What remains is to account for Pound's attacks on "taozers." In the China Cantos, Pound is parroting de Mailla. The Neo-Confucians who informed de Mailla and Pound bombarded the "taozers" while holding Laozi and Zhuangzi in high esteem. Neither interpreters seem to have grasped their point. Students of Chinese thought really must distinguish the philosophy of Laozi and Zhuangzi from the religion of "taozers." Of the latter, Wen Fong offers a lucid account: "Founded as an organized religion by the Celestial Master Chang Tao-ling in the late second century A.D., religious Taoism, as opposed to philosophical Taoism, played an important role in popular rebellions and secret societies in China from the end of the Han period."[53] Not to make this conceptual distinction was one of Pound's most serious misrepresentations.[54] However, as William McNaughton testifies, in the mid-1950s, at St. Elizabeths Hospital in Washington, D.C., Pound owned up to his oversight: "There's no doubt I missed something in Daoism and Buddhism. Clearly, there's something valid, meaningful, in those religions."[55]

FIVE

Stevens and
Chan Art

WALLACE STEVENS'S connection with Chan Buddhism was taken up by Robert Aitken and Robert Tompkins in the early 1980s and treated in greater detail by William Bevis in *Mind of Winter: Wallace Stevens, Meditation, and Literature* (1988).[1] In my examination of this relation, I would like to stress one thing that has not been stressed enough: Stevens's Chan-like notions are directly linked to his lifelong interest in Chan art. Since we have barely begun to see art as a powerful medium for transmission of ideas and since some important evidence has remained hidden, this point often gets lost in discussions of Stevens and Chan Buddhism.

Like the Dao, Chan is beyond logic, reasoning, and verbal definition. Yet Chan masters will seek to help others discover and understand its spirit. A traditional way of doing this is inviting students to share the meditative insights of Chan poets and painters. Daisetz T. Suzuki (1870–1966), Japan's foremost authority on Chan (Zen) Buddhism, for instance, would find it futile to proceed with his Chan discourse without making use of illustrations. His reliance on Chan poetry and art to clarify the "ungraspable" and the "unattainable" is characteristic of the Chan tradition.

Chan started in China in the early sixth century with the semilegendary Indian master Bodhidharma as its first patriarch.[2] In due course it took root among former students of Laozi and Zhuangzi because its system corresponded to theirs in many ways. From the time of its flowering in the eleventh century, Chan Buddhists seemed to look upon their idiosyncratic painting and poetry as a dynamic media through which to convey their message. In the early thirteenth century, when groups of Chan monks voyaged from Southern Song China to Japan,[3] many carried with them Chan paintings and calligraphic objects. Chinese Chan works soon found ardent admirers in Japan, thus giving rise to a constant flow of such works from one side of the waters to the other. It was largely through the medium of Chan art and verse that Chinese Chan culture traveled speedily to Japan in the Kamakura period (1192–1333) and blossomed in the Muromachi and Edo periods (1338–1573; 1603–1867).

In the late 1870s and early 1880s, when New Englanders Ernest Fenollosa and William Sturgis Bigelow (1850–1926) arrived in Japan,[4] the renown of Chan art was nonetheless on the decline. Yet the two men, one a professor of philosophy and one a physician, were both captivated by the peculiar Chan taste. Shortly they became fervent collectors of centuries-old treasures preserved in Buddhist temples. As they grew more and more absorbed into Chan art, they were initiated into its cultural set and became avowed Buddhists.[5]

The bulk of the valuable Chan objects assembled by Fenollosa, Bigelow, and other pioneers eventually found their home in the Museum of Fine Arts, Boston.[6] In 1890, upon his return to America, Fenollosa was appointed the first curator of Oriental art at the MFA, managing his friends' as well as his own art collections. His five-year tenure coincided with the period during which Harvard professor Charles C. Everett was offering a course in "Comparative History of Religions," a trial effort to acquaint American students with Buddhism and other Eastern religions and philosophies.[7] By mounting a series of excellent exhibitions in 1892–95,[8] Fenollosa triumphed where Professor Everett failed. He firmly established the MFA as a center for introducing Americans to the culture of the Orient. Bernard Berenson (1865–1959) chronicled one of his exhibitions' startling effects. After viewing forty-four Chinese Buddhist paintings loaned from Kyoto's temple Daitoku-ji to the MFA, December 1894 through March 1895,[9] the renowned art historian commented: "To begin with they had composition of figures and groups as perfect and simple as the best we Europeans have ever done. . . . I was prostrate. Fenollosa shivered as he looked, I thought I should die, and even Denman Ross who looked dumpy Anglo-Saxon was jumping up and down. We had to poke and pinch each other's necks and wept. No, decidedly I never had such an art experience."[10]

The forty-four loan pieces that gave Berenson and others a hard "thrust" were part of a set of one hundred Chinese Luohan paintings that had been the property of Daitoku-ji for centuries. According to Kojiro Tomita, curator of Asiatic art at the MFA from 1931 to 1962, the set produced by two Southern Song artists, Zhou Jichang and Lin Tinggui, was taken to Japan in the thirteenth century and transferred to Kyoto's Daitoku-ji in the late sixteenth century.[11] In 1895, when the exhibition came to a close, Daitoku-ji sold ten of the loan scrolls to the MFA and two of them to Charles Freer.[12] What this suggests is that Stevens had opportunities, during and after his Cambridge years, of contemplating a part of Fenollosa's last exhibition.[13]

In a recent discussion of Buddhist art transferred to the West, Bernard Faure stresses that "the aura—which is perhaps not irreversibly lost, but often ignored or eclipsed—is an important aspect of these artworks."[14] Buddhist art placed in a new cultic context will indeed have "aura," or "speak." As Berenson has testified, the forty-four Luohan paintings "spoke" to him. Berenson had studied countless European masterpieces; yet he said that he "never had such an art experience." In front of the Buddhist images, he "thought [he] should die."

According to Suzuki, enlightenment is central to the teachings of all schools of Buddhism.[15] While other sects try to make this state of consciousness appear complex, Chan simplifies it by urging the disciples to practice meditation in the Chan manner and let the rest take care of itself. As empirical studies of Chan meditation, the Buddhist paintings in Fenollosa's last exhibition illustrate how certain Luohans do this and what visions they are granted.

One of the ten Luohan scrolls purchased by the Museum of Fine Arts, *The Transfiguration of a Luohan* (fig. 16), shows what is meant by the Buddhist saying that "the Buddha is nowhere to be found except in yourself." In the painting one of the five Luohans is portrayed as transformed into the Buddha as he sits deep in meditation. From a halo he bears behind his head and shoulders we know that he has attained the spirit of the Buddha. The smoke rising from his head indicates that he has obtained Chan energy from the transfiguration, a triumph to which the other Luohans are all paying homage.

A similar Chan-related moment is depicted in *Luohan Manifesting Himself as an Eleven-headed Guanyin,* another Luohan painting acquired by the MFA. Here one of another group of five Luohans appears to have put on a mask of an eleven-headed Guanyin. Nevertheless, as Fenollosa describes in *A Special Exhibition* (1894), the Luohan has in fact "pulled aside the bronze skin of his face, as if it were a mask, and revealed beneath the luminous features of the eleven-headed Kwannon."[16] His interpretation is based on an account given by the fourteenth-century Buddhist monk Nianchang. While posing for a portrait in the court of

16 *(left)*. Zhou Jichang (active second half of 12th century), *The Transfiguration of a Luohan,* ca. 1178. General Funds, 95.3. © 2000 Museum of Fine Arts, Boston. All Rights Reserved. (Courtesy, Museum of Fine Arts, Boston)

17 *(right)*. Zhou Jichang (active second half of 12th century), *Luohan in Meditation Attended by a Serpent,* ca. 1178. Denman Waldo Ross Collection, 06.288. © 2000 Museum of Fine Arts, Boston. All Rights Reserved. (Courtesy, Museum of Fine Arts, Boston)

Emperor Wu of Southern Liang (r. 502–49), the Buddhist saint Bao-zhi "scratched his face with his fingernails" to reveal the image of the multiheaded Guanyin.[17]

The demeanor in which a Luohan sits in meditation is nowhere more manifest than in *Luohan in Meditation Attended by a Serpent* (fig. 17), yet another Luohan painting in the Museum of Fine Arts. Here one of the five Luohans is seated motionless outside a grotto and upon surging water. As he shuts his eyes and other organs of senses, he ceases to see or hear or feel the serpent in front of him and the leaves by his side. This makes it possible for him to perceive "the thing itself" in the waves, as is shown in the halo he bears. He gives the perception no thought, no interpretation, no emotion. "Only with a state of no-mind can one attain a flash of insight into human nature and the cosmos," the painting seems to be claiming.

What connection can we make between Chan art and Stevens's poetic use of meditative experience, then? In *Mind of Winter,* after a summary of the structure of Middle Way Buddhist meditation, William Bevis states, "A number of Stevens' poems seem not only to use meditative issues and points of view, but also to imitate the structure of meditative experience, an advanced, sensate, meditative experience that follows the middle way."[18] Bevis does an impressive job in identifying the various stages of Chan or Middle Way meditation in "The Snow Man," "The Course of a Particular," and other poems. Moreover, in accounting for Stevens's use of meditative experience, Bevis sensibly attributes it first to his own meditative nature. The poet's delight in solitary walking, "just sitting," and "merely gazing" certainly explains why other modernists read the same books and he alone should have "come to grips with meditative detachment."[19] For Bevis, however, Stevens's use of meditation is no proof for direct exchange with Chan. To quote his words, "Stevens seems to have arrived at his knowledge without significant help from Buddhists, scientists, or orientalists."[20]

In my view, Stevens's innate meditative detachment not only clarifies his well-known fascination with Chan art, but also multiplies the likelihood of an intimate transaction with its message. Chan art is designed to invite viewers to enter into it and lose themselves to its outlook. Those with meditative inclinations are expected to be more profoundly affected. Stevens's habit of looking at things with meditative detachment almost ensures his entry into the nothing or the no-mind state (*śūnyatā* in Sanskrit) of Chan art with the thing itself perceived. In the 1910s he took a leap to a higher form of meditative consciousness.

The channel through which he attained the greatest insight, I believe, was Chan culture.

Bevis offers two reasons for his reluctance to connect Stevens's admiration for Chan art to his musings on the nothing in poems such as "The Snow Man." One is the lack of evidence that in 1900–1920 Chan art was "appreciated as Buddhist."[21] But there is evidence for this. Many of the early exhibitions at the MFA were prepared with a mind to acquaint Americans with Buddhist insights. Fenollosa's catalogue, *Special Exhibition,* available in 1894–1911, for instance, labeled all the Luohan paintings as executed "for the Zen sect in China," particularizing that "They represent the magical deeds of the great Rakan [Luohan], in contemplation, in transfiguration, in their power over nature, animals, and men."[22] John Gould Fletcher, like Stevens a frequenter of the MFA, got the message from similar shows. He stated in 1917 that in the Southern Song period "Chinese landscape art reached its high water mark" precisely because the artists "were trained in the Zen Buddhist doctrine."[23]

The other reason given is the lack of known pre-1920 Chan studies to inform "The Snow Man."[24] It is true that works on Chan by Arthur Waley and D. T. Suzuki were not published until the 1920s,[25] but Stevens had read Okakura, Binyon, and perhaps also Fenollosa.[26] Okakura's *The Ideals of the East* offers accounts of the origin of Chan, its emphasis on meditation, its disrespect for rituals, and, above all, what it means by "suchness": "The mind is like a great lake, clear to its bottom, reflecting the clouds that hover over it, sometimes ruffled by winds which make it foam and rage, but only to settle down into the original calm, never losing its purity, or its own nature."[27] Binyon's *Painting in the Far East* similarly elaborates on Chan art (120–45). Further, we must not forget exhibition catalogues and newspaper articles. The essay on "The Noble Features of the Forest and the Stream," which Stevens read in 1911, for instance, gives a superb insight into the Chan belief that people can enjoy "the luxuries of nature" even "without stepping out of their houses."[28]

Neither Okakura, Binyon, nor the author of "The Noble Features of the Forest and the Stream" counted too much in articulating Chan aesthetic to Stevens, however. Rather, it was Chan painting that played a principal role in elevating the poet's detachment to a higher level of meditative experience. This claim is supported by a statement Stevens made in 1950. In response to Earl Miner's question about the Oriental effects in "Thirteen Ways of Looking at a Blackbird," Stevens wrote, "While I know about haiku, or hokku, I have never studied them and certainly I did not have them in mind when I wrote THIRTEEN WAYS ETC. I have been more interested in Japanese prints."[29] Despite the 1917 poem's haiku-like stanzas, we have no reason to doubt the poet's stress on Oriental art as an inspiration for his poetic development.

Critics such as Robert Buttel and Walton Litz have long acknowledged the importance of Oriental art to Stevens's early poetry.[30] Our task now is to identify and analyze the precise Oriental or Chan elements appropriated. In saying this I am aware that what seems like Chan in certain poems by Stevens may be derived in part from Chan art and in part from other traditions. To clarify the Chan aspects, I have to suspend other contributing factors. What I attempt to do here is not to replace the way we read Stevens but to provide a valid addition to the way we interpret him.

Miner remarks that the title of Stevens's 1917 poem is reminiscent of Hiroshige's *Eight Views of Omi,* Hokusai's *Thirty-six Views of Fuji,* or Utamaro's *Seasons.*[31] For me "Thirteen Ways" recalls not only Japanese prints but various Chinese copies of the *Eight Views* whose subjects captivated Stevens about 1909. The poem clearly provides multiple perspectives that are Chan-like. Cubism could also have served as a model after which to build sensations into juxtaposed stanzas. However, its multiple perspectives, as Wendy Steiner explains, are simultaneous on a single graphic surface,[32] rather than on eight or thirteen or fifty separate planes. Further, it does not present a beauty that is profoundly associated with Chan aesthetic.

To justify my last remark it is necessary to define beauty from the Chan point of view. In *Zen and the Fine Arts,* Hisamatsu Shin'ichi clarifies this question by identifying seven characteristics of Chan art: asymmetry, simplicity, austere sublimity or lofty dryness, naturalness, subtle profundity or deep reserve, freedom from attachment, and tranquility.[33] By "asymmetry" he means negation of "perfection, grace, and holiness" (*Zen,* 30). Chan is for informality as opposed to formality, irregularity as opposed to regularity, odd numbers as opposed to even numbers. By "simplicity" he suggests avoiding elaboration. In color Chan prefers monochrome or black and white (30–31). By "austere sublimity" he is speaking of adherence to the pith or essence only. It also means being "bony" and well-seasoned in age (31). By "naturalness" he implies being unstrained and unforced. "'Intentional' Naturalness," he argues, "results when the artist enters so thoroughly into what he is creating that no conscious effort, no distance between the two, remains" (32). By "subtle profundity" he really designates a presence that is implied,

18. Unidentified Chinese artist (14th century), *White Heron on a Snow-covered Willow*. William Sturgis Bigelow Collection, 11.6161. © 2000 Museum of Fine Arts, Boston. All Rights Reserved. (Courtesy, Museum of Fine Arts, Boston)

"an endless reverberation, which comes from a never completely revealed, bottomless depth" (34). By "freedom from attachment" he hints at obeying no rule (34–35). And by "tranquility" he refers to composure and "rest amid motion," not being disquieted or disquieting (36).

A summary of the seven characteristics is not helpful enough in defining the Chan concept of beauty. To have a real appreciation of Chan aesthetic we must see how these characteristics are reflected in Chan paintings. For our purpose, the best thing to do is to look at some winter scenes available in the MFA during Stevens's formative years. Three of these come to mind: the hanging scroll *White Heron* (fig. 18), the fan piece *Winter Forest* (fig. 19), and the square album leaf *Winter Riverscape*.[34]

Readers will find that these pictures, painted six hundred to eight hundred years ago by unknown Chan artists, share a common rule without rule. They all appear irregular ("asymmetric"), sparse ("simple"), and "aged" ("austere/sublime"). The white heron, the mountains,

19. Unidentified Chinese artist (mid-12th century), *Winter Forest*. Chinese and Japanese Special Fund, 14.53. © 2000 Museum of Fine Arts, Boston. All Rights Reserved. (Courtesy, Museum of Fine Arts, Boston)

the rivers, and the trees all have rugged, sturdy, and ancient faces. Instead of situating in the center, they each occupy a corner with plenty of empty space around them. There are no glaring colors, no feelings of crowdedness, nothing that Chan detests.

As we wander deeper into the pictures, we are struck by the other characteristics of Chan art. All the subjects here appear unstrained ("natural"), deceptively artless ("subtle/profound"), "non-dependent" ("free from attachment"), and infinitely serene ("tranquil"). The white heron looks common and spontaneous in the sense of having "no-mind." So do the mountains and rivers. So do the trees and rocks. Further, there is a darkness pervading the scenes, a darkness that implies calmness instead of fear. Indeed, the overall impression one receives from these and other pictures of the tradition is infinite tranquility.

If Stevens had not viewed the above paintings, he had at least gazed at works similar to them by 1917. He seems to have translated their common characteristics into "Thirteen Ways." Speaking of the series in 1928, Stevens insisted that it was "not meant to be a collection of epigrams or of ideas, but of sensations" (L, 251). After citing that remark, Litz comments that the group was meant to isolate and identify "the 'sensations' prompted by different landscapes."[35] Stevens's "sensations," we can add, were prompted mostly by different Chan landscapes and their unique attributes.

Read with the seven characteristics in mind, "Thirteen Ways" becomes, first of all, an excellent illustration of the Chan preference for "informality over formality, irregularity over regularity, odd numbers over even numbers." Some would argue that the series has a form, that of the Japanese haiku. Yes, quite a few of its poems resemble the haiku in both form and subject matter, but many more appear too long. The line numbers vary from 2, 3, 4 to 5, 6, 7, betraying an irregularity that is typical of Chan art. And the total number of its poems, thirteen, is a Chan-endorsed odd number. For Helen Vendler "thirteen is the eccentric number" that reveals Stevens's medievalism "in his relish for external form."[36] Stevens is "almost medieval," medieval in Chan in this case.

"Thirteen Ways" also exemplifies what Chan means by "simplicity." Like the Chan landscapes we have pondered, the poems here reject crowdedness, complexity, and bright colors. The series begins with a poem like a simplified Chan spatial arrangement in black-and-white: "Among twenty snowy mountains, / The only moving thing / Was the eye of the blackbird" (CPWS, 92). And it ends with a verse like a simplified Chan spatial arrangement in black-and-white: "It was evening all afternoon. / It was snowing / And it was going to snow" (CPWS, 95). In between, the remaining poems all resemble simplified Chan monochromes.

Of the third characteristic, "austere sublimity," Hisamatsu remarks that it "means the disappearance of the sensuous—of the skin or the flesh—and becoming bony" (Zen, 31). In the verbal sketches of "Thirteen Ways" we witness nothing but the pith, that is, just blackbirds with their eyes, trees, mountains, rivers, snow, winds, icicles, a glass coach, and so on with no sensuous details added. Whereas previous critics have spoken of this style in terms of modernist abstraction, we might call it "lofty dryness" in the vocabulary of Chan Buddhism.

The group can no doubt serve as a superb example of the fourth characteristic, "naturalness." Going through the thirteen poems we see that everything presented is far from being forced or strained. Despite the shift of perspectives, the blackbirds consistently appear impulsive in their movement and stillness. The thin men of Haddam look totally absorbed in their imagination of golden birds, so absorbed that they pay no heed to the blackbird around them. The river keeps moving whether or not it is snowing. As we go over the poems, we are encouraged to experience the state of no-mind that warrants perception of the thing itself in ordinary things.

Further, underneath superficial simplicity there is "subtle profundity," the fifth characteristic, in these poems. So much is implied in the unadorned statements of, say, IV ("A man and a woman / Are one / . . ."), IX ("When the blackbird flew out of sight / . . ."), and X ("At the sight of blackbirds / . . .") that readers have kept speculating about their meaning without having exhausted the depth of their reserve.

Likewise, the sixth characteristic, "freedom from attachment," is evident throughout the series. All the poems here refuse habit, formula, rule, and custom—in short, conventional way of looking at things. So instead of catching sight of golden birds, the speaker sees only blackbirds. Instead of just noticing that "A man and a woman / Are one," he notices also that "A man and a woman and a blackbird / Are one." Instead of just saying that "I know noble accents / And lucid, inescapable rhythms," he bewilders and amuses us by adding that "the blackbird is involved / In what I know." Everywhere in the group is unorthodoxy of this sort.

Finally, the sequence illustrates the characteristic of "tranquility" very clearly. As Hisamatsu notes, the Chan quality of composure is "excellently expressed in the phrase 'rest amid motion'" (*Zen,* 36). It may be said that this attribute is present at its best in poems I, II, III, VI, XII, and XIII. These turn out to be the pieces that are most reminiscent of the paintings considered above. Poem III ("The blackbird whirled in the autumn winds. / It was a small part of the pantomime."), in particular, articulates the Chan notion mutely suggested by the winter scenes; there is endless reverberation in the infinite tranquility of the universe.

Hisamatsu attests that the seven characteristics arise from the nature of Chan itself (*Zen,* 53). This shrewd statement clarifies why Chan art necessarily possesses these qualities. It also illuminates how it is possible that viewing different Chan landscapes should enable Stevens to translate their shared traits into his work perhaps without knowing it.

Remarkably, the same Chan attributes are present in "The Snow Man," where the meditative detachment sharpens into an overpowering vision of the nothing in the thing itself:

> One must have a mind of winter
> To regard the frost and the boughs
> Of the pine-trees crusted with snow;
>
> And have been cold a long time
> To behold the junipers shagged with ice,
> The spruces rough in the distant glitter
>
> Of the January sun; and not to think
> Of any misery in the sound of the wind,
> In the sound of a few leaves,
>
> Which is the sound of the land
> Full of the same wind
> That is blowing in the same bare place
>
> For the listener, who listens in the snow,
> And, nothing himself, beholds
> Nothing that is not there and the nothing that is.
>
> (*CPWS,* 9–10)

This widely anthologized piece is unique among *Harmonium* poems in its use of a single long sentence, broken into tercets, to present a meditative experience. Its imagery, like that of "Thirteen Ways," is reminiscent of Chan landscapes. Unlike the series, the short poem appears to be a synthesis of their multiple perspectives. Put together "Thirteen Ways" and "The Snow Man" may serve to illustrate the Chan belief in "the One in the Many and the Many in the One."[37]

It is not surprising that "The Snow Man" can accompany any of the above Chan landscapes and clarify their implications. On the other hand, these Chan landscapes may be used to illuminate this famous poem of winter. Viewed with "The Snow Man" in mind, the *White Heron* turns into "the listener, who listens in the snow, / And, nothing himself, beholds / Nothing that is not there and the nothing that is."

No such listener is physically present in the other pictures. Nonetheless, Stevens's poem will cause the beholder to recognize that the winter landscapes are meant to change himself or herself into the listener who beholds "Nothing that is not there and the nothing that is."

Readers have often found the poem's abrupt shift from the thing itself—"the pine-trees crusted with snow" or "the junipers shagged with ice"—to "the nothing" puzzling, shocking, disturbing, or even distasteful. Many have trouble apprehending what the poet actually means by "a mind of winter." It is hard to grasp how one can become nothing and behold the nothing. Bevis suggests that in Western theories there is no suitable language for interpreting "The Snow Man."[38] Such a reading can be found in Chan Buddhism, a system that disregards reason in favor of intuition.

For Chan Buddhists, to achieve enlightenment one must be stripped of all desire, all thought, all fantasy, all acquired acknowledge. Only when one ceases to think and becomes nothing, one perceives the thing itself and the nothing in enlightenment. "Before one is enlightened," Chan masters often say, "one sees a mountain as a mountain and a river as a river; in the process of attaining enlightenment, mountains are no longer mountains, rivers no longer rivers; but when one has finally achieved enlightenment, mountains are once more mountains, rivers once more rivers."[39] What they mean is that before enlightenment one tends to confuse seeing/hearing with cogitating, whereas with enlightenment one loses all cogitating (misery, joy, and so on), hence perception of the thing itself and the nothing.

"The Snow Man," while paralleling the Emersonian figure in "Nature," who on a bare common "[becomes] a transparent eyeball," and who asserts, "I am nothing; I see all,"[40] also seems to echo the Chan zeal for becoming nothing to perceive only the thing itself (the Particular) and the nothing (the Absolute). To an extent, the poem may be an attempt to invoke the process of achieving enlightenment in three steps. Whereas in stanzas 1–2 readers are apt to picture the frost as the frost, the snow as the snow, and the ice as the ice, in stanzas 3–4 the frost is no longer the frost, the snow no longer the snow, and the ice no longer the ice. In stanza 5, readers may perceive that the frost is once more the frost, the snow once more the snow, and the ice once more the ice.

To return to the question about the poem's "abrupt shift," it should be stressed that it is not a shift from the thing itself to the nothing but one from the thing itself to the unity of the thing itself and the nothing. The vision of the thing itself and the nothing, joined in stanza 5 ("Nothing that is not there and the nothing that is"), is brought about through negation of cogitating ("not to think") in stanzas 3–4.

Stevens makes a start at perceiving the thing itself in "Thirteen Ways." It is in "The Snow Man" that he first succeeds in uniting the thing itself and the nothing. The motif of the poem of 1920–21, as Robert Aitken insists, recurs in its companion piece "Tea at the Palaz of Hoon," where Hoon's descent "in purple" might be compared to that of the Buddha "from his profound experience under the Bodhi tree":[41]

> Out of my mind the golden ointment rained,
> And my ears made the blowing hymns they heard.
> I was myself the compass of that sea:
>
> I was the world in which I walked, and what I saw
> Or heard or felt came not but from myself;
> And there I found myself more truly and more strange.
>
> (CPWS, 65)

The theme of the suchness/nothingness is to be rehearsed again and again in Stevens's poetry, in "Autumn Refrain" (1931), "The Latest Freed Man" (1938), "The Course of a Particular" (1951), and "A Clear Day and No Memories" (1955).

Around 1920 Stevens was decades ahead of his fellow Americans in appreciation of the spirit of Chan.[42] Besides his innate meditative detachment, he perhaps most owed this advance to Chan art. Pictures, according to J. Hillis Miller, are apt to conceal and misrepresent while they illuminate (Illustration, 150). Nevertheless, such visual "blurs" tend to clarify in the context of words. Is it possible, then, that Stevens was reading Buddhist literature in 1919–20, and that the insights he acquired from it had joined relevant pictures in prompting "The Snow Man" and "Tea at the Palaz of Hoon"?

Evidence reveals that Stevens was reading a guide to Buddhism, the Reverend Samuel Beal's Buddhism in China, in 1919. His copy of the book in the Huntington Library bears his inscription in the upper left of the front endpaper: "W. Stevens / Boston / Feb. 12, 1919." With aid of his markings throughout the volume, we can identify Stevens's moments of puzzle, recognition, appreciation, and awakening. One of the marginal markings he entered is on page 198. It shows a certain eagerness with which he read about Chan Buddhism's emphasis on "quietism." The paragraph that follows outlines that their "definition of destruction as a part of the formula for Nirvāna alludes to the destruction of every part of the being called 'man.'"[43]

Another marking he entered is on page 215. It pins down a moment at which his attention was captured by an account of how Bodhidharma of India, the semilegendary founder of Chan Buddhism, bewildered the emperor of South China (Emperor Wu of Southern Liang) by a peculiar way of demonstrating "emptiness" and "nothingness." In the passage marked out by a bold line, we read that "The emperor then asked: 'Which is the most important of the holy doctrine?' To which the monk replied: 'Where all is emptiness, nothing can be called 'holy.' The emperor rejoined: 'Who then is it that replies to me?' The patriarch: 'I do not know.'"[44]

Finally, a notation at the end of the book's index—"The Awakened 83"—points to Stevens's own moment of "awakening." The section singled out for attention describes how after long meditation Śākyamuni attains the state of no-mind and no-feeling, the "great awakened state of 'perfect light'":

> Then, passing through successive stages of rapt ecstasy, he traces back all suffering to the one cause of ignorance (*avidyā*), that is, absence of light, and then himself attains the great awakened state of "perfect light." Thus did he complete the end of "self"; as fire goes out for want of grass, thus he had done what he would have men do; he first had found the way of perfect knowledge, then lustrous with all-wisdom, the great *rishi* sat, perfect in gifts, whilst one convulsive throe shook the wide earth. This is the condition of the Buddha, or the awakened, and by this name henceforth he is to be called.[45]

We might compare this description with its visual counterpart in a pair of scrolls by Liang Kai often reproduced together in books about Chan, although they do not appear in Beal's work. Of one of the two scrolls, *Śākyamuni Emerging from the Mountains,* Hisamatsu writes, "The entire figure of Śākyamuni unmistakably tells us that he has attained the serenity of *nirvana*" (*Zen,* 61). "The eyes, unlike those looking *at* something, are very introspective," he specifies. "They are the eyes, we may say, of depth itself, or of Nothingness" (62).

Śākyamuni and its companion piece, *Landscape in Snow,* now preserved in the National Museum, Tokyo, are held in very high esteem by Chan devotees. Ironically, to those with no knowledge of Chan the two relics probably mean as little as Beal's passages marked out by Stevens. Some may ask, "How do you know Śākyamuni's eyes are of nothingness?" Others, "What makes you think *Landscape in Snow* is from the perspective of one with no-mind?" Nevertheless, if the two paintings are put together and accompanied by Chan commentary, picture and word may cause each other to shine. Precisely because of their recognition of this effect, Hisamatsu in *Zen and the Fine Arts* and Suzuki in *Zen and Japanese Culture* both include the pair as illustrations.

Now, it should be clear that the passages Stevens found to be delightful, engaging, and significant may not appear so to other readers of *Buddhism in China*. Unlike most of his peers, Stevens read these passages with illuminating pictures and meditative conditions in mind, which made all the difference. At age nineteen he was already musing on a question that betrayed Chan leanings: "why people took books into the woods to read in summertime when there was so much else to be read there that one could not find in books" (*L, 22*). The poet, according to Peter Lee, acknowledged "a strong taste for Oriental paintings."[46] By 1919 he most probably had viewed quite a few pictures in the style of Liang Kai's masterpieces. Several of them would remain dormant in his memory until they blended with words and meditative experiences to incite "The Snow Man."

It is tempting at this point to risk a few general remarks. One is offered three ways to grasp Chan: visual, verbal, and actional. Stevens was involved in all three during his formative years. It was his own meditative nature that inspired him to pursue Chan art. From there he moved on to read about Chan Buddhism. Almost certainly, his Chan pictures glowed when combined with corresponding words and consciousness. Nevertheless, Chan did not become realized until Stevens took the action of composing poems such as "The Snow Man."

Chan does not fade away in late Stevens as some have claimed. Instead, it recurs in his poetry of the 1930s to the 1950s. To that concern I shall return in chapter 13.

PART 3

Picturing

the

Other

SIX

Stevens's "Six Significant Landscapes"

IN *Picture Theory*, W. J. T. Mitchell offers an engaging examination of ekphrasis, or verbal representation of visual representation, beginning "not at origin" but with Stevens's "Anecdote of the Jar."[1] This 1919 poem certainly is not Stevens's first experiment with ekphrasis. Several of his earlier poems—section 1 of "Six Significant Landscapes" (1916), "Thirteen Ways of Looking at a Blackbird" (1917), and section 3 of "Le Monocle de Mon Oncle" (1918)—may serve as equally fine examples of the literary mode whose central goal, according to Mitchell, is "the overcoming of otherness," that is, "those rival, alien modes of representation called the visual, graphic, plastic, or 'spatial' arts."[2] One thing strikes us at once: All three earlier poems signify Stevens's aspiration to represent otherness in a more intricate way. What he seeks to explore includes not only the passage to another medium but the passage to another age and another culture as well. His endeavor to cross medium, age, and culture simultaneously is best exemplified by section 1 of "Six Significant Landscapes," a verbalized depiction of Chinese landscape painting:

> An old man sits
> In the shadow of a pine tree
> In China.
> He sees larkspur,
> Blue and white,
> At the edge of the shadow,
> Move in the wind.
> His beard moves in the wind.
> The pine tree moves in the wind.

Thus water flows
Over weeds.   (*CPWS*, 73)

In this "verse-panel" (Walton Litz's phrase), Chinese landscape painting is represented in several ways: by focus on a single point of sight
("An old man" gazing out forever at those gazing at him); by choice for
subject all that is elemental in nature and in Chinese landscape painting ("a pine tree," "wind," "water," and so on); by reliance on a few
simple strokes of description (five simple sentences); and by an almost
monochrome tonality of gray and blue and white that is known to have
dominated Chinese landscape painting in the twelfth to the fifteenth
centuries. The repetition of "Move in the wind" in the last five lines
emphasizes only too obviously the painting's peculiar power of showing "rest amid motion" and turning every object, including the lone
figure, into an integral part of the immense cosmos. The verse panel,
like the landscape it represents, portrays a single impression: consciousness of the unity of all created things. In Litz's description, "Here nothing is wasted: the mosaic of images, one superimposed upon the other
in the mind of the reader, makes a complex statement on the paradox
of permanence within change."[3]

For those immersed in Chinese art, the style and sentiment presented
here really recall a particular school of Chinese landscape painting—
the "Ma-Xia school" of landscape painting, which flourished in the late
twelfth to the early thirteen centuries. Landscape rose as an independent genre of painting in China at least a millennium earlier than in
Europe. It attained maturity in the Northern Song (960–1127). After
the collapse of the Northern Song the discourse continued to thrive
in Southern Song China (1127–1279).[4] Although most of the aesthetic
interests we now associate with Chan had arisen in the Northern Song,
according to Li Zehou, "they reached their acme in the academic style
of the Southern Song."[5] Ma Yuan (active before 1189 to after 1225) and
Xia Gui (active ca. 1180–1224)[6] were the cofounders of this school—
note the fact that their simple, concentrated treatments contrast sharply
with the elaborate, panoramic views of their predecessors. Their exem-
plary works, the paintings of fragments of hills and streams and trees,
are prized today especially for their faculty for bringing to light the
"inexpressible" spirit of Chan.

Prior to 1916, when "Six Significant Landscapes" first appeared, a
considerable number of works of the "Ma-Xia school" had already
made their way into the Museum of Fine Arts, the Metropolitan Mu-

seum, and the Freer Collection. These paintings are characterized precisely by impressionistic and fragmentary depiction of lone figures and natural objects, by sweeping strokes of the brush that suggest the most with the simplest means, by the faintest application of color, and by means of expression for the artist's sentiment. A single man in the midst of rippling pine trees, weeds, and waters in a Ma Yuan or a Xia Gui, as Suzuki remarks, is enough to awaken in the mind of the beholder a sense of ease, leisure, and contentment, the Chan-Buddhist sense of "the Alone."[7]

In 1919, as we have noted, Stevens was to read Samuel Beal's *Buddhism in China* and to mark out a passage that deals with the Chan Buddhist ideal of "the Awakened." To our amazement, in his 1916 version of a Chinese landscape painting, this sense of "the Awakened" or "the Alone" is well captured; we as readers are given an opportunity to feel the breathing of nature and to become one with it.

If Chinese landscape painting aiming to communicate the spirit of Chan or the Dao has a traditional scene, this is it. First of all, the old man in Stevens's ekphrastic poem, as in the kind of Song landscape painting it endeavors to emulate, appears sitting in meditation, that is, in a state of active tranquility that opens the way to enlightenment. Second, the figure is shown to be perfectly in harmony with nature. The larkspur he gazes at may provide the shock that brings enlightenment. The man who sees the larkspur moving in the wind suddenly, in the flash of a single thought, is no longer aware of himself. He is that larkspur, the larkspur that reveals universal reality: "Thus water flows / Over weeds." When the artist paints the landscape, the essential breath is discharged through his brush; he captures it in its dazzling "suchness." Third, the flowing water in the scene is a perfect symbol of the Dao. As the *Daode jing,* the single most important text of Daoism, teaches, "The sage's way, Tao, is the way of water. There must be water for life to be, and it can flow wherever. And water, being true to being water, is true to Tao." Finally, the wind in the scene is just another symbol of the Dao. According to the *Daode jing,* "The Great Tao goes everywhere past your left hand and your right—filling the whole of space. It is breath to every thing, and yet it asks for nothing back; it feeds and creates everything, but it will never tell you so."[8]

In this light, it is not surprising that Stevens's image is to be seen in numerous Chinese landscape paintings of the Southern Song period and thereafter. The New York collector C. C. Wang, for instance, owned an album leaf by Ma Yuan, which was later sold to Mr. and Mrs. A. Dean

Perry of Cleveland, showing a scholar with a servant beneath a pine tree watching a deer bend to flowing waters (fig. 20).[9] He sees bamboo leaves, gray and white, at the edge of the water, move in the wind. The pine tree moves in the wind. Thus water flows over rocks. In the Bigelow Collection at the Museum of Fine Arts are sixteen Southern Song Buddhist paintings, one of which portrays the Luohan Fanaposi sitting

20. Ma Yuan (active before 1189–after 1225), *Watching the Deer by a Pine-shaded Stream.* Gift of Mrs. A. Dean Perry, 1997.88. © The Cleveland Museum of Art, 2002. (Courtesy, Cleveland Museum of Art, Cleveland)

in the shadow of a willow tree contemplating a lotus pond (fig. 21).[10] He sees lotus, pink and white, in the pond, move in the wind. The willow tree moves in the wind. Thus water flows in the lotus pond. Evidently there is Buddhist lyricism in both masterpieces.

Additional examples of landscape paintings repeating this theme are to be found in books on Far Eastern art. In *Epochs of Chinese and Japanese Art,* a work Stevens might have gone through, Fenollosa presents two: one ascribed to the Northern Song emperor Huizong and the other to

21. Lu Xinzhong (active late 12th–early 13th century), *The Fourteenth Luohan Fanaposi.* William Sturgis Bigelow Collection, 11.6129. © 2000 Museum of Fine Arts, Boston. All Rights Reserved. (Courtesy, Museum of Fine Arts, Boston)

Xia Gui.[11] It is worth quoting Fenollosa's version of a little poem given below Xia Gui's image: "Where my pathway came to an end by the rising waters covered, I sat me down to watch the shapes in the mist that over it hovered."[12] Also, in *The Illustrated Tao Te Ching,* a 1993 version of Laozi's treatise, the illustration for the saying "The Tao is the breath that never dies" is precisely an old man in the shadow of a pine tree gazing out onto a flowing stream.[13]

One painting that matches Stevens's poem to the smallest detail, however, is the album leaf *Viewing the Moon under a Pine Tree,* a thirteenth-century imitation of a masterpiece formerly attributed to Ma Yuan (fig. 22). This painting has been in the Metropolitan Museum ever since 1923. Though the treasure is not publicly displayed except on rare occasions, its image appears in numerous books on Chinese art. Indeed, many may recognize it as the cover art for a volume of the Norton series of anthologies, *Masterpieces of the Orient,* edited by G. L. Anderson.

As can be seen, in the painting the wind really becomes "visible" with the rhythmical movements of the pine tree, the weeds, the water, and the old man's beard. The flower that captivates the figure does not look like larkspur, though, but Stevens could have taken it as such. On 25 July 1915, it may be remembered, Stevens was attracted to some larkspur from China in the Botanical Garden of New York, and in a letter of that evening to his wife, he remarked, "I was able to impress on myself that larkspur comes from China. Was there ever anything more Chinese when you stop to think of it?" (*L,* 184).

22. After Ma Yuan, 13th century, *Viewing the Moon under a Pine Tree.* Rogers Fund, 1923 (23.33.5). (Courtesy, Metropolitan Museum of Art, New York)

However, according to the records of the Metropolitan Museum, the album leaf *Viewing the Moon under a Pine Tree* entered its collection in 1923.[14] Research uncovers no evidence that the work was ever on loan to it prior to that date. The poem is therefore more likely to have been inspired by what James Heffernan calls "memory-pictures,"[15] that is, Stevens's reminiscence of other Chinese landscape paintings echoing Ma Yuan's favorite theme. He might have seen one example of this tradition with admiration, and then another and another, in books and in art galleries. As he observes in his 1951 article on "The Relations between Poetry and Painting," "The mind retains experience, so that long after the experience . . . that faculty within us of which I have spoken makes its own constructions out of that experience" (*NA*, 164). Here his insight sounds like Chan. Several facts appear to point to the truth of this assumption. First, Stevens attended numerous exhibitions of Far Eastern art during the years 1897–1916. Second, his admiration for Oriental art spurred him to study the subject extensively in 1909–11. Third, in pursuit of Chinese art, his taste appeared especially for Song landscape painting that illustrates the Dao with "magical" clarity.

In 1905–13, with Okakura in charge of Chinese and Japanese art, a large number of paintings attributed to Ma Yuan and his followers entered the MFA. Among these were *Scholar with Attendants under a Tree,* ascribed to Ma Yuan, and *Landscape,* a fifteenth-century Japanese imitation of the motif (fig. 23).[16] Since Stevens traveled to Boston so frequently during that period (September 1906, October 1907, September 1909 with his bride, and so on), we have reason to believe that he had seen Ma Yuan and his imitators with fresh eyes.[17]

While in New York, Stevens kept going to various art shows. By 1913 the Metropolitan Museum had acquired Xia Gui's *Landscape,* Tan Song's *Landscape in the Style of Guo Xi,*[18] and *Scholar under a Tree in Autumn,* a fifteenth-century imitation of Ma Yuan's timeless theme. As a frequenter of the Metropolitan Museum, Stevens might have viewed some of these works in the Asiatic Room. In March 1916 the Met staged an exhibition of early Chinese pottery and sculpture, while the Bourgeois Gallery in New York mounted a show of Chinese, Japanese, and Persian paintings. As chapter 2 indicates, Stevens probably went to both. If he really attended the Met exhibition, he most likely saw a Song vase adorned with an image of an old man seated under a pine tree. And if he indeed visited the Bourgeois Gallery show, he could not have missed a large Song painting portraying several scholars viewing waterfalls under trees.

23. Bunsei (Japanese, active mid-15th century), *Landscape*. Chinese and Japanese Special Fund, 05.203. © 2000 Museum of Fine Arts, Boston. All Rights Reserved. (Courtesy, Museum of Fine Arts, Boston)

Further, prior to 1916, Stevens did considerable reading about Chinese art. Among the books he went through were Okakura's *The Ideals of the East* and Binyon's *Painting in the Far East*. In *Painting* Binyon refers to Ma Yuan, Xia Gui, and their precursor, Guo Xi, as the three "preeminent landscape masters of Sung" (136). Just as Fenollosa in *Epochs* presents several images in the style of Ma and Xia, Binyon in his volume includes a reproduction of Ma Yuan's *Pines and Rocky Peaks*.[19]

Also, in *Painting* Binyon calls attention to a little poem by the Song reformer Wang Anshi. The piece struck Stevens as more beautiful and more Chinese than anything he had seen anywhere, and so he copied it out for Elsie on 18 March 1909: "It is midnight; all is silent in the house; the water-clock has stopped. But I am unable to sleep because of the beauty of the trembling shapes of the spring flowers, thrown by the moon upon the blind" (*L,* 138).[20] What is represented here is a verbal version of a traditional Chinese scene—a Chinese seated in darkness enjoying the shapes of spring flowers move in the wind. Stevens could have in mind this poem along with Song pictures while painting his significant landscapes in words. A look at the verse panels that follow reveals that Wang Anshi's images—the serene night, the full moon, the flower silhouette—get involved almost everywhere. His trembling flowers appear to have changed into a bracelet in panel 2: "A pool shines, / Like a bracelet / Shaken in a dance." His bright moon has become Stevens's image of the moon in panel 4: "When my dream was near the moon, / The white folds of its gown / Filled with yellow light." And more important, the moonlight that recurs in panels 2 and 4 seems to have contributed to Stevens's Cubist image of the starlight in panel 5:

> Not all the knives of the lamp-posts,
> Nor the chisels of the long streets,
> Nor the mallets of the domes
> And high towers,
> Can carve
> What one star can carve,
> Shining through the grape-leaves.

It is apparent that panels 1–5 are all variations "on the 'anti-rational' theme of [panel 6]":

> Rationalists, wearing square hats,
> Think, in square rooms,

Looking at the floor,
Looking at the ceiling.   (*CPWS*, 74–75)

So, Litz is precise in suggesting that Stevens's first five verse panels are meant to mock "those habits of mind and language which screens us away from new perceptions of things as they are."[21]

In *Mind of Winter*, Bevis demonstrates at some length how Stevens was attracted toward notions that bring our mind closer to "new perceptions of things as they are," notions best illustrated in Chinese and Japanese art. He aptly points out, "One of Stevens' most distinguishing and pervasive characteristics, his detachment, is meditative and therefore experiential in origin, and difficult to perceive from within our culture." Further, he notes, "If one distinguishes Western and Eastern artists along the lines of interest in cause-effect events, assertion, anxiety on the one hand, and consciousness, negation, serenity on the other, then Stevens would seem at least half oriental."[22] There is no need to go over all the evidence Bevis adduces to build up his argument. One incident toward the end of Stevens's Cambridge years, however, is worth repeating.

In composing the verse panel, Stevens probably recollected two summer evening scenes in Reading, Pennsylvania. After a long walk on the afternoon of 17 July 1899, he went through a garden "in a half enchantment over the flowers." Larkspur, "generally purple, or mixed purple and pink"; bergamot, "a big husky flower"; and mignonette, "a little vigorous flower," caught his eye, and he was mesmerized by "The least breath of wind shimmer[ing] over them." "[T]he impression of them is daffodylic," he noted in his journal. "It is impossible to say more— they are so splendid" (*L*, 28). The next evening, as his journal entry of 19 July 1899 reveals, he "lay in a field on the other side of the creek to the S. E. of the house and watched the sunset. . . . The moon was very fine. . . . [He] felt a thrill at the mystery of the thing and perhaps a little touch of fear" (29). The two summer evening scenes struck him as so beautiful that for days he tried to find words for what these had meant to him. A week later he concluded, "Diaries are very futile. It is quite impossible for me to express any of the beauty I feel to half the degree I feel it; and yet it is a great pleasure to seize an impression and lock it up in words: you feel as if you had it safe forever" (30).

This incident should help illuminate two essential facts. First, in early youth Stevens developed an interest in "consciousness, negation, serenity," which Bevis has described as the "other aspect" in his nature.

Second, he apparently had a strong desire to express this aspect "difficult to perceive from within our culture." In his search for forms, Chinese landscape painting, particularly Southern Song landscape painting, displayed in galleries, naturally had an appeal for him, as it appeared to be the best means of expression for clarifying the otherness in his character.

Stevens has evidently translated certain Song (or Chan) tastes, along with the "other aspect" in his nature, into section 1 of "Six Significant Landscapes." The verse panel, despite its surface simplicity, exemplifies Southern Song landscape painting in its most complex and articulate status. Its image might be seen as a labyrinth of Southern Song painters'—and Stevens's own—reflections on the relations of art, artist, model, and observer. As the poem opens, the "old man" appears unequivocally as an object, a model, a part of a painting; he "sits / In the shadow of a pine tree / In China." At this moment, when he is classically posed, he is perfectly identified with other objects—the pine tree, larkspur, weeds, and water. Like everything else the figure is being gazed at, studied, and portrayed. This image, however, is capable of turning itself (or himself) into an active observer/seeing artist: "He sees larkspur, / Blue and white, / At the edge of the shadow, / Move in the wind." Here he is no longer identified (at least not completely identified) with seen objects such as the pine tree and the larkspur. With the action of seeing and imagining, his image as a model/seen object is subverted or deconstructed. His role has shifted from that of a passive model to that of an active observer/seeing artist. In other words, the viewer *in* the landscape has metamorphosed into the viewer *of* the landscape. At this moment we might as well question our own identity as the reader/observer/artist: Is it possible that the image has turned the table on us and changed us also into the gazer/object, who at once gazes and is gazed at? This ambivalence intensifies in the final four meditative lines, where all the distinctions among art, artist, model, and observer disappear and everything in and beyond the poem (or the painting it depicts) becomes one, moving along with the motion of the great "cosmic rhythm": "Thus water flows / Over weeds."

This is the perfect experience of the Dao or "the Alone," the perfect condition of Chan or "the Awakened." In the hanging scroll *The Luohan Fanaposi,* the Luohan pays no heed to the servant who has been standing there, tray in hand, for a long while. In the album leaf *Viewing the Moon under a Pine Tree,* the old man is oblivious to this world, so oblivious that he never notices a servant boy playing around him. (In fact, in Ma Yuan and his most faithful imitators' treatment of their timeless theme, the lone figure is also oblivious of being gazed at/portrayed. He sits characteristically with his face turned away from the artist/viewer.) Likewise, Stevens in his verse panel never mentions a boy who is always there in the background of the Southern Song landscape. Like the old man in the Chinese painting, he is oblivious of *this* world and he sees nothing but larkspur, blue and white, move in the wind.

Section 1 of "Six Significant Landscapes" may not be a very important poem in Stevens's canon, but ironically it provides the fullest case for approaching Stevens's ways of crossing medium, age, and culture, his peculiar way of modernizing his poetry. In his formative years, Stevens evidently was attracted to Southern Song landscape painting, which at once stood for visual otherness, historical otherness, and cultural otherness. The influence comes down to his recognizing Chinese artists' power of getting the unsayable message of the Dao or Chan said. This power made it possible for Stevens to build a model of values dependent not so much on "cause-effect events, assertion, anxiety" as on "consciousness, negation, serenity." Out of this model some of Stevens's most memorable lines emerge:

> The river is moving.
> The blackbird must be flying.   (*CPWS*, 94)

> For the listener, who listens in the snow,
> And, nothing himself, beholds
> Nothing that is not there and the nothing that is.   (10)

SEVEN

Moore and
Ming-Qing Porcelain:
"Nine Nectarines"

TO SHIFT FROM Stevens's "Six Significant Landscapes" to Moore's "Nine Nectarines" is to shift from nonclassical ekphrasis to mock-classical ekphrasis, from the verbal representation of a Chinese landscape painting to appealing designs on Chinese porcelain pictured in words. In Western literature, the origin of ekphrasis goes back to Homer's account of Achilles's shield in *The Iliad*,[1] a passage Mitchell characterizes as "an imagetext that displays rather than concealing its own suturing of space and time, description and narration, materiality and illusionistic representation."[2] From Homer's "Shield" there has arisen a long tradition of ekphrasis, concentrating first and foremost on serviceable implements with scenes and figures fixed on them. The most noteworthy English example of classical ekphrasis, "Ode on a Grecian Urn," is a Romantic poet's meditation on a relic that shares distinguishing traits with Homer's shield. Their common features are captured in Moore's objects of aesthetic contemplation. Like Homer's shield and Keats's urn, her plate and vase are circular, utilitarian articles that happen to bear ornamental pictures.[3] Unlike them, however, her objects of art were wrought not in Greece but in China.

Written in the early summer of 1934—what is sometimes considered the bloom of Moore's poetic career—"Nine Nectarines" offers a conspicuous instance of modernist ekphrasis that challenges the Homeric model under the guise of imitation. As various critics have seen, Homer's famous ekphrastic passage places a great emphasis on the forging of Achilles's protective weapon. In reading Homer's "subtle allusions to sculptural stasis and to the inorganic conditions of the figures on the shield," James Heffernan further points out that Homer deliberately registers in his language "the difference between the medium of visual

representation and its referent." "In the ploughing sequence," he remarks, "we are told that 'the earth darkened behind [the ploughmen]
and looked like earth that has been ploughed / *though it was gold.* Such
was the wonder of the shield's forging.'"[4] Comparison of Moore's verbal reconstruction of a nectarine motif on a "much-mended plate" veri-
fies that she echoes Homer's focus on the fashioning of the ekphrastic
object and his signal of the subtle opposition between the representation of a natural thing and the natural thing itself. Moore is certainly
not paying homage to Homer, but the opening passage of her poem testifies her familiarity with Homeric ekphrasis. She begins in this manner
only to deviate from Homer.

> Arranged by two's as peaches are,
> at intervals that all may live—
>   eight and a single one, on twigs that
>   grew the year before—they look like
> a derivative;
>   although not uncommonly
> the opposite is seen—
> nine peaches on a nectarine.
>   Fuzzless through slender crescent leaves
>   of green or blue or
>   both, in the Chinese style, the four
>
>   pairs' half-moon leaf-mosaic turns
> out to the sun the sprinkled blush
>   of puce-American-Beauty pink
>   applied to bees-wax gray by the
> uninquiring brush
> of mercantile bookbinding.   (*CPMM,* 29)

Notice that the act of painting the picture on porcelain is accentu-
ated by verbs such as "Arranged" and "applied" in the passage. Where
Homer gives the clause "though it was gold" to undermine a figment of
the imagination he has just created, Moore uses the above verbs alongside phrases such as "in the Chinese style" and "by the / uninquiring
brush" to dissolve an illusion of reality built up by another set of verbs:
"live," "grew," and "turns." Furthermore, the last line of the passage, "of
mercantile bookbinding," discloses that what is represented is in fact a
photographic reproduction of an illustrated Chinese plate, or to put it
simply, representation of representation.

Moore's echo of Homeric ekphrasis in "Nine Nectarines" stops at these outer edges, however. Homer's whole point, as most critics agree, is to unite a circular image with a linear text, lend voice and movement to a silent and stilled icon, and turn a permanent descriptive scene into an impermanent narrative action. Thus, in his account of the shield, we witness not only landscapes and personages on the gold piece, but more significantly, a rich variety of Hellenic activities associated with them, activities ranging from the domestic to the civil, from the military to the agricultural, from the festive to the ritualistic. As Murray Krieger remarks, in his ekphrastic masterpiece, "Homer seeks to give us at once both the elaborately ornamented metal artifact and the routine material life of ancient Greece (together with its mythological divine overseers) that he both represents and *mis*represents."[5] Homer's urge to extract stories from stilled figures on implements seems repeated in most examples of ekphrasis from ancient times to postmodernism. Nevertheless, it is absent in Moore's response to illustrated Chinese porcelain. Except for her reference to "the peach *Yu*" which may allude to Chinese legend, her account has no narrative. In her adherence to the quietness and stillness of the visual arts, she is closer to Keats, whose "Urn," in Heffernan's words, "*resists* the traditionally ekphrastic impulse to narrate."[6] Further scrutiny reveals, moreover, that "Nine Nectarines" plays a theme similar to "Urn"'s. The ekphrastic aspiration is said to lend action to art. Surprisingly, in her tribute to art from China, Moore expresses a yearning for its ability to translate imagined movement into permanence. While this is in "Urn," we'll see a moment later that Moore goes far beyond Keats in her modernist ekphrasis.

Having implied Moore's refusal to disparage art's strength in "Nine Nectarines," it is nevertheless necessary to add that the notion of rivalry is inherently embedded in her attempt to represent in words the graphic designs of Chinese wares. A question arises: Has Moore seen, in addition, the nectarine and peach painted on actual porcelain? Laurence Stapleton remarks that Moore's "rapt attention to the nectarine and peach arose from seeing them in a beautiful design on a rare piece of Chinese porcelain."[7] To this we can add: Moore's equally rapt attention to the *qilin* must have stemmed from observing it in beautiful designs on other pieces of Chinese porcelain. We can safely say so partly because such wares from China were easily accessible in New York in the early 1930s and partly because Moore's description appears far richer than if it were drawn on a single photographic representation.

In June 1934, when she sent her ekphrastic poem to *Poetry* to be pub-

24. Qing dish (Yongzheng period, 1723–35) decorated inside with five peaches and three bats and outside with three more peaches and two more bats. (Courtesy, Shanghai Museum, Shanghai)

25. Qing oblated pot (Qianlong period, 1736–95) decorated with nine peaches on a tree. (Courtesy, Shanghai Museum, Shanghai)

lished together with "The Buffalo," Moore offered the title "Imperious Ox, Imperial Dish" for both pieces. Evidently she was aware that her objet d'art adorned with a nectarine or peach motif was once a dish reserved in China for imperial use. It is worth noting here that the center for China's outstanding ceramic art was the ancient porcelain metropolis of Jingdezhen in the province of Jiangxi.[8] During the Ming period (1368–1644) this establishment made impressive wares with peach and *qilin* motifs at different times to be sent to the imperial palace. The Archaeological Museum, Tehran, is one of the fortunate art institutions outside China that houses a group of such enameled porcelain. John Pope, in *Chinese Porcelains from the Ardebil Shrine* (1981), surveys this fine collection of early Chinese porcelain brought together by Shah Abbas the Great of Persia (r. 1587–1629).[9] Among its Ming wares illustrated in the volume is a dish with a formal design of nine peaches or nectarines "Arranged by two's . . . and a single one" on a potted tree. On its base are inscribed the characters *da ming xuande nian zhi:* "Made under the auspices of Emperor Xuande [r. 1426–35] of Great Ming."[10] Another piece illustrated is a ewer with a prancing *qilin* in a landscape as the main design. A matching ewer has the characters *da ming xuande nian zhi* on its base.[11]

In the first half of the seventeenth century, owing to skirmishes between the Ming and the Qing, there was a marked decline in China's production of porcelain. It was the second Qing (Manchu) emperor, Kangxi (r. 1662–1722), who salvaged this industry by appointing a competent man as director of the Jingdezhen imperial factory.[12] The making of wares continued to grow under the patronage of his son Yongzheng (r. 1723–35) and grandson Qianlong (r. 1736–95), who both showed personal interest in ceramic art.[13] A study of Qing porcelain in the Shanghai Museum (edited by Qian Zhengzong) shows that the peach and the *qilin* are among the most popular motifs of the early Qing. Some of the specimens illustrated are a Yongzheng dish adorned with eight peaches and five bats (fig. 24), a Qianlong pot adorned with nine peaches and five bats (fig. 25), and a Kangxi vase adorned with two *qilin* unicorns and a lion (fig. 26).[14]

It is unsurprising that wares with the peach-bat motif remain popular in China today. For the Chinese, the oval peach (*pan tao*) traditionally symbolizes long life, and the bat, pronounced the same way as fortune (*fu*), naturally embodies good fortune. Accordingly, of the curios in a Chinese living room, not the least precious is a porcelain piece

26. Qing long-necked vase (Kangxi period, 1662–1722) decorated with three creatures. (Courtesy, Shanghai Museum, Shanghai)

decorated with a *fu shou tu* (a "fortune-longevity" picture). That explains why imitations of such Ming-Qing wares sell so well in China. During my March 1998 visit to Shanghai, I purchased from the Jingdezhen Artware Service their last vase adorned with nine peaches, an imitation of a Yongzheng ware. In my graduate seminar in modernism and the visual arts offered that summer, the vase served as an illustration for Moore's nectarines "through slender crescent leaves / of green or blue or / both, in the Chinese style."

China's infatuation with the peach is rooted in a belief that the fruit prolongs life symbolically if not practically. In the Chinese mind, the peach is associated with the god of longevity (*Shouxing*). In fact, in 1911 Moore might have viewed in the British Museum a Chinese picture of the god of longevity bending to let a small boy in his arms receive an offer of oval peaches. For young people in China the oval peach is more naturally linked with an episode in Wu Cheng'en's *Journey to the West*. In that episode, Monkey King, the charming hero of the sixteenth-century novel, was put in charge of the Emperor of Heaven's Peach Garden. Upon arrival at his post, he

> asked the local spirit, "How many trees are there?" "There are three thousand six hundred," said the local spirit. "In the front are one thousand two hundred trees. . . . These ripen once every three thousand years, and after one taste of them a man will become an immortal enlightened in the way, with healthy limbs and a light-weight body. In the middle are one thousand two hundred trees. . . . They ripen once every six thousand years. If a man eats them, he will ascend to Heaven with the mist and never grow old. At the back are one thousand two hundred trees. . . . These ripen once every nine thousand years, and if eaten, will make man's age equal to that of Heaven and Earth, the sun and the moon."[15]

Similarly, the Chinese attachment to the *qilin* has its origin in mythical animal lore. To my knowledge, the earliest reference to the imagined creature is in a song in the sixth-century B.C. *Book of Songs (Shi jing)*:

> The *qilin*'s hoofs!
> The horde of the duke's princes.
> Alas for the *qilin*!
>
> The *qilin*'s scalp!
> The horde of the duke's kinsmen.
> Alas for the *qilin*!
>
> The *qilin*'s horn!
> The horde of the duke's clansmen.
> Alas for the *qilin*!

While most critics believe this to be an ancient dance song, Gao Heng suggests that it might be the "long-lost" elegy in which Confucius grieved over a *qilin* slaughtered by a prince and his attendants.[16] Whether or not this is true, the "rarely seen" *qilin* has been regarded as an auspicious animal. Indeed, Confucius is said to have been born after the appearance of a *qilin* to his mother. According to the Han historian Sima Qian, the sage once compared himself to the humane animal. He was traveling to Wei to seek public office. Halfway there he was told of Duke Wei's execution of two scholars. Turning back he said, "I have heard that when you destroy unborn animals or kill young game, the unicorn will not come to the countryside."[17] So, the *qilin* on a Qing vase has a political implication; it displays the early Qing (Manchu) emperors' zeal for appealing to Confucianism and Confucian scholars.[18]

We are now in a better position to appreciate "Nine Nectarines." Moore begins by describing a photographic representation of what are meant to be peaches but to her look like nectarines.[19] That her image is enriched by what she has seen on actual Chinese porcelain and in other representations is plain enough. Her image goes beyond a single picture to include features of several peach motifs on Ming-Qing wares. She recaptures the minute detail of a bat on the wing whose "eyes / are separate from the face" apparently without knowing its association, for she drops this feature along with other things in later printings.[20] Although nine peaches are occasionally seen on Ming dishes, they do not share Moore's rich, soft colors suggestive of the *famille-rose* ware developed in the Yongzheng-Qianlong era.[21] In layout and pigmentation, Moore's image corresponds most closely to those on Yongzheng porcelain. However, according to Lu Minghua, as a rule only eight peaches are painted on Yongzheng dishes as opposed to nine on Qianlong wares.[22] Keats's urn, as Ian Jack has shown, is forged from a variety of real objects of art from Greece.[23] Moore's plate, we can say, mixes features of a number of actual porcelain motifs from China.

We have seen previously Moore's rapture over things Chinese in her formative period. In the years shortly before "Nine Nectarines," this delight was reanimated by several factors. In the spring of 1930 the world-famous Beijing opera singer-dancer-actor Mei Lanfang (1894–1961) toured the United States. Moore saw a program of four short plays by him and his company.[24] She was so overwhelmed by Mei Lanfang's performance in female roles that she wrote to Monroe Wheeler, stating: "I liked him so much the one time I saw him in New York, that I was well satisfied not to go to anything else at the theatre afterward that season" (*SLMM,* 302). In November of 1932 Wheeler got a chance to visit China. In a letter of congratulations, Moore openly expressed her bias for the "classic land" in the East: "Japan I am sometimes interested in, but China is the magic place" (281). While in Paris, Wheeler graciously sent Marianne and her mother some Chinese handkerchiefs and writing paper with matching envelopes. Amusingly, she admired the gifts in the same enamored tone in which she would admire the Chinese porcelain motifs:

> The handkerchiefs almost frighten us by their perfection. . . . This
> paper was a piquant sight to western eyes—the etched red dog

on the green cover sheet not being the least feature. I think the two red gum leaves are perhaps the masterpiece, though one has leanings toward the frog—& toward both envelopes. To think of hazarding two such birds near P. Office cancellation marks seems blasphemy. Accuracy and liveness so remarkable—presented freely in this way as if it were an everyday affair, make one breathe easier having set up for a writer rather than as a painter (*SLMM*, 302).

This is the background against which Moore composed "Nine Nectarines." Her notebook of 1930–43 reveals that her earliest entries of the Chinese oval peach and the *qilin* were made in March 1931.[25] Three years later, on 1 June 1934, she told her brother John Warner Moore that "I am writing like a demon with canton-flannel horns, on my Nectarines poem" (*SLMM*, 252). Thus, the incentive for the piece is traceable not only to Chinese porcelain designs but also to those of the Mei Lanfang show and those on the handkerchiefs and writing paper from China. Nevertheless, before composing the poem, Moore almost certainly had, aside from consulting the *Encyclopedia Britannica,* Alphonse de Candolle, and the *Illustrated London News,*[26] examined a number of Ming-Qing porcelain pieces in galleries and in art books. Oddly, her view about late imperial Chinese wares was not changed in nearly eighteen years after "Critics and Connoisseurs." For Moore, the nectarine picture by an "uninquiring brush" was just another unnaturally flawless Ming product. Such pieces were "well enough in their way" but lacked a spontaneity or "unconscious / fastidiousness" that she liked better.

If Moore's praise of the nectarine design includes an unfavorable remark ("by the / uninquiring brush"), her homage to the image of the *qilin* is without reservation. The imagined creature on porcelain receives attention only in the final stanza of the poem. However, no one will overlook the vigilance bestowed. The stanza begins with the speaker's emphatic comment that "A Chinese 'understands / the spirit of the wilderness'" and ends with her passionate statement that "It was a Chinese / who imagined this masterpiece." In between is the image of

> . . . the nectarine-loving kylin
>   of pony appearance—the long-
> tailed or the tailless
>   small cinnamon-brown, common
> camel-haired unicorn

with antelope feet and no horn,
    here enameled on porcelain.   (*CPMM*, 30)

What quality distinguishes the *qilin* on porcelain as a masterpiece
Moore does not tell. But is there a need to tell? It is shown exactly
the way Moore (mis)represents the image. As Bernard Engel notices,
Moore's *qilin* "scarcely conforms in detail to the creature described in
her notes to the poem."[27] Where Frank Davis, Moore's asserted source,
characterizes the *qilin* as having "the body of a stag, with a single horn,
the tail of a cow, horse's hoofs, a yellow belly, and hair of five colours"
(qtd. in *CPMM*, 266), Moore (mis)represents it as having the body
of a pony, with no horn, long-tailed or tailless, antelope's feet, and
cinnamon-brown, common camel-haired.

Intriguingly enough, although Chinese written texts frequently describe the *qilin* the way Davis describes it,[28] it is not unusual that we see
a somewhat changed image of the mythic creature in a Chinese picture.
This should happen because Chinese artists, especially those inspired by
Daoism, favor spirit over physical likeness. For them the very purpose
of art is to go beyond representation. Thus, in a Southern Song Luohan
painting displayed in the British Museum 1910–12 exhibition, one of
the *qilin* unicorns portrayed has a long tail unlike that of a cow's and
another has its tail concealed. Similarly, the two *qilin* unicorns imagined by a Qing painter for a vase are not in five different colors,[29] but
in the uncommon color of "cinnamon-brown" (fig. 26). By calling attention to these details I do not mean to indicate that the final stanza
of "Nine Nectarines" is modeled after an actual Chinese picture. The
final stanza of the poem is imitation of Chinese imagination. Donald
Hall is precise in asserting that "What we have, finally, is imagination
itself, not talk about imagination."[30]

I began by noting that Moore shares with Keats an interest in art's
silent detail. In turning to this focal point, Moore actually turns from
description of an art object to description of creativity behind an art
object. In confronting the image of the *qilin* "of pony appearance . . . /
with antelope feet and no horn, / . . . enameled on porcelain," we are
not enticed to ponder any isolated trait. Rather, we are enticed to marvel at the genius of a Chinese who imagined a creature that combined
features of different real animals; and further, to marvel at the genius of
other Chinese who refreshed the imagined creature's spirit by simultaneously representing and misrepresenting its prototype. It is no accident that Moore should want to salute the Chinese talent for "making

it new." "Make it new" is a hallmark of both modernism and Daoist aesthetic. In remaking in language the visual image of a *qilin* unicorn on porcelain, she eloquently demonstrates that her creativity can be at once modernist and Chinese.

Moore's impulse to thematize creativity behind objects of art leads to her "museological focus," a more striking characteristic of modernist ekphrasis. "Museological focus" is a term used by Heffernan in his account of what William Carlos Williams does in his Breughel poems.[31] What he means to suggest is that Williams follows certain principles of the modern museum in organizing his Breughel poems. However, comparison of Williams's poems about Breughel and "Nine Nectarines" reveals that Moore's piece is structured more like a modern museum. First, Moore's illustrated plate and vase are neatly juxtaposed within the frame of a single poem, whereas Williams's Breughel pictures are presented piece by piece in a volume of verse (*Pictures from Breughel*).[32] Initially, in the *Selected Poems* version ("Nine Nectarines and Other Porcelain"), Moore presented more than just two porcelain pieces. She removed all other porcelain from this "gallery of words" perhaps because of a distaste for its possibility of blurring the "Chineseness" of Chinese art.[33] Second, Moore has brought far more curatorial information to her poem than Williams has to his. Above I have argued that in "Nine Nectarines" Moore's objects of art are voiceless. By this I do not mean to say that there is no voice at all in the poem. Moore's silent objects are in fact perpetually accompanied by a voice—a museum curator's—now informing that "Like the peach *Yu,* the red- / cheeked peach . . . / . . . eaten in time prevents death," now commenting that "It was a Chinese / who imagined this masterpiece."

Like a museum curator, Moore is acutely aware of her audience's needs. The Western viewer unfamiliar with Chinese culture will depend on a label here to know what association the image has for a Chinese, and a label there to understand that the peach or nectarine "as wild spontaneous fruit was / found in China first." Once such labels are provided, the beholder will desire to know the sources of the information. Moore's references will satisfy such interest. Indeed, in one of her endnotes, she quotes the French botanist Alphonse de Candolle, who quotes a certain Chin-noug-king: "The Chinese believe the oval peaches which are very red on one side, to be a symbol of long life. . . . According to the word of Chin-noug-king, the peach *Yu* prevents death. If it is not eaten in time, it at least preserves the body from decay until the end of the world" (*CPMM,* 265). Moore has a habit of inserting quotations in poetry and appending endnotes in which she acknowledges her out-of-the-way sources. Such mechanisms in "Nine Nectarines" nevertheless play a peculiar role; they serve as curatorial notes on museum walls or entries in an exhibition catalogue.

Since Moore is so attentive to the curiosity of her audience, why doesn't she furnish a clue to the folklore of the *qilin* in her representation? Her knowledge of the mythical creature is apparently beyond a portrayal of its outward appearance. Frank Davis, who informs her of the official Chinese description of the animal, also informs that for the Chinese it is "a paragon of virtue."[34] For Moore, "Omissions are not accidents." Why then does she choose to omit Davis's account of the creature's symbolic meaning while quoting his description of the creature's appearance? A possible answer is that allusion to its symbolic meaning would inevitably divert our attention away from her intended focus on rivalry/discrepancy between versions of the imagined animal. On the other hand, reference to the standard image of the creature in China, a contrast to her own, will underscore her admiration for the Chinese race, which sustains its imaginative power by way of continuously imitating and rivaling its supreme models.

My last statement brings us back to my emphasis on the silent status of Moore's ekphrastic objects. Like her nectarines, Moore's *qilin* remains voiceless throughout, but paradoxically, it "speaks" louder than its accompanying voice: "It was a Chinese / who imagined this masterpiece." It is after all the image itself rather than the accompanying curatorial voice that convinces us that the hope for creating or re-creating a masterpiece lies not in copying the model but in capturing its spirit and challenging its appearance.

EIGHT

Pound's
Seven Lakes
Canto

To this point we have considered only notional ekphrasis of "memory objects of art." Pound's Canto 49, generally designated as "The Seven Lakes," is a rare instance of modernist ekphrasis that represents a group of privately owned, actual paintings from the Orient. The story of what Pound's Canto 49 owes to the screen book he received from his parents in early 1928 has been told and retold many times.[1] A relic from Japan,[2] the fourteen-fold screen book consists of two endpapers, two covers, eight ink paintings, eight poems in Chinese, and eight poems in Japanese, mutually representing eight classic views about the shores of the Xiao and Xiang Rivers in central South China. In a 1977 essay, Sanehide Kodama points out that the Seven Lakes Canto "significantly pins down the essential quality of the original manuscript poems and paintings."[3] His statement implies that the greater part of the canto is based on exchanges with both verbal and visual representation. Needless to say, all the items of the source book require careful examination. Yet, curiously, few have paid serious attention to the eight painted scenes, of which four appear in facsimile in Daniel Pearlman's *The Barb of Time*.[4] No one has tried to appreciate Pound's Seven Lakes Canto as a modernist instance of ekphrasis.

It is so easy to overlook the power of the visual. For decades we have spoken of Pound's translations from Chinese as reworkings of others' versions, so we take it for granted that Pound relied on a verbal source to paint Chinese scenes in words. True to this assumption, something of that nature was found apropos of the first part of Canto 49.[5] In May 1928, as a series of Pound letters reveal, a Miss Zeng from the Xiao-Xiang River region, descendent of Confucius's disciple Zeng Xi,[6] offered Pound an oral translation of the eight Chinese poems. Pound copied out these paraphrases in an unmailed letter he wrote to his father on 30 July. Is most of Canto 49 made of nothing but Miss Zeng's text?[7] Apparently not. The poems and paintings of Pound's source book are versions of each other doubly or triply representing a traditional Chinese theme in waterscape. "[F]rom the *semantic* point of view," Mitchell contends, "from the standpoint of referring, expressing intentions and producing effects in a viewer/listener, there is no essential difference between texts and images."[8] In Pound's case, his source book's "images" must have impressed him long before Miss Zeng had made its Chinese "texts" readable, or he would not have requested the book. What's more, when he set out to compose the canto, these "images" continued to interact with the "texts." Some thirty lines of the canto, therefore, must have registered Pound's response to both visual and verbal representation of the eight scenes. Without recognizing Pound's creative response to the painted scenes, I argue, the achievement of his Seven Lakes Canto cannot be appreciated properly.

To those familiar with Chinese and Japanese masterpieces of the eight views, the first part of Canto 49 may appear as more than ekphrasis of eight privately owned ink paintings from Japan. It can be taken as ekphrasis of an ekphrastic tradition in the Far East. To see this we must dwell a little on the origin of this nine-hundred-year tradition.

As in Europe painting and sculpture relieved themselves of a reputation lower than literature during the Renaissance, so in China art achieved a position equal to poetry during the Song period.[9] Where Leonardo da Vinci refers to painting as "a poetry that is seen and not heard" and poetry as "painting which is heard and not seen," the Song poet Su Shi (1037–1101) calls great poems "pictures without forms," and great paintings "unspoken poems."[10] Painting and poetry were able to thrive side by side in Song China partially because the Song rulers took a great interest in art. To give an extreme example, the eighth Song emperor, Huizong (r. 1101–25), turned government over to his ministers in order to spend more time on artistic activities. His neglect of state affairs eventually led to his capture by the invading troops of the Jin and loss of half of China. It was in this era, an era of political impotence and creative vigor, that the primal works on the eight views were born.

Song Di (ca. 1015–ca. 1080), a Northern Song painter-scholar and a friend of Su Shi, is known to have initiated the theme of the eight views. We owe our knowledge of his lost masterpiece to Su Shi, who recalled watching Song Di "working with facility forgetting brush" in "Three Poems on Song [Di] Painting Evening Views on the Xiao-Xiang,"[11] and to Shen Kuo (1031–95), another Song scholar, who entered the subjects into his *Mengxi Jottings* (*Mengxi bitan*) (1088–93):

Wild Geese Descending to Sandbar (*ping sha yan luo*);
Sailboats Returning from Distant Shore (*yuan pu fan gui*);
Mountain Town, Clear with Mist (*shan shi qing lan*);
River and Sky in Evening Snow (*jiang tian mu xue;*
Autumn Moon over Lake Dongting (*Dongting qiu yue*);
Night Rain on the Xiao and Xiang (*Xiao-Xiang ye yu*);
Evening Bell from Mist-shrouded Temple (*yan si wan zhong*);
Fishing Village in Twilight Glow (*yu cun luo zhao*).[12]

From yet another source we have learned when and where Song Di created his masterpiece. In 1063 Song Di was assigned a post in Changsha, Hunan. Shortly after reporting to his position, he traveled by boat to Mount Tanshanyan, situated at a point where the Xiao and Xiang Rivers converged, and returned to paint the eight views on a terrace wall in Changsha.[13] To Song Di the region's appeal must have been from the beautiful scenes as well as from their rich associations. In the third century B.C. China's first great poet, Qu Yuan, was exiled there. The local scenery and Shamanist culture inspired him to make the remarkable *Nine Songs,* of which the ninth song, *Shan gui* or "The Mountain Spirit," yielded Pound his Imagist "After Ch'u Yuan."

Su Shi's three poems on Song Di's eight views and Shen Kuo's listing of the subjects inaugurated a poetry-painting competition destined to cross the boundaries of age and culture. Shortly after the poetic titles of the eight views appeared in *Mengxi Jottings,* a Chan monk-poet called Huihong (1071–1128) was challenged by a fellow monk to compose eight poems on the same theme, following the sequence given by Shen Kuo. His set of poems of eight lines of seven characters each turned out to outdo the three poems by Su Shi, his mentor and a master of ekphrasis.[14] These poems and Song Di's paintings stimulated more artists and poets to work on the eight scenes. The rivalry soon caught the attention of Emperor Huizong. He is said to have first commissioned his court painters to try their hands at the theme and then himself painted a set of the eight views.[15]

The vogue for making paintings and poems on the eight views culminated in the sets of Southern Song painters Ma Yuan, Wang Hong, Yujian, and Muqi. While Ma Yuan's version has not passed down to us,[16] that of Wang Hong has entered the Metropolitan Museum of Art in

New York. In a meticulously researched study, Alfreda Murck demonstrates how this set translates Huihong's poems back into paintings in a rearranged order.[17] Where Wang Hong tried to follow his precursors, the Chan artists Yujian and Muqi endeavored to break away from them. Not only did they treat the motif in unorthodox ways but they also improvised a calligraphic style now associated with Chan art. Yujian, moreover, initiated a tradition of adding poems to pictures on the eight views, which brought about many latter-day fine examples, including Yunqiao Zhuren's in the British Museum (figs. 5, 14).

Perhaps because most of their significant works have been transferred to Japan, Yujian and Muqi have for centuries enjoyed a greater reputation abroad than in China. Their treatments of the eight views now housed in museums in Tokyo and elsewhere were largely responsible for the Japanese passion for the subject.[18] Among artists in Muromachi and Edo Japan who made remarkable copies of the theme were Soami (1472–1525),[19] Sesson Shūkei (1504–89), and Kano Tōun (1624–94). Sesson and Tōun's versions found their way into the British Museum and were displayed in its 1910–12 exhibition.[20] Like Sesson's "Wild Geese," Soami's "Autumn Moon" encapsulates the style that influenced Postimpressionism. We now know that they owe their "ink-splash" technique to Yujian and Muqi.

Pound's familiarity with this tradition is evident in a letter he wrote to his father on 30 May 1928: "They are poems on a set of scenes in Miss Thseng's part of the country = sort of habit of people to make pictures & poems on that set of scenes."[21] Presumably Miss Zeng addressed the topic in her oral translation. But Pound had learned about the eight views much earlier. In the "British Museum era," he lunched with Binyon, attended his slide lectures, went to his exhibition of Chinese and Japanese paintings, and reviewed his *The Flight of the Dragon*. The series was Binyon's favorite subject. If the slide images Binyon threw on the screen did not impress Pound, those in the exhibition—Yunqiao Zhuren's scenes and Sesson's set—surely did. The catalogue to the exhibition described the eight views as "a traditional series of landscape subjects . . . originally associated with the scenery of Lake Tung-Ting [Dongting] in China" (Binyon, *Guide,* 37). A note to that effect should be enough to rouse Pound's interest, and in *The Flight of the Dragon* he was to take in more information. The topic is covered in chapter 10, where Song Di is characterized as having advised painters to throw silk over a rugged wall and "fancy travellers wandering among [mountains, streams, and forests]," a strategy favored also by Leonardo. In the eight views, we are then told, "the painter of the Vesper Bell from a Distant Temple would evoke the mellow sound of the evening bell coming over the plain to the traveller's ears" (*Flight*, 61).

From *Painting in the Far East*, Pound could have learned more about the tradition. In that earlier work Binyon seeks to explain why generation after generation of Chinese poets and artists should be interested in repeating a commonplace theme. His comment made after a discussion of Muqi's "Evening Bell" is revealing: "It is by the new and original treatment—original, because profoundly felt—of matter that is fundamentally familiar, that great art comes into being" (134). For Binyon the success of Muqi's "Evening Bell" offers the West a good lesson. "The subject is essentially the same as that which the poetic genius of Jean François Millet conceived in the twilight of Barbizon," he writes. But "our foolish and petty misconceptions of originality would cause all the critics to exclaim against any painter who took up the theme again as a trespasser on Millet's property" (135).

To return to Canto 49, it must be stressed that Pound's source book represents a Far Eastern tradition of making pictures and poems side by side on a theme of great masters. In this kind of "mixed arts," to borrow a term from Mitchell, the viewer/reader's attention is split between the two media.[22] What eventually impresses him or her will be the interplay of visual and verbal representation. This should describe Pound's experience of conceiving most of the canto. He had easy access to all parts of the book—eight ink paintings and sixteen poems, half of which he could read with the aid of Miss Zeng's "paraphrases." Moving between the two media he should have noticed both echoes and discrepancies in representation.

A question may be raised: Isn't it possible that Pound had put aside his source book? He could be simply following the "paraphrases" in composing the canto. Let us assume that that was how he began. Still, Pound would have to return every now and then to the source book. He would have to do so because the "paraphrases" were far from comprehensible. Translating a poem from Chinese to English was painstaking enough. When one had to deal with the handwriting of a Japanese artist, the task was doubly strenuous. Here is Pound's typescript for Miss Zeng's version of the opening scene "Night Rain":

Rain, empty river,
Place for soul to travel
    (or room to travel)

27. Unidentified Japanese artist, "Night Rain," a scene accompanied by a poem in Chinese (right) and a poem in Japanese (left) from Ezra Pound's screen book. (Courtesy of Mary de Rachewiltz, Brunnenburg, Italy; courtesy of Richard Taylor)

> Frozen cloud, fire, rain damp twilight.
> One lantern inside boat cover (i.e., sort of
>   shelter, not awning on small boat)
> Throws reflection on bamboo branch,
>   causes tears.[23]

Without substantial aid one simply cannot comprehend what the translator means by "Place for soul to travel / (or room to travel)" or "Throws reflection on bamboo branch, / causes tears." Luckily, Pound had his "picture book" to turn to at his moment of puzzle. Viewing the painted scene "Night Rain" (center of fig. 27), he could easily decipher curls as waves stirred up by rain in an empty river, three bold strokes in the middle as small boats amid bent reeds, and blankness across distant hills as chilled cloud. So, "Place for soul to travel" should signify a "voyage" even though no characters could verify it; and "reflection on bamboo branch, / causes tears" should imply a poetic reading of nature's response. Consequently lines 2–6 in Canto 49:

> Rain; empty river; a voyage,
> Fire from frozen cloud, heavy rain in the twilight
> Under the cabin roof was one lantern.

The reeds are heavy; bent;
and the bamboos speak as if weeping.   (*C,* 244)

Surprisingly, the lines evoke the same sort of emotion the painted scene
and original poem in Chinese combine to evoke. Kodama is not exag-
gerating when he remarks that Pound's version "is closer to the original
Chinese poems than to the paraphrases." For him Pound's success was
due to the fact that he "went over the original himself, or had someone
re-examine them."[24] This is doubtful. To begin with, the opening poem
in Chinese (right of fig. 27) is one of the three that are legibly written
out in regular script (*kai shu*).[25] Pound's failure to drop the word "fire,"
for which there is no matching character, proves that neither he nor any
helper reexamined it. As for how the error could have slipped into the
"paraphrases," Kodama's explanation is acceptable: "[S]he might have
said 'adhere' for the ideogram meaning 'stick,' which Pound might have
heard as 'fire.'"[26] Besides, until 1936, as Kenner testifies, "Pound's forte
was haruspication of the single ideogram, not the tracing of sequen-
tial connections western syntax specifies."[27] Pound's large debt, therefore, was not to the original poem. His guide had to be the painted
scene.

Turning to the "Autumn Moon" scene, we shall find more eloquent
evidence that Pound deliberately reexamined the paintings after he acquired the "paraphrases" and before he composed the canto. In chapter 3 I argued, following J. Hillis Miller (*Illustration,* 68), that in "mixed
arts," in which picture and word are set side by side, their respective
elucidating force is at once reinforced and subverted. If in the above
example we have focused only on how picture and word illuminate
each other, here we are to observe more of their disruptive dynamics.
A glance from the draft version of "Autumn Moon" to the corresponding ink painting (right of fig. 28) designates that each contains some
striking features that disrupt striking features in the other. Thus in the
text the most remarkable details are "evening clouds," "Ten thousand
ripples," and "cinnamon flowers."[28] By contrast, the picture presents
a high mountain with a cloud across it, a tall pine tree with an upward point, and no stretch of water with ripples or "cinnamon flowers."
Juxtaposed, the visible images of the picture tend to darken those of
the text. Pound evidently examined both the pictorial and verbal representation of "Autumn Moon," and it was the interaction of the two
that yielded lines 7–12 of Canto 49:

Autumn moon; hills rise about lakes
against sunset
Evening is like a curtain of cloud,
a blurr above ripples; and through it
sharp long spikes of the cinnamon,
a cold tune amid reeds.   (C, 244)

In discussing *Cathay,* I suggested that Chinese painting may "serve as a secondary source clarifying settings, situations, and states of mind essential to [one's] comprehension of [Chinese] poems" (56). In conceiving Canto 49, Pound used the painted scenes not as a secondary source but as a principal guide. Since the Seven Lakes Canto is not, and never was intended to be, a translation, I see nothing wrong with Pound's drifting away from the awkward "paraphrases" toward the versions that brought to light the visual aspects of the eight views.

Nowhere is Pound more removed from his verbal text than in lines 13–17 of the canto, where he defies what is elaborated in word and freely responds to his fancy evoked by visual detail from his source book. Lines 13–14 are said to have come from the paraphrase of "Evening Bell":

28. Unidentified Japanese artist, "Autumn Moon" (right), "Evening Bell" (center), "Sailboats Returning" (left), three scenes from Ezra Pound's screen book. (Courtesy of Mary de Rachewiltz, Brunnenburg, Italy; courtesy of Richard Taylor)

Cloud shuts off the hill, hiding the temple
Bell audible only when wind moves toward one,
One can not tell whether the summit is near or far,
Sure only that one is in hollow of mountains.[29]

There is evidently Chan illumination here in the contrast between what is far off and what is near at hand. For those who intuitively interpret the bell sound as a symbol of distance/immediacy, the last two lines of the poem are superfluous. In turning from the paraphrase to the picture, we turn from verbal redundancy to visual simplicity: A pagoda top and a temple roof are barely visible behind mountaintops (center of fig. 28). Many of us will wonder how we are to hear the temple bell. It is the view of Walter Benjamin that original works of art "will have aura, or 'speak.'" In identifying this potential in van Gogh, Miller explains, "this power is associated with distance. Van Gogh's painting takes us 'somewhere else [*jäh anderswo*]'" (*Illustration,* 80). The bell scene Pound held before him was not a masterpiece, but it was hand painted and could be linked to Muqi's "Evening Bell," praised by Binyon. The pagoda in ink and light color could have taken Pound "somewhere else," where through the subtle playing of association he envisioned a temple bell and heard it sound. Lines 13–14—imitation of an actual painting's mute language—register his response:

Behind hill the monk's bell
borne on the wind.   (*C,* 244)

The unique pictorial speech of "Evening Bell" brings about more dynamics in "Sailboats Returning." The sight is rendered thus in the paraphrase:

Touching green sky at horizon, mists in suggestion of autumn
Sheet of silver reflecting all that one sees
Boats gradually fade, or are lost in turn of the hills,
Only evening sun, and its glory on the water remain.[30]

It is again in the corresponding painted scene that we witness the actual spectacle at fixation, what Wendy Steiner terms the "frozen moment of action"[31]—three boats in rapids in broad daylight (left of fig. 28). The boats, delineated as in full sail, do not exactly indicate return, however. In Yujian's treatment one catches sight of masts instead.[32] (The word *qiang,* or "mast," actually occurs in the third line of the Chinese poem: *gui qiang jian ru lu hua qu* or "Returning masts slowly disappear into reeds.") Pound may well have picked this misleading detail, discarded "green sky," "mists in suggestion of autumn," and "hills" in the paraphrase, and dashed off lines 15–17:

> Sail passed here in April; may return in October
> Boat fades in silver; slowly;
> Sun blaze alone on the river.   (C, 244)

We can pause for a moment now to reflect on the overall design of the sequence. As in the paintings, so in the poems, water path and shore take turns to occupy the center; ripples, reeds, boats, hills, and clouds that appear and disappear in the previous scenes continue to do so in "Mountain Town," "Snowy Evening," "Wild Geese," and "Fishing Village" (figs. 29–32). Put together, the pictures signal a continuous flow, a journey by boat through seasons. The figure "Under the cabin roof" who hears "the bamboos speak as if weeping" reappears in subsequent scenes to catch glimpses of a "wine flag," "a world . . . covered with jade," and "Wild geese" (C, 244), and listen to "the young boys prod

29 and 30. Unidentified Japanese artist. 29 *(right)*, "Mountain Town"; 30 *(left)*, "Snowy Evening." Scenes from Ezra Pound's screen book. (Courtesy of Mary de Rachewiltz, Brunnenburg, Italy; courtesy of Richard Taylor)

stones for shrimp" (245). While the duplication of such a subject is implied in the poems, it is physically presented in the pictorial sequence in the form of a repeated small boat (see figs. 27, 32).

The preoccupation of multiscened painting with continuity has been examined by various critics. Steiner establishes "repetition of a subject" and "continuity of the road" as two chief strategies of European masters in their attempt to secure pictorial narrativity.[33] For her the latter is a metaphor, "shopworn" in the picaresque novel, but "in particular pictorial manifestations can be very powerful."[34] Wu Hung describes a continuous long handscroll as a Chinese art medium painted section by section and viewed section by section. "In terms of both painting and viewing," he writes, "a handscroll is literally a moving picture, with shifting moments and loci."[35] Allied to this is a painted screen, an art medium like a long handscroll but with separately zoned scenes. What Pound had was precisely that last format: a fourteen-fold screen with four Chinese scenes on the front and four more on the back, each set between two poems, Chinese to the right and Japanese to the left.[36]

When photographs of the eight pictures are arranged in the original

31 and 32. Unidentified Japanese artist. 31 *(right)*, "Wild Geese"; 32 *(left)*, "Fishing Village." Scenes from Ezra Pound's screen book. (Courtesy of Mary de Rachewiltz, Brunnenburg, Italy; courtesy of Richard Taylor)

order without interruption of the poems, a multiscened long hand-scroll emerges.[37] Viewing it from right to left, as a Chinese or a Japanese connoisseur would, the eight separate views appear as a continuous waterscape with a connected outline of hills in the background and a now wide, now narrow water path in the foreground. The moorings at the left of "Night Rain" join those of "Autumn Moon." A slope of "Autumn Moon" lengthens into the left of "Evening Bell." With imposing peaks, "Evening Bell" marks a transition in the progression of design. Looking both ways one recognizes a change in color: from the gray of the views on the right to the green and bright orange of those on the left. The shift in color gradation certainly signals a shift in mood. While in "Night Rain" and "Autumn Moon" the dominant atmosphere is gloom, in "Snowy Evening" and "Wild Geese" it is serenity and leisure, and in "Mountain Town" and "Fishing Village," calm and gaiety. Accordingly, it would be insensible to interpret the water path here as a "path of life" through hardship. In the Chinese tradition it is more reasonably interpreted as a woeful scholar's retreat into nature, where he attains the Dao or Chan, and with it bliss.

Now, there are unquestionably differences between painting the eight views and writing poems about them: differences between visual presentation of scenes and presentation of them in a figurative sense. In writing these poems in Chinese, moreover, the Japanese artist labors to represent the views in a fixed form of four seven-character lines.[38] Often after presenting a scene he still has space left for moralizing or speculating. This of course goes against Pound's Imagist credo: "Direct treatment of the 'thing'" and "Don't be 'viewy'" (LE, 3, 6). Pound is not interested in Chinese or Japanese verse form. He just desires to recapture the essential quality of the eight views. Hence his disregard of all personal reflection for "Evening Bell." Hence his omissions of all stretched imaginings: "A few country people enjoying their evening drink" for "Mountain Town" and "Fisherman calls his boy, and takes up his wine bottle" for "Fishing Village."[39] By ignoring such musings he succeeds in producing a version nearer to the "mute speech" of painting, an ideal of modernist ekphrasis.

My last remark reinforces my position that the first part of Pound's Seven Lakes Canto is better understood as ekphrasis of his source book's painted scenes than as translation of its Chinese poems. Pound does make use of the paraphrases provided by Miss Zeng. The services they render are more like those of captions, however. Without a clue from the text for "Mountain Town," Pound wouldn't have been able to identify in the corresponding picture (fig. 29) a "wine flag" sticking out behind a roof, thence giving line 18: "Where wine flag catches the sunset" (*C,* 244). Nor could he have imagined line 28, "Rooks clatter over the fishermen's lanthorns" (244), if not for the text's hint of "birds" stopped around a small boat in the last picture "Fishing Village."[40] Nonetheless, despite the texts' importance, Pound never seems to have permitted them to influence his direct treatment of the pictures. Indeed, in the canto he mimics the pictorial language so intensely that his lines do not become "audible" unless a source image shows "aura," or breaks muteness. When this occurs first in reference to "Night Rain," his response, "the bamboos speak as if weeping" (line 6), communicates sorrow suggested in the first two painted scenes. Next, when line 12, "Behind hill the monk's bell" (244), turns "audible," again it is "audible" like its source picture; its resonance awakens us to a sense of peace and contentment that is supported by subsequent silent views such as "wine flag," "a people of leisure," and "Wild geese." When line 30 — "the young boys prod stones for shrimp" — "speaks," it echoes the sequence's final note of bliss. Thus, by way of translating the changing tones of the pictorial composition, the canto signifies its Daoist theme of joyous liberation after withdrawal into nature.

The way I have described Pound's source book's pictures as having "aura" or power to "speak" might have sounded as if they were masterpieces. I must point out that the term "aura" has been used here solely for the sake of stressing the representational power of the visual. As for my enthusiasm, it is really for the eight views tradition in China that has generated numerous works of art and poetry in the Far East, of which Pound's screen book is a very late and common example.

It should be clear now why Pound inserts a version of the eight views in the middle of his modernist epic. The subject is a monument of Chinese culture, an example of how poets and artists in China (and in Japan) have continuously made an old theme new. All remarkable copies of the eight views have been accepted as such because of their originality. For Pound, modernism also demands originality, originality allowing him to interweave texts and make statements about history and politics.

To make Canto 49 modernist, Pound must not stop at the eight views. A quick search through de Mailla's *Histoire générale* yields him lines 31–32: "In seventeen hundred came Tsing to these hill lakes. / A light moves on the south sky line." The reference to the Qing is fitting because it brings Chinese history to its last imperial dynasty. Indeed,

it prefigures the conclusion of the China Cantos—the signing of the
Nipchou Treaty with the Tsar "Year 28th of KANG HI" (*C*, 327), which
was a decade before Kangxi's journey to "hill lakes."[41] Kangxi would
not have been able to travel to South China by boat without a canal
built by an "old king." Pound owed his knowledge of this to Fenollosa, who entered Mori's comment on Emperor Yang of Sui (r. 605–18)
into a notebook: "[H]e made a canal from Benrio (Kaifong [Kaifeng]
of Kanan [Henan]) to Yosingo [Yangzhou], and they say that he did this
for his own pleasure."[42] He simply substitutes "TenShi" for "Kaifong"
and proceeds:[43] "This canal goes still to TenShi / though the old king
built it for pleasure" (*C*, 245).

Still, Pound has not tracked down the origin of China's ideal system.
Two ancient songs, *Qing yun ge* ("Auspicious Clouds Song"), supposedly
from the sage ruler Shun, and *Ji rang ge* ("Clod Beating Song"), supposedly from the sage ruler Yao, are then incorporated into the canto to
recall a golden age. Both songs are derived from a notebook in which
Fenollosa recorded Mori's lectures on Chinese poetry, and, in fact, the
first song, *Qing yun ge*, is given in Japanese sound, in Kenner's words,
a way to remind us that "the Chinese had come to [Pound] by way of
Japan."[44]

Pound has certainly added dimensions to his Chinese material. This
he does first in lines 33–34: "State by creating riches shd. thereby get
into debt? / This is infamy; this is Geryon." And then again in the ter-
minal lines: "Imperial power is? and to us what is it? // The fourth;
the dimension of stillness. / And the power over wild beasts" (*C*, 245).
These abrupt comments serve to place his eight views in a pre–World
War II Euro-American context. Rereading the first part of the canto,
we begin to see the traveler differently; he becomes a Westerner seeking a way out of political chaos. From the outset he has a vision of Yao
and Shun. The rustling sounds he hears from the bamboo are the sobs
of Yao's daughters mourning the death of their husband, Shun. Legend
says that their tears stained the bamboo all the way, and it also says
that they were drowned and metamorphosed into the twin goddesses
of the Xiang.[45] Pound might have heard the tale from Miss Zeng, or
he would not have been able to produce a line so approximate to the
original in effect. Nor would he have closed his canto with *Qing yun
ge* and *Ji rang ge*, which echo the opening scene's nostalgia for the lost
leaders. But Pound could also have picked the story first from Fenollosa. At one point, Fenollosa had Ariga copy out in Chinese five songs
from Qu Yuan's *Nine Songs*. A note to the third song, "Lord of the

Xiang," indicates: "The two wives of Shun died on the banks of the river Sho [Xiang]; since that time this river became a good topic of poets. Kutsugen [Qu Yuan] lived near this river and wrote this ode to the god of Sho."[46]

So the two ancient songs are not digressions from representation of the eight views but an integral part of an instance of modernist ekphrasis. What makes ekphrasis modernist, what distinguishes ekphrasis of the twentieth century from its predecessors', according to Heffernan, are a self-sufficient quality and kinship to the museum. "The ekphrastic poetry of our time," he writes, "represents individual works of art within the context of the museum, which of course includes the words that surround the pictures we see, beginning with picture titles."[47] Pound's Canto 49 is not representation of a museum piece of art. Given its modernist nature, however, it is hardly surprising that it incorporates art-historical commentary, informing us of the making and viewing of his ekphrastic masterpiece.

PART 4

The Poets
as Critics
and
Connoisseurs

NINE

Pound, Fenollosa,

and *The Chinese*

Written Character

POUND'S, MOORE'S, and Stevens's creative response to Chinese art, which is my focal point in chapters 1–8 and 12–14, goes hand in hand with their reception of the latest on the subject. The three poets' critical writings assume a no less important place in the modernist canon. An examination of their reactions to Far Eastern art events will deepen our understanding of their Orientalism.

A key text on the Orient by Pound is his 1915 review of Binyon's *The Flight of the Dragon* (1911). By 1915 Pound's aesthetic outlook had undergone profound transformations. He had by then completed the transition from Imagism to Vorticism, brought out *Cathay,* initiated "Three Cantos,"[1] and above all, plunged into Fenollosa's drafts for *The Chinese Written Character.* In short, by 1915 Pound could no longer look at Binyon's book in the same way he would have looked at it in 1911–13.

Binyon was no doubt enthusiastic about the Orient. Nevertheless, he would not embrace it as a revolt against the Occident. As a "Man of 1914" Pound was dissatisfied. He could in no way tolerate his mentor's folly of trying to link an ancient yet very modern art in the Far East to some nineteenth-century English poetry. For him Chinese and Japanese art embodied an aesthetic system opposed to Anglo-American traditions. To grasp the spirit of such an art required breaking from Western preconceptions. Consequently, it jarred his ears to hear someone pay high compliments to both Far Eastern art and nineteenth-century poetry. Speaking on behalf of the modernist rebels, Pound thus opens his review: "We regret that we cannot entitle this article 'Homage to Mr. Lawrence [*sic*] Binyon,' for Mr. Binyon has not sufficiently rebelled. Manifestly he is not one of the ignorant. He is far from being one of the outer world, but in reading his work we constantly feel the influence upon him of his reading of the worst English poets. We find him in a disgusting attitude of respect toward predecessors whose intellect is vastly inferior to his own. This is loathsome" (*P&P*, 2:99).

Surely Pound is repelled by the way Binyon deals with the Orient in *The Flight of the Dragon,* by "his mind constantly hark[ing] back to some folly of nineteenth century Europe" (99). Edward Said's generalization of Orientalism as "a Western style for dominating, restructuring, and having authority over the Orient" does not hold for *everyone* in nineteenth-century England and France.[2] In *The Flight,* however, we can trace some, if not all, of the symptoms of the Orientalism in Said's sense. Alluding to Laozi's belief in inaction, therefore, Binyon must link it to Wordsworth's "doctrine of 'wise passiveness'" (*Flight,* 28–29). More unpleasantly, in discussing the Chan doctrine of contemplation, he feels it necessary to bring up George Meredith, who, he says, shares with the Chan sages the conviction that the contemplation of nature is "no sentimental indulgence, but an invigorating discipline" (30).

Understandably, Pound finds his friend's forced connections absurd. "We can see him as it were constantly restraining his inventiveness," he writes, "constantly trying to conform to an orthodox view against which his thought and emotions rebel, constantly trying to justify Chinese intelligence by dragging it a little nearer to some Western precedent" (*P&P*, 2:99). In his view, Binyon's "recurrent respect for inferior, very inferior people" has obnoxiously defaced the otherwise wholesome subject of *The Flight.* Admittedly, Pound is not free from all Western biases, but his refusal to think of the West as the cultural center of the world and his allusion to "Chinese colours" as an antidote to European "evil" (*P,* 95), have, in the main, separated his Orientalism from what we now call Saidian Orientalism.

Despite his disgust with an attitude of visionless allegiance to "inferior, very inferior people," we must recognize that Pound nevertheless admires Binyon's acuteness to certain Far Eastern values. After noting that "Mr. Binyon has, indubitably, his moments," he cites a number of passages from *The Flight,* the very passages he rehearses in *Gaudier-Brzeska,* stressing that "They bear on much of Gaudier's work" (134–35):

> P. 17. Every statue, every picture, is a series of ordered relations, controlled, as the body is controlled in the dance, by the will to express a single idea.
> P. 18. In a bad painting the units of form, mass, colour, are

robbed of their potential energy, isolated, because brought into no organic relation.

    P. 19. Art is not an adjunct to existence, a reproduction of the actual.

    P. 21. FOR INDEED IT IS NOT ESSENTIAL THAT THE SUBJECT-MATTER SHOULD REPRESENT OR BE LIKE ANY-THING IN NATURE; ONLY IT MUST BE ALIVE WITH A RHYTHMIC VITALITY OF ITS OWN.

    On P. Fourteen he quotes with approbation a Chinese author as follows: — As a man's language is an unerring index to his nature, so the actual strokes of his brush in writing or painting betray him and announce either the freedom and nobility of his soul or its meanness and limitation. (*P&P*, 2:99)

The first passage (page 14 in the 1959 reprint) is part of a formulation of a relational aesthetic, with its roots in Daoist thinking but queerly striking an intimate chord with modernism. A look at what is omitted between this and the next quoted passage will increase our suspicion that Binyon's summary of this notion might have contributed some insight to Pound's Vorticism, what Kenner characterizes as "patterned energies":[3] "A study of the most rudimentary abstract design will show that the units of line or mass are in reality energies capable of acting on each other" (*Flight,* 15).

Another key Chinese sensitivity captured by Binyon is the Daoist concept of "beyond representation." Chinese artists' disregard of physical likeness in favor of spiritual transmission is difficult to grasp. But Binyon sums it up in a succinct statement on page 21 (page 17 in the 1959 reprint). Apparently Pound views this as his friend's shrewdest and most radical moment, for the capital letters have registered his approval and exhilaration.

To illustrate what is meant by "RHYTHMIC VITALITY," Binyon offers a Japanese example, which Pound cites as another instance of his friend's brilliance: "You may say that the waves of Korin's famous screen are not like real waves: but they move, they have force and volume."[4] Just as the art of China and Japan has served as a crystallizing model for modernist experiments, so its principles elucidated by Binyon help justify their claim to an antirepresentational aesthetic.

It is here, as elsewhere, Pound witnesses Binyon "restraining his inventiveness . . . trying to conform to an orthodox view against which his thought and emotions rebel . . . trying to justify Chinese intelligence by dragging it a little nearer to some Western precedent." It is this Eurocentric prejudice that has irritated Pound, causing him to retrieve his homage and state in the review that "Mr. Binyon has not sufficiently rebelled" (*P&P,* 2:99).

With some knowledge of Pound's activities in 1915 we can better understand the kind of intention and mental drive that prompted his review of *The Flight.* In that crucial year he was not only promoting the Vorticist cause but also pushing for the launch of Fenollosa's essay on *The Chinese Written Character as a Medium for Poetry.* Evidently Pound went through Fenollosa's drafts for that essay in the winter of 1914–15. In a February 1915 article on "Imagisme and England," he alluded to Fenollosa's theory for the first time: "As for Chinese, it is quite true that we have sought the force of Chinese ideographs *without knowing it*" (*P&P,* 2:19). Four months later, in a letter to Professor Felix Schelling, he hailed the essay as "a whole basis of aesthetic, in reality," adding caustically that "the adamantine stupidity of all magazine editors delays its appearance" (*SLEP,* 61). The impact of Fenollosa's essay proved to be far-reaching. In fact, we have reason to believe that Pound's ambivalence toward Binyon around 1915 had more to do with his exchanges with Fenollosa than with his engagement in the Vorticist enterprise. This leads to Pound's enthusiasms for *The Chinese Written Character* and his ideogrammic method.

In the 1950s the theory Fenollosa proposed and Pound staunchly stood by received much criticism. Without the questioning of some sinologists, many of us perhaps would not have taken their philological blunders seriously. Clearly, anyone is justified in blaming Fenollosa and Pound for disregarding the phonetic value of the Chinese script and for suggesting more metaphoric overtones than are perceivable to the native Chinese speakers. But should scholarship stop at that? In a letter of 20 July 1955 to Pound biographer Noel Stock, the renowned sinologist and fellow Pound scholar Achilles Fang hinted at a necessity to go beyond philology. He stated: "It is easy enough to demolish the id. method philologically; by no means so when it comes to write on its operation on poetic levels where it works like a fugue."[5] More than four decades have elapsed and, oddly, much of our discussion of the essay and Pound's ideogrammic method still remains at the philological level.

Moving beyond philology, it becomes apparent that not all Fenollosa and Pound are nonsense. Their subject has a valid place in Chinese art history. For Chinese poets, artists, and art historians, the Chinese script is not just speech on record; it is, in addition, a form of art executed with the instrument of both painting and writing. We learn from Wen Fong that the script, "rather than painting, was the natural medium for the [Chinese] scholar-artist."[6] Reviewing "Embodied Image," an exhibition of the John B. Elliott Collection of Chinese Calligraphy at the Met (2000–2001), Holland Cotter stresses that "in China . . . writing has traditionally been the highest art form of all, and a source of profound political and emotional power."[7]

Chinese etymology generally identifies six techniques regarding character formation: *xiangxing* ("mirroring the form"), *zhishi* ("embodying the thing"), *huiyi* ("suggesting the meaning"), *xingsheng* ("harmonizing the form and the sound"), *zhuanzhu* ("mutually defining"), and *jiajie* ("borrowing").[8] In presenting these techniques, James Liu dismisses the last two on the grounds that they are "concerned with the extended *use* of already existing characters and not with the *formation* of new ones." He refers to the other four as "Simple Pictograms" (日 "sun"; 月 "moon"), "Simple Ideograms" (一 "one"; 二 "two"), "Composite Ideograms" (明 "bright"), and "Composite Phonograms." The fourth type, he notes, "usually consists of a phonetic (p) and a significant (s), while the phonetic and the significant in themselves could be Simple Pictograms, Simple Ideograms, Composite Ideograms, or other Composite Phonograms."[9] Two instances of this category he gives are 忠 ("loyalty"), "which consists of a phonetic *chung* 中 and a significant *hsin* 心 ('heart')"; and 寶 *bao* ("treasure") (Archaic pronunciation *pog*), "which consists of a phonetic *fo* 缶 (Archaic pronunciation *piog*), and three significants: 'roof' 宀, 'jade' 玉, and 'mother-of-pearl' 貝."[10]

Fenollosa made a terrible mistake in shrinking from the fourth group, which comprises 80 percent of the Chinese characters. One can hardly construct a natural-sounding sentence without them. Fenollosa's insistence on dodging this class results in his infamous example: 人見馬 "Man sees horse." It is not surprising that the average speaker of Chinese does not see as much as he sees: "First stands the man on his two legs. Second, his eye moves through space. . . . Third stands the horse on his four legs."[11]

It is misleading to characterize the Chinese script as pictographic or ideographic. But it is also improper not to recognize any such elements. Users of Chinese, like users of any other languages, tend to take familiar signs for granted. It is in the unfamiliar that one notices things. So it is not unusual that native speakers of Chinese do not catch sight of the tree in the character for "tree," the bird in the character for "bird," or the fish in the character for "fish." However, they are by no means blind to the tree, the bird, or the fish within composite phonograms, that is, in those with 木, 鳥, 魚 radicals (significants). In fact, the average speaker of Chinese tends to rely on radicals such as these to figure out the category of unknown characters. Thus, 橡, 榕, and 楠, like 松 and 柏, are all trees. 鳩, 鶄, and 鵬, like 鴿 and 鴉, are all birds. And 鯧, 鱸, and 鱒, like 鯉 and 鯽, are all fish.[12]

Fenollosa could have profited from acknowledging the composite phonograms and selecting examples from great Chinese poems. After all, Song 167 (Pound's "Song of the Bowmen of Shu") illustrates more aptly the mind of the early Chinese favoring the concrete over the general and the verb over the noun. The notation for its title, 采薇 (*Cai wei*) ("Pick Ferns"), first depicts three fingers clutching something and then a kind of grass that is called *wei*. Likewise, the title of the ancient folk song 擊壤 (*Ji rang*) ("Beat Clod") shows a hand holding a tool and some clod. The top of 擊 and the right side of 壤 denote their respective sounds.[13] When we move to the song itself, we are struck by an abundance of verbs:[14]

ri chu er zuo	Sun rises and [we] work;
ri ru er xi	Sun sets and [we] rest.
zao jing er yin	[We] dig wells and drink;
geng tian er shi	[We] plough fields and eat.

Yes, it is true that not many speakers of Chinese are aware of a hand holding a tool in the character 擊 (*ji*). In fact, the abridged version of that character (now in common use) consists of only a part of the phonetic *ji*. Awareness of etymology varies considerably from person to person among users of Chinese. The title *Yu cun xi zhao* ("Sunset Glow over a Fishing Village") for a poem in Chinese in Pound's screen book, for instance, is said to be a series of pictures caught at dusk (right-hand column of fig. 33). While some marvel at the calligrapher's depiction of fish and water (topmost character) and sunset glow (bottom two characters), others are totally blind to this embodiment.

Today's users of Chinese seem more conscious of the phonetics of their language than of its etymology. This may have to do with a series of government campaigns since the 1950s to standardize Chinese, notably popularization of the *putonghua* or Mandarin, simplification of difficult characters, and adoption of the pinyin spelling system.[15] The global spread of digital technology is beginning to impair the practice of Chinese calligraphy. Is China going to lose the written character? I

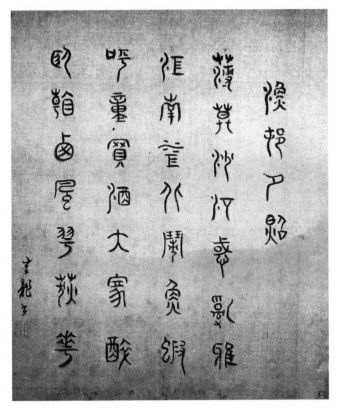

33. Unidentified Japanese calligrapher, *Yu cun xi zhao* ("Sunset Glow over a Fishing Village"), a poem in Chinese from Ezra Pound's screen book. (Courtesy of Mary de Rachewiltz, Brunnenburg, Italy)

do not think so.[16] But will the rich *phanopoeia* in traditional Chinese poetry fade away?[17]

Some educators in China seem to be aware of the predicament and are therefore devoting attention to etymology in teaching the Chinese language. In 1998, China's leading newspaper, *Renmin Ribao* (overseas edition), started a *Xue zhongwen* section ("Learning Chinese") for overseas Chinese learners. What interests me most in this section is a column called *Hanzi suyuan* ("Etymologizing Chinese"). Every Wednesday a different Chinese character is presented along with its three primitive forms—bone inscription (*jiagu*), bronze inscription (*jin*), and seal script (*zhuan*)[18]—accompanied by commentary and illustration. So, week after week, we are picking up something interesting regarding

34. Lao Wu, Chen Zheng, and Chen Rong, forms of the characters for "mother" (upper left); "child" (lower left); "give birth," "raise," or "educate" (upper right); "man" or "husband" (center right); "clutch" or "clutching hand" (lower right). From Xie Guanghui, *The Composition of Common Chinese Characters* (1997). Reproduced in *Renmin Ribao,* 24 October 1998, 5 December 1998, 28 November 1998, 22 August 1998, and 8 June 2000. (Courtesy, Beijing University Press; courtesy of Xie Guanghui)

ancient Chinese writing, some lost verbal overtones in etymology. The Chinese character for "mother" or "female" (*mu*), for example, is traced to forms portraying a nursing woman, her arms folded beneath her breasts (upper left of fig. 34). The Chinese character for "child" (*zi*) is shown to have its origin in forms depicting a newborn baby in swaddling clothes, his or her arms jiggling outside (lower left of fig. 34). Combining a "nursing mother" and a "newborn baby" are the ancient forms of the character for "give birth," "raise," or "educate" (*yu*) (upper right of fig. 34). The three dots beneath the strokes for "baby" represent fetal fluid. Ancient Chinese rites required that when a boy reached the age of twenty he wear a hairpin to indicate coming of age. The early forms of the character for "man" or "husband" (*fu*), therefore, imitate a male standing upright with a pin thrust in his hair (center right of fig. 34). The bone inscription form of the character for "clutch" or "clutching hand" (*zhua*) delineates three fingers clutching something. The fingers are garnished with nails in the bronze inscription form of the character, giving way to its simplified seal script form, and thence to its present form (lower right of fig. 34).

This column, launched in April 1998, is still under way. Beyond doubt, it is based on scholarship.[19] So scholarship concurs with Kenner that "Fenollosa's sinological mistakes . . . owed their right intuitions . . . originally after all to China."[20] Compare what the project implies to say to Fenollosa's statement: "The earlier forms of these characters were pictorial, and their hold upon the imagination is little shaken, even in later conventional modifications. It is not so well known, perhaps, that the great number of these ideographic roots carry in them *a verbal idea of action*" (*Character*, 9).

Pound seized on Fenollosa's central theme in his initial engagement with the essay—namely, the emphasis on juxtaposition of active elements. Where else was he to find an equally absorbing theoretical basis for his poetics of "patterned energies"? His rapture over this thesis is manifest in his June 1916 letter to Iris Barry: "To primitive man, a thing only IS what it *does*. That is Fenollosa, but I think the theory is a very good one for poets to go by" (*SLEP*, 82).

Fenollosa made this point emphatically in the course of lectures he was drafting about 1904: "Chinese poetry demands that we abandon our narrow grammatical categories, that we follow the original text with a wealth of concrete verbs" (*Character*, 21). In poetry, "We need . . . thousands of active words, each doing its utmost to show forth the motive and vital forces" (28).

Nevertheless, he digressed from this theme in long sections. Despite his claim at the outset that he was speaking "not as a professional linguist nor as a sinologue" (*Character*, 5), he kept straying onto the sinologist scene: "In nature there are no negations . . . in Chinese we can still watch positive verbal conceptions passing over into so-called negatives" (14–15). He dismissed the copula ostentatiously: "In Chinese the chief verb for 'is' not only means actively 'to have,' but shows . . . something even more concrete, namely 'to snatch from the moon with the hand'" (15). And he was diverted to a discussion of the parts of speech in Chinese, knowing perfectly well that "We import into our reading of Chinese all the weakness of our own formalisms" (17).

Why couldn't Fenollosa keep closely to his key insights? They lack convincing supporting facts, data from Chinese poetry available in his notebooks. Li Bo could be used effectively to illustrate the force of juxtaposition of active words. In the poem Pound calls "The Jewel Stairs' Grievance," each of the four lines contains a verb phrase that "concretely and vividly . . . express[es] the interactions of things" (*Character*, 28): *sheng bai lu* ("gather white dew"), *qin luo wa* ("soak gauze stockings"), *xia shuijing lian* ("draw the crystal curtain"), and *wang qiu yue* ("watch the autumn moon"). Without a subject in the last two lines the reader might wonder who performed the actions.[21]

Similarly, the poem Pound calls "The River-Merchant's Wife: A Letter" would be a superb example exhibiting the "dominance of the verb" (*Character*, 29). In the poem, a character denoting the subject often takes a succession of characters expressing concrete actions. Thus in lines 1–2 the character meaning "I" is followed by characters meaning "wear hair," "cover forehead," "pluck flowers," and "play about gate," respectively. In lines 3–4 the character for "you" is followed by characters meaning "play horse," "come," "walk about bed," and "play blue plums," respectively. Juxtaposing active words without linking words is commonplace in classical Chinese. The usage affords Chinese poets and prose writers great freedom to transfer material energies into language.

Fenollosa cited "Farmer pounds rice" as "the normal and typical sentence in English as well as in Chinese" (*Character*, 13). He at least oversimplified Chinese syntax, which allows an endless piling of active words and the omission of the subject. We have seen how Li Bo violates Fenollosa's "typical" construction in the above poems. A more revealing example of his continuous use of words of concrete actions is in the poem Pound calls "Exile's Letter." Consider the lines *fu zhou nong shui xiao gu ming / wei bo long lin suocao lu* (float a boat   stir water   flutes drums sound / gentle ripples   dragon scales   grass green) within a longer chain of juxtaposition. At first glance, one is likely to regard the first line as the juxtaposition of words of actions and the second line as the juxtaposition of words of things. Such a reading does Li Bo little justice, for *wei bo long lin suocao lu* really imitates a succession of processes—the speaker's vision of the water "rippling gently, turning dragon-scales and going grass green."

Because of its resemblance to bamboo growing upward node after node, the above structure is sometimes referred to as *zhujie ju,* or a "bamboo-nodal sentence."[22] Li Bo and other Chinese poets owed their gift for making such continuous, vigorous sentences to Qu Yuan. An extended example of the third-century B.C. poet's art is in *Shan gui,* or "The Genius of the Mountain." Giles's version gives one some idea of what it is like: "Methinks there is a Genius of the hills, clad in wisteria, girdled with ivy, with smiling lips, of witching mien, riding on the red pard, wild cats galloping in the rear, reclining in a chariot, with banners of cassia, cloaked with the orchid, girt with azalea, culling the perfume of sweet flowers to leave behind a memory in the heart."[23]

Chinese poets' habit of piling words of concrete actions calls to mind the modernist experiment with repeated juxtaposition of words in the present tense. The prototypical innovator of English prose in the continuous present tense was of course Gertrude Stein. Among modernist poets, Pound, Williams, Moore, and Stevens also contributed to this style. In accounting for a source of influence, Charles Altieri is correct in attributing it to modern art.[24] While modernist writers tried to borrow Cubist and Surrealist strategies, they would surely appreciate a verbal model that justified their attempt. And this they could find in suitable translations of Qu Yuan, Li Bo, and their descendants.

To return to *The Chinese Written Character,* some critics like to call Fenollosa's theory Fenollosa-Pound's theory. It is true that by devoting many years to editing, publishing, and promoting the essay, Pound virtually became a collaborator. However, we still must distinguish his view from Fenollosa's and, moreover, be wary of the changes in his understanding of the Chinese character. These changes are reflected both in various editions of the essay and in his comments over a considerable period of time.

In 1976 Ronald Bush was the first critic to alert us to the fact that early on Pound's enthusiasm was for "the spirit of Fenollosa's remarks about oriental logic" rather than for "their letter."[25] Bush's evidence was a 1919 note to the essay (later removed): "These precautions should be broadly conceived. It is not so much their letter, as the underlying feeling of objectification and activity, that matters."[26] From the beginning, Pound did not seem to think much of Fenollosa's "Man sees horse." In *Indiscretions* (1920), as Bush observes, he insisted that Henry James offered a more useful "poetic tool": We have "long since passed the stage when 'man sees horse' or 'farmer sow[s] rice,' can in simple ideographic record be said to display anything remotely resembling our subjectivity" (*P&P,* 4:60).

Pound's reservations regarding Fenollosa's "typical" Chinese sentence were based on his own investigation. In 1916–17, spurred by his ecstasies about the essay, he renewed his study of Chinese poetry in Fenollosa's notebooks.[27] Although at that stage he still could not see for himself the alleged pictorial qualities, he discerned Chinese structures that are far more involved than "Man sees horse." A version of Wang Wei's "Farm Field Pleasure," rendered in the summer in which he urged Iris Barry to read the essay, may illuminate his failed effort to recapture juxtaposition of verbs in pithy Chinese.[28]

Elsewhere I have argued that the example of Wang Wei eventually joined those of de Gourmont, James, Lewis, Eliot, Joyce, and Picasso "to supply the material and technique for the mode of presentation that gradually grew to be known as the 'ideogrammic method.'"[29] By this I do not mean to downgrade the essay's key role in forging the method. It surely afforded *The Cantos'* sustaining theoretical framework, while other factors contributed the substance.

In the mid-1930s Pound gave Fenollosa the credit for his ideogrammic method: "He did not proclaim his method as a method. He was trying to explain the Chinese ideograph as a means of transmission and registration of thought" (*ABCR,* 19). Following Fenollosa he used "rose-cherry-rust-flamingo = red" as a prime example to define the way the Chinese form their characters, which he believed was the way a poet should go about his or her poetry (22).[30] While the "rose-cherry-rust-flamingo" bit does not represent an actual Chinese character for "red," it does point to the mechanism for making a large number of Chinese characters, say, the character for "bright" ("sun-moon") or the character for "treasure" ("roof-jade-*piog*-mother-of-pearl").

Pound obviously did not care, at that point, whether he represented the Chinese character correctly or Fenollosa correctly. His preoccupation was to get his method correct, the method for *The Cantos* and for modernist poetry. It is true that Fenollosa resisted facts about Chinese sounds as much as he could, but he at least did not openly deny their existence.[31] Pound went completely overboard, so that by *ABC of Reading* (1934), he described the Chinese character as "the picture of a thing," which does not even "try to be the picture of a sound, or to be a written sign recalling a sound" (*ABCR,* 21).

By 1934 Pound ought to have known as well as Fenollosa that ancient Chinese poems were created first and foremost as songs to be sung, and that their notations (later made) registered sounds while putting together some shorthand pictures. On 4 June 1901 Fenollosa transcribed

in Japanese syllables one of China's oldest lyrics: "*KEI MEN RAN KEI /*
KIU MAN MAN KEI." Pound would soon incorporate this transcript
into his Canto 49. Besides, both men are supposed to have learned
that Confucius selected 305 *songs* for a compilation (of which one had
yielded Pound his "Song of the Bowmen of Shu"), and that Qu Yuan in
exile made his *Nine Songs* (of which one had yielded Pound his "After
Ch'u Yuan").

In due course, Pound would pay high tribute to the *melopoeia* in Chinese. "Whatever a few of us learned from Fenollosa twenty years ago,"
he wrote in 1935 for a separate edition of the essay (London: Stanley
Nott, 1936), "the whole Occident is still in crass ignorance of the Chinese art of verbal sonority. I now doubt if it was inferior to the Greek.
Our poets being slovenly, ignorant of music, and earless, it is useless to
blame professors for squalor" (*Character,* 33).

What happened between 1934 and 1935 that prompted Pound to extend credit to something he had slighted for so long? A fragmented
typescript in the Beinecke Library of Yale University furnishes a clue
to this puzzle.[32] While preparing the essay for the Stanley Nott edition,
Pound revisited Fenollosa's three notebooks for Mori's lectures on the
history of Chinese poetry. On Thursday, 28 May 1901, in a discourse
on the Chinese character, Mori presented the six principles regarding
formation and paid sound due respect: "3. Kei Sei [xingsheng]; form
noise. Characters of sound and form; the sound is made the base and a
certain form combined with it also called Shosei [xiesheng]. . . . e.g. Ko
(Kiang I. Ku) Ka (Ho i) names of two rivers in China. The first radical
of both is water, the 2nd part of word not for meaning but to represent
sound of flowing water, great many."[33] Referring to this and other paragraphs, Pound noted in 1935: "Red pencilings show me that I did read
and at least mark certain passages, some of which I had certainly for-
gotten fairly completely."[34] What had failed to stir Pound's imagination
twenty years earlier now caught his eye: "They contain considerable
more wisdom than I noticed when I first read through them 20 or so
years ago. . . . In 1914 I was in no shape to penetrate his rapid note on
the sound of the various verse forms even as far as I now have."[35]

So, if we take Pound's words on faith, in 1914–15 he read Mori's
comments on the Chinese character and red-penciled certain passages
without noticing their wisdom. But is it also conceivable that about
1935 he copied the Japanese syllables of an ancient Chinese poem into
Canto 49 without thinking of correcting his misrepresentation in *ABC
of Reading*? At any rate, no change was made even in 1951 when the book

was reissued. Critics perhaps would never concur as to whether prior to 1935 Pound had intentionally ignored Chinese sound in its notation or he had simply overlooked its *melopoeia* because he had been too overwhelmed by its *phanopoeia*.

Pound did not finish retyping Fenollosa's notes for Mori's lectures in 1935, however. Nor did he publish any part of his 1935 typescript. In November 1958, in his tower room at Brunnenburg, he resumed the task: "I now tackle Fenollosa's penciled record of Mori's lectures on the History of Chinese Poetry, with the intention of transmitting them as *his* view of the subject."[36] The typescript ran on for thirty-seven sheets, and then it was dropped.

During his thirteen years of incarceration in Washington, Pound heard harsh criticisms of the essay and his ideogrammic method.[37] He chose in the middle of retyping Mori's lectures to put up a defense. When Mary de Rachewiltz's publisher in Milan requested a note to her bilingual (English-Italian) edition of *Cathay* (*Catai*, 1959), he had his chance: "Non asseriva che il giornalista cinese medio usasse questo strumento come 'mezzo di poesia,' ma che può essere ed è stato usato come tale. I denigratori non hanno saputo leggere il titolo del suo saggio" or "He [Fenollosa] did not claim that the average Chinese journalist uses this instrument as 'a medium for poetry' but that it can and has been so used. The belittlers have failed to read the title of his essay."[38] Cheadle, who urges attention to this statement, calls it "a valid defense of the continuing interest and validity of Fenollosa's essay." However, she also observes that its closing remark—"È falsa l'idea che si possa tradurre senza compensare ciò che naturalmente va perduto nella versione in una diversa lingua," or "The false idea that you 'translate' by making NO compensation for what is necessarily lost in the transfer to a different language"—shows that "he still did not fully understand or accept what is meant by the place of phonetics in Chinese words."[39]

Pound's excessive use of Chinese in *Rock-Drill* (1955) and *Thrones* (1959) will make evident both his belated interest in Chinese sound and his unchanged misconception about its place in the script. This duality will be tackled fully along with Pound's late Confucianism in chapter 14.

TEN

Stevens

as Art

Collector

ON THE OTHER SIDE of the Atlantic, Stevens followed Oriental art news as attentively as Pound. Although Stevens published no reviews of Binyon or Fenollosa, he was by no means reserved on the topic. Indeed, his correspondence documents not only his interest in Binyon's *Painting in the Far East* and Guo Xi's "The Noble Features of the Forest and the Stream," but also his rapture over Oriental art displayed in diverse galleries. Seldom did an important event of Far Eastern culture escape Stevens's attention. So in October 1919, upon the appearance of the second installment of Fenollosa's essay in the *Little Review,* Stevens asked Harriet Monroe, "Have you seen this month's *Little Review* with the quotation from the Chinese?" (*L,* 215) In December 1935, when an enormous exhibition of Chinese art opened in Burlington House, he wrote to Miss Monroe again: "The exhibition of Chinese works of art that has just opened in London must be a marvelous thing. I get as much satisfaction from reading well-written descriptions of an exhibition of that sort and of the objects in it as I do from most poetry" (299).[1] Most probably he had been reading Binyon's *Chinese Art* (1935), a volume "intended to serve as a help to those who wish to profit from the unique opportunity offered by [that exhibition]."[2]

To say that Stevens became increasingly interested in Far Eastern art from the early 1920s onward is an understatement. Stevens had an avid collecting interest, which Pound never developed. This was partly due to the influence of his Harvard friends, Walter Arensberg, Witter Bynner, and Arthur Davison Ficke. Glen MacLeod suggests that Stevens "may well have been comparing his own very small collection of [modern European] paintings with his memories of the Arensberg salon."[3] We might suppose, further, that Stevens probably had been estimating his few objects from the Far East against his impressions of Bynner's pink abode in a Chinese style and Ficke's apartment filled with Japanese prints.

Both Bynner and Ficke had traveled to the Far East and acquired their pretty things firsthand. So had Harriet Monroe. This Stevens learned in late March 1918 during a visit to her home in Chicago.[4] Miss Monroe's sister Lucy married William J. Calhoun, an Illinois lawyer, in 1904, who later became U.S. minister to China. In 1910, on the eve of the collapse of the Qing imperial house, Miss Monroe sailed to Europe and then took the Trans-Siberian Railway to China, where she spent two months in Beijing with her sister. One day, as she related in a letter home, she "went out with a man from Tientsin [Tianjin]—something of an expert—through Book Street and into some picture shops, and at one dingy old place . . . bought a 'genuine Ming dynasty picture.'" After that purchase, she reminisced much later, she "made a sudden and very deep plunge into Chinese art, guided partly by Charles L. Freer, the Detroit collector whose beautiful museum in Washington, bequeathed to the nation at his death in 1919, perpetuates his fame."[5] Mr. Calhoun died in 1917. After a sojourn in Paris, Lucy Calhoun visited her sister in Chicago for a few weeks. She may well have just left for Beijing when Stevens called on Miss Monroe. This possibility leads us to suspect that on that occasion Miss Monroe spoke of Lucy and her own adventures in China.

The conversation, carried out in an atmosphere of the milieu that reminded one of the host's voyage to the Orient, presumably awakened Stevens's own collecting interest. It was after much hesitation and delay, however, that Stevens plucked up his courage to make a request: He would like Miss Monroe to arrange for her sister to send him one or two art objects and some Chinese tea from Beijing.

In late August 1922, a matter of days after an agreement with Alfred A. Knopf for the publication of *Harmonium,* he got the first of several "pleasant surprises"—a card from Miss Monroe at Hendersonville, North Carolina, with good news from Beijing: "My sister writes from Peking: 'I shall be delighted to fill the delicate commission for Mr. Stevens—it is a seductive one.'"[6] "One of these days," Stevens told Miss Monroe, the harbinger of the good news, "when the different things on their way to Hartford from Peking, Paris, Geneva, London, Mexico (cigar), actually arrive I shall have exhausted the possibilities of life within my scope" (*L,* 228).

True to Miss Monroe's notice, the first package from Beijing, "containing two packages of jasminerie," arrived a month later. Stevens pried open one of them and smelled "the good smells, out of China." In a letter he wrote to Miss Monroe he expressed his thanks: "Nothing could please me more. Do, please, tell your sister, la belle jasminatrice, how grateful I am." He also noted in the letter that he was looking forward to "some subsequent marvel." In describing his anticipation he made a comment that would remind one of Guo Xi's belief in art's power of bringing nature home: "For a poet to have even a second-hand contact with China is a great matter; and a desk that sees so much trouble is blessed by such reversions to innocence" (*L,* 229).

Another month later, the much yearned for box from Beijing reached Stevens's Hartford home. Packed in it were not two but five "really delightful things." Stevens gave a full description of these items in his next letter to Miss Monroe:

> Of these, the chief one is a carved wooden figure of the most benevolent old god you ever saw. He has a staff in one hand and in the other carries a lotus bud. On the back of his head he has a decoration of some sort with *ribbons* running down into his gown. The wood is of the color of dark cedar but it is neither hard nor oily. And there you are. But the old man, Hson-hsing [Shouxing], has the most amused, the nicest and kindliest expression: quite a pope after one's own heart or at least an invulnerable bishop telling one how fortunate one is, after all, and not to mind one's bad poems. He is on a little teak stand as is, also, each of the other things. The other things are a small jade screen, two black crystal lions and a small jade figure. The jade pieces are white. We have placed the screen behind the prophet, so that if he desires to retire into its cloudy color he can do so conveniently and we have set the lions in his path, one on each side. The heads of these noisy beasts are turned back on their shoulders, quite evidently unable to withstand the mildness of the venerable luminary. The other figure precedes the group as handmaiden and attendant casting most superior glances at the lions meaning, no doubt, to suggest that it would be best for them to put their tails between their legs and go about their business" (*L,* 230–31).

Fittingly, Stevens mentioned after the account that Mrs. Stevens would take a photograph of the group for Miss Monroe. The promised photograph is nowhere to be seen. However, with the exception of the jade screen, all the tokens from Beijing have survived in the collection of Stevens's grandson, Peter Hanchak.[7] Stevens called the carved wooden old man *Shouxing* (fig. 35). In China *Shouxing* may refer either to the god of longevity or to a very old man. As a rule, the Chinese god of longevity is bareheaded, showing a protruding forehead, and he normally holds a staff in one hand and an oval peach in the other hand. Stevens's fourteen-inch *Shouxing*, with a very large hat on his head and with no peach in his left hand, appears just an old saintly man. Mrs. Calhoun had no doubt gone to a great deal of trouble to find things such as a pair of jade lions and a small brass dancer to go along with the old man. She probably believed the figure to be the Chinese god of longevity, although traditionally *Shouxing* as a god is accompanied not by lions but by *Fuxing* (the god of happiness) and *Luxing* (the god of fortune).

Stevens had bought art objects from abroad through other people as well, but as he put it, this was the first time the thing shipped back had been after his own heart. The reason he gave—the *Shouxing* "is so humane that the study of him is as good as a jovial psalm" (*L*, 231)—revealed his continued interest in Chan Buddhism. Perhaps the image of Buddha in Beal's *Buddhism in China* remained confused with other

35. Wallace Stevens's Chinese carved wooden *Shouxing*. (Courtesy of Peter Hanchak, Charlottesville, Virginia; photographs by Jackson Smith)

Chinese saints to offer him meditative vision. Stevens could not resist planning to buy more: "I must have more, provided he is not a solitary." Soon, in November 1923, he would have an opportunity to compare his treasures with Bynner's in Santa Fe. Nonetheless, he decided to "let that rest for the moment" (*L*, 231), for he sensed that he had troubled Mrs. Calhoun more than enough.

The center of Stevens's outside world was after all France. During the week when he received two packages of jasmine tea from Beijing, "a batch of large photographs after the Poussins in the Louvre" also arrived (*L*, 229). In the 1930s he arranged for Anatole Vidal, a proprietor in Paris, to send him paintings by Amédée de La Patellière, Henri Lebasque, and other French artists.[8] After the senior Vidal died in 1944, his daughter, Paule Vidal, continued to buy French pictures and books for Stevens. It was to Mme. Vidal that Stevens made the now famous comment: "I have a taste for Braque and a purse for Bombois" (*L*, 545). And it was to her also that he offered a candid description of his personal taste: "I like things light and not dark, cheerful and not gloomy, and that above everything else I prefer something real but saturated with the feeling and the imagination of the artist" (545).

Stevens obviously delighted as much in Lebasque's *Paysage avec femme* as in the cheerful *Shouxing* from Beijing.[9] His peculiar sensibility urged him to keep an eye on Chinese art objects mostly in catalogues while pursuing more French works of art from Paris. Shortly after the publication of *Harmonium,* he sent Mrs. Calhoun an inscribed copy of the volume. She had done him a huge favor, and some day he would ask her to repeat it. His untold plan explains why he appeared upset to learn in October 1934 that Miss Monroe had gone to China for another reunion with her sister without notifying him.[10] What Miss Monroe said in a letter she wrote upon return—"I wish you could see Peking, and live for a while in my sister's beautiful temple home"—only made him feel worse.[11] His idea of her being in Beijing, he replied on 13 March 1935, "instead of suggesting temple roofs, suggested tea and other things" (*L*, 277). Figuring that it would be a good opportunity to renew his request, he went on, "Do you suppose your sister would care to do a little shopping?" At the moment he did not have money, he wrote, but in a few months he would definitely be able to wire a sum enough "to buy, say, a pound of Mandarin Tea, a wooden carving, a piece of porcelain or one piece of turquoise, one small landscape painting, and so on and so on" (278).

Stevens's subtle complaint instantly brought a package of Chinese tea from Chicago. In his next letter to Miss Monroe, a letter of thanks, dated 5 April 1935, he explained that the list of things he gave "was merely an improvisation." He would rather leave everything to Mrs. Calhoun, so long as she remembered that what he wanted were not things to place on the mantelpiece, but things to do him good, things similar to the wooden *Shouxing,* which he saw as "a religious pilgrim" and "one of the most delightful things" he ever owned. Consequently, after all the politeness and ambiguity, he added, "A small landscape by a scholarly painter, or that sort of thing, would do me more good, picked up by chance, than anything that I could ask for specifically" (*L,* 280).

Summer passed and autumn came. Stevens put together another list of items for Miss Monroe and then tore it up because he realized that it would amount to much more than he could afford. On 4 December 1935, after reading the descriptions of the Chinese art exhibition in London, he wrote Miss Monroe again: "[I]f I had carried out my plans, I should about now be receiving several crates of ancient landscapes, rare Chinese illustrated books, Chun Yao ware, Tang horses, and so on" (*L,* 299). That turned out to be his last letter to reach Miss Monroe, for she was to die in September 1936. And he was to regret forever that he had not acted more quickly.

With Miss Monroe gone, Stevens could not bother Mrs. Calhoun anymore. He had to look elsewhere for such favors. By then his fondness for things Oriental had grown so great that he would make use of business associates' contacts. Thus on 20 December 1935, he wrote to Benjamin Kwok, a college student in South China: "Hearing about Central China and about Hankow, and now about Macao . . . somehow or other brings me in much closer contact with these places than I ever have had before" (*L,* 303).[12] On 14 September 1937, he contacted Leonard van Geyzel, a young poet and a longtime resident of Ceylon: "I hope to hear that what I am going to ask you to do can be done without bothering you. It involves getting together a few things from Ceylon and sending them to me here so that they may arrive in time for Christmas" (323–24).[13] In due course, he received from Macao, China, three boxes of teas, including "some of the best Kee-Moon" (303); and from Ceylon a Buddha statue, some Hindi jaggery, and tea. Of the second group, he liked the Buddha best and so placed it in his own room. "At night, when my windows are open and the air is like ice," he wrote, "this particular Buddha must wish that I put a postage stamp on him and send him back to Colombo" (328).[14] Whereas the tea from Ceylon surfaces in "Connoisseur of Chaos" (*CPWS,* 215), the Buddha unites with the *Shouxing* from Beijing to become "the speechless, invisible gods / . . . from over Asia" in "Montrachet-le-Jardin" (262). Moreover, Stevens's sympathy for the Buddha in his cold room goes into "A Weak Mind in the Mountains" with references to "The wind of Iceland and / The wind of Ceylon, / Meeting, gripp[ing] my mind" (212).

A little earlier, in his search for connections in the Far East, Stevens had even written to Mrs. Cary, a mere acquaintance of Elsie's. In 1931 Elsie and their daughter, Holly, met Mrs. Cary and her daughter, Mary Alice, in a program for young children at Vassar. The Carys had since gone to Otaru, Japan, where Mary Alice's father served as a missionary. An unanswered postcard from Mrs. Cary to Elsie afforded Stevens an excuse in May 1935: "I thought it might be amusing to send you a little money, and ask you to make up a box of things that you thought that Holly might like." What he said next makes evident what he was after: "Of course, I don't know what sort of a place Otaru is. Japanese peasant pottery is often quite delightful; there may be other things that I could suggest" (L, 281).[15]

Beyond doubt, Stevens would not rely totally on mere acquaintances to satisfy his collecting needs. During one of his trips to Baltimore, he hunted out a Chinese antique store specializing in the late imperial periods—"Ming: Hung Wu 1368–1398; Yung Lo [Yongle] 1403–1424; and Ching [Qing]: Shun-che [Shunzhi] 1644–1662; Kang Hsi [Kangxi] 1662–1723; Yung Cheng [Yongzheng] 1723–1735; Chien Lung [Qianlong] 1736–1795." A business card that was given to him is kept in a large envelope labeled "addresses & phone numbers saved by Stevens" in the Huntington Library Stevens Collection:[16]

Chao Ming Chen
Antiques
Established in the U.S. in 1920
339–341 E. 29th St.
Baltimore, MD
Telephone: University 3206

What might Stevens have purchased from this antique store? No one can tell. Nonetheless, in his collection is a portrait of a Chinese figure in red robe whose origin remains unidentified (fig. 36). Could it be from Chao Ming Chen? The inscription at the upper right designates it as a portrait of the ninth Ming emperor (r. 1464–87). However, the official portraits of Emperor Chenghua show him to be a stouter man.[17] Another indication that the subject of the painting may not be the em-

36. Unidentified Chinese artist, *Portrait of Emperor Chenghua*. (Courtesy of Peter Hanchak, Charlottesville, Virginia; photograph by Gail Hanchak)

peror is the man's posture. Typically, Chinese emperors pose with hands on laps. With hands in sleeves over the belly, this figure looks more like a Ming high official.

Of the Oriental objects Stevens collected, the most conspicuous are a pair of Hiroshige prints, *Fireworks at Ryojoku* and *Foxes Assembling under the Shozoku Enoki Tree at Ojion, New Year's Eve.* Hiroshige prints, as Ficke acknowledges, "have been more greatly admired in Western lands than the prints of any other artists except Hokusai."[18] In *Epochs,* Fenollosa hails the printer as "a painter of night . . . without a rival, save Whistler."[19] One of his works illustrated is precisely *Foxes.*[20] Where Stevens acquired the two prints remains unknown.

Since art objects from China and Japan were difficult to get, Stevens often had to cure his thirst for them by going to exhibitions and ordering catalogues. In June 1909, he told Elsie that he "would give last winter's hat" for the illustrated catalogue of an exhibition of Japanese prints in London with notes by Arthur Morrison (*SP*, 235).[21] His copy of that volume is now in the Huntington Library. On 23 November 1920, he spoke to a friend of a "manual on Japanese prints published by [the V & A Museum in London]" in his possession.[22] In December 1935, he probably obtained a copy of Binyon's *Chinese Art* with descriptions of Chinese paintings, sculptures, and bronzes shown at Burlington House. In addition, his collection at the Huntington Library includes a catalogue of Chinese sculpture exhibited at museums in San Francisco, Santa Barbara, Pasadena, Portland, and Minneapolis, 1944–45.[23]

We do not know if Stevens saw that exhibition. What we do know is that in late June 1945 he spent some time in Harvard's Fogge Museum (*L*, 508) while it was showing Chinese jades, bronzes, and sculptures from the Winthrop Collection; Ming-Qing porcelains from the Davis Bequest; pottery from the Han to the Song loaned by Charles Hoyt; and Ming-Qing porcelains from the John Coolidge Collection.[24] On a visit to Boston in late November 1953 he missed a Japanese art show at the MFA.[25] It was the Fogge again that cheered him up.[26] The revisit prompted him to recommend the museum to Barbara Church on 8 December: "an extremely pleasant place, open to the public, whose only real public are the students at Harvard and visiting parents, brothers and sisters and young persons of honorable intentions" (*L*, 804).

No less than three times Stevens expressed to Miss Monroe his desire for a small Chinese landscape painting.[27] His wish did not come true until 1952, when something near to that—a large flower-and-bird scroll by a Korean artist—unexpectedly arrived. The giver of the scroll, Peter H. Lee (b. 1929), was then a twenty-two-year-old Korean student at Yale. In 1955 Stevens was to give an official account of how their friendship had budded a year before the hanging scroll: "When he was at New Haven, he used to come up to Hartford and the two of us would go out to Elizabeth Park, in Hartford, and sit on a bench by the pond and talk about poetry. He did not wait for the ducks to bring him ideas but always had in mind questions that disclosed his familiarity with the experience of poetry" (*OP*, 285).[28] Clearly Stevens was very fond of the young poet with Chan impulse. The first advice he offered him after reading his poems was "to forgo the familiar for the unfamiliar" (*L*, 711).

Lee would not have been able to offer Stevens scrolls if he had not been from an art collector's family. As Lee recalled, his father used to invite local painters and calligraphers to his house in Seoul to drink and chat and collaborate in making pictures. Till this day, Lee, poet and

37. Kim Kyongwon (Korean, 1901–67), *Flowers and Birds.* (Courtesy of Peter Han-chak, Charlotteville, Virginia; photograph by Gail Hanchak)

professor of East Asian languages and cultures at UCLA, keeps a scroll executed by ten painters and two calligraphers. The flower-and-bird scroll was just another one of the many art objects Lee received from his father, which he graciously gave Stevens in early 1952.[29]

It proved to be a perfect gift. Never had Stevens received a token as pleasant as this. As expected, he at once put it up in his own room. In a lyrical mood, he began describing to Peter Lee what he saw in the picture: "I don't recognize the birds with their crests and strong feet. They are probably birds very well known in your part of the world, but I do not recall them. On the other hand, the flowers with the reed-like stems around the rocks are what are called Chinese lilies here. They might be white jonquils." Next were his thoughts, things he was more eager to tell his Korean friend: "All this seems to be part of an idyllic setting in some remote past, having nothing to do with the tormented constructions of contemporary art. The scroll made the same impression on me when I first looked at it that a collection of Chinese poems makes: an impression of something venerable, true and quiet" (*L*, 741–42).

Kim Kyongwon (1901–67), the artist who made the picture, would be elated to hear all this. As Ch'oe Sun-u remarks, Korean landscapists normally trained themselves by copying Chinese albums.[30] According to Lee, Kim Kyongwon studied with Yi Toyong (1884–1933), a landscape master.[31] He probably went through such training. In any event, the way his *Flowers and Birds* (fig. 37) combines lyricism and observation of nature recalls a Chinese masterpiece, *Grass, Flowers, and Wild Birds* by Lu Zhi (1496–1576), reproduced in *Time* magazine (6 May 1957), which captured Moore's interest.[32] Note close parallels between the two pictures in motif, composition, and color tones.

Lu Zhi's *Grass, Flowers, and Wild Birds* is a splendid example of Chinese literati painting whose true aim is delineating the mind. To make the "Images of the Mind" (Wen Fong's phrase) evident, the scholar-artist would often inscribe a poem that more directly depicts his intellect. The proof for Kim's familiarity with this genre is his inscription of a poem in Chinese that offers no objective description of his berries or birds. The four lines may be rendered as this:

From the Crystal Palace, unshut at night,
Issue sea fairies, reaching white waves;
For playing with the moon's reflection, my head lowered
I am unaware that dew has soaked my clothes.

These things—the moon, the waterscape, flowers, birds, and a seen or unseen gazer—prevail in Chinese poetry and painting. Stevens had encountered them hundreds of times. So he was able to read the scholar-artist's mind even without having to learn about his inscription. He made this evident when he remarked that the picture "made the same impression on me when I first looked at it that a collection of Chinese poems makes: an impression of something venerable, true and quiet."

From *Harmonium* to *The Rock,* much of Stevens's lyricism manifests a preoccupation with blending meditative detachment into simplified spatial arrangements. From the very beginning, Lee seems to have discerned a connection between this mode of poetry and Chan art. His gifts appear to point to this understanding. The flower-and-bird scroll he sent Stevens echoes "Thirteen Ways" in both motif and method of presentation. It illustrates, say, "Do you not see how the blackbird / Walks around the feet / Of the women about you?" (*CPWS,* 93).

In the early summer of 1954, Lee turned up in Fribourg, Switzerland. In a letter he told Stevens that he was to offer him another scroll painting, perhaps as a way of thanking the older poet for commenting on his translation of Korean poetry, which would in 1964 go into his *Anthology of Korean Poetry.*[33] Stevens's reply was explicit: "If you want to send one of your Korean paintings to me, don't hesitate because there is nothing that I should like more" (*L,* 839). When asked about the second scroll, which has not surfaced, Lee remarks that it "must be a painting of Daoist sages or Confucian scholars in retirement."[34] Could this be a landscape with old men under trees that somewhat recalls the first poem of "Six Significant Landscapes" or the third poem of "Le Monocle de Mon Oncle"?

Stevens's own description of the second scroll seems to confirm this assumption: "The scroll is delightful. . . . It represents my ideal of a happy life: to be able to grow old and fat and lie outdoors under the trees thinking about people and things and things and people" (*L,* 865).

So, after decades of unsuccessful searches for "A small landscape by a scholarly painter" from the Far East, Stevens ended up receiving two large ones without much effort on his part. And that concluded his limited experience as a connoisseur of Far Eastern art.

ELEVEN

Moore and
The Tao of
Painting

IT IS TO HER REVIEWS for *The Dial* that Moore owes her reputation as an ardent, serious, and witty critic of the latest in print. Her April 1928 "Briefer Mention" piece on *Guide-Posts to Chinese Painting* by Louise Wallace Hackney (Houghton Mifflin, 1927) may bear witness to her accuracy of perception.

> That a delighted consideration of art should be less than delightful; that as writing and as thinking it should be occidentally "prompt" is in this survey compensated for by illustrations such as "Winter Landscape," "Narcissus," a "Ming Ancestral Portrait"; and one is as attentive as the author could wish one to be, to the "ideals and methods" of Chinese painting, to "influences and beliefs reflected in it," and the influence exerted by it. Any lover of beauty may well be grateful to a book which commemorates the blade of grass as model for the study of the straight line, the skill of calligraphers, with "hog's hair on finely woven silk," "methods of treating mountain wrinkles," "tones of ink to 'give color,'" the thought of genii, winged tigers, and Emperor crossing "'weak waters' on a 'bridge made of turtles,'" or a theme so romantic as that of Yang Kuei-fei [Yang Guifei] "going, 'lily pale, between tall avenues of spears to die.'" (*PrMM*, 255)

This reveals to us something Moore was always happy to have—a guide to Chinese art. As to the Eurocentric way Hackney handles the subject, Moore finds it "less than delightful." Nonetheless, she suggests that one should be grateful to the book for providing authentic illustrations and for bringing to light the calligraphic nature of Chinese painting.[1]

After *Guide-Posts,* Moore continued to watch for something counter-hegemonic on the subject. In 1961, she declared in the foreword to *A Marianne Moore Reader* that she had written on such a book: "What became of 'Tedium and Integrity,' the unfinished manuscript of which there was no duplicate? A housekeeper is needed to assort the untidiness" (*MMR*, xiii). The greater part of the manuscript for "Tedium and Integrity" has survived among the Moore papers (see appendix), thanks to her keepers at the Rosenbach Museum and Library in Philadelphia.[2] Of the typescript, Linda Leavell remarks, "[T]his may have been one of Moore's most important essays along with 'Feeling and Precision' and 'Humility, Concentration, and Gusto' had she not lost the first four pages."[3] In discussing this potentially important Moore essay, we must account for what gave rise to its composition.

On the evenings of 3 and 5 October 1956, at the request of the UCLA Department of English, Moore inaugurated its Ewing Lectures by offering a seminal talk in two parts, to be published in 1958 under the title of *Idiosyncrasy and Technique*. A year later, in October 1957, she was invited to give another lecture on the West Coast, which afforded the occasion for "Tedium and Integrity." "This whole theme—the thought of integrity," she says, "—was suggested to me by THE TAO OF PAINTING, with a translation of THE MUSTARD SEED GARDEN MANUAL OF PAINTING 1679–1701, by Miss Mme Mme [Mai-mai] Sze; published by the Bollingen Foundation, 1956" (see appendix). So in plain terms, "Tedium and Integrity" is Moore's homage to *The Tao of Painting*, a Chinese painter's account of the ritual disposition of Chinese painting, with an English translation of a seventeenth-century handbook of Chinese painting.

Moore received her complimentary set of *The Tao of Painting* from the Bollingen Foundation perhaps in January 1957. Just how she was enraptured by this two-volume work may be seen first from what she states in her letter of 22 January 1957 to Mr. John Barrett of the Bollingen Foundation: "[Y]ou cannot imagine my excitement in possessing these books.[4] The exposition of subjects and the terminology in discussing 'The Elements of a Picture' in the Chinese text is pleasure enough for a lifetime."[5]

Her extraordinary reaction is also reflected in the fact that on 5 September 1957, a matter of weeks prior to her second lecture tour to the West Coast, she wrote Mr. Barrett again, ordering five more sets of *The Tao of Painting*: "Now!—I need some copies of the TAO and for two, enclose a check for fifty dollars and a memorandum of what I owe for conveyance will have to be made. I seem to make a salesman of you, but may I explain. I am going to California to give a talk to students and some readings, and in November I shall be able to pay for 3 other sets."[6]

Having said this, she goes on to specify that the first two sets are for Dr. James Sibley Watson at Rochester, New York, and Mr. David Playdell-Bouverie at Glen Ellen, California; and that the other three are for Mr. Monroe Wheeler of the Museum of Modern Art; Bryher [Winifred Ellerman], in Switzerland; and Mrs. Marion Doren Kauffer, the widow of the noted illustrator E. McKnight Kauffer, in New York.[7] With regard to her gift for Bryher, Moore makes clear why she wants her to have it: "I have been talking to my friend Bryher about my so-called lecture in California TEDIUM AND INTEGRITY about how the Tao makes study charming and I cannot rest till she has this treatise—of all my friends the one perhaps who deserves it most."[8]

A quick glance through the book will clarify some of its pleasure given to Moore. According to the *Times Literary Supplement* (*TLS*) (31 October 1958), the book was "one of the most beautifully printed and produced publications on Chinese art ever to appear in the West." It provides an introduction, a chronology, and a valuable twenty-page appendix in which the basic terms of Chinese painting are analyzed and illustrated by means of their characters and, in many cases, the earlier and more pictographic forms. In addition, the first volume offers eleven plates of beautiful Chinese painting and calligraphy. Leafing through that volume, Moore was apparently enchanted by two color plates. At any rate, she refers to one—a plum branch (fig. 38)—as a symbol of integrity in the foreword to *A Marianne Moore Reader* (xiv), and passionately admires the other—an insect-and-frog picture (fig. 39)—in her letter of 22 January 1957 to Mr. Barrett:

If I were in a decline mentally, the insect and frog color-print in Volume I of the Tao would, I think, help me to regain tone. The accuracy without rigidity of the characterizations is hard to credit; the emerald of the leopard-frog and its watchful eye, the dragon-flies, sanguine, brown and greenish gray against the fragile beetle of some kind, the climbing katydid and grasshopper on the move, the plausibility of all this life above the pumpkin-leaves and lace of lesser leaves, the bumble-bee so solid despite frail violet wings and trailing legs with thorny rasps, are something, I suppose, that one could learn by heart but never become used to.[9]

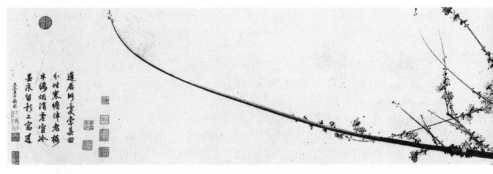

38 *(top)*. Zou Fulei (active mid-14th century), *A Breath of Spring,* 1361. Purchase, F1931.1. (Courtesy, Freer Gallery of Art, Smithsonian Institution, Washington, D.C.)

39 *(bottom)*. Qian Xuan (1235–1305), *Early Autumn.* Founders Society Purchase, General Membership Fund. Photograph © 1994. (Courtesy, Detroit Institute of Arts, Detroit)

The exhilaration with which Moore recounts the details in the insect-and-frog painting is reminiscent of her eulogy of "mandarins and insects painted upon silk" by a Chinese hand in a 1925 *Dial* "Comment" piece (*PrMM,* 151), and of her tribute to the artistry of an enameled *qilin* in "Nine Nectarines." It was Chinese, Moore appears to be reasserting, "who [created these] masterpiece[s]" (*CPMM,* 30), in which one perceives "imaginary gardens with real toads in them" (267).

Chinese artworks definitely had their appeal. Yet *The Tao*'s value for Moore lay less in its illustrations—which are meticulously chosen and

beautifully reproduced—than in its account from a Chinese painter's perspective of "certain ideas that have motivated and governed Chinese painting, and of the methods used to express them."[10] Moore's admiration for *The Tao* was rooted in her abiding fascination with the Chinese aesthetic, a fascination that had only deepened over the course of four decades since her initial brush with Chinese art in London and New York museums. In her years of pursuing the subject, she nonetheless regretted having to put up with the Orientalist thinking of books that had to be "occidentally 'prompt'" (*PrMM*, 255). After *Guide-Posts, The Tao* proved to be such an eye-opener for Moore. Mai-mai Sze, the author of *The Tao,* was, in Kenneth Rexroth's opinion, "probably one of the two best living Chinese painters working in anything resembling contemporary Western idiom."[11]

Born in Tianjin, China, Mai-mai Sze (1902–92) grew up in England and attended college in America because her father Sao-ke Alfred Sze (1877–1958) served as Chinese minister to London and Washington.[12] At

Wellesley College, 1927–31, she studied English literature and painted traditional Chinese pictures.[13] By 1945 she was known as a columnist ("East-West") for the *New York Post,* as author of an autobiographic novel *Echo of a Cry: A Story Which Began in China,* and as a painter with pictures exhibited in London, Paris, and New York.

As if knowing that her favorite poet Marianne Moore was to lecture on *The Tao,* Mai-mai Sze wrote her a brief letter on 28 September 1957. Enclosed was her clipping from *The Listener* 12 September 1957 of a review of Moore's new book, *Like a Bulwark.* Later that year she informed Moore that she had "taken the liberty of sending [her] a subscription" for the *TLS.*[14] The friendship grew as the two women corresponded during the next eleven or more years.[15] Moore was absolutely sincere in her repeated acknowledgments of the importance of *The Tao* to her career, especially during the years stretching from the composition of *O to Be a Dragon* to the appearance of *A Marianne Moore Reader.* In a letter of 18 April 1959, she tells Sze, "my universe [is] enlarged and ever expanding by receiving from Mr. Barrett, the Tao OF PAINTING."[16] And in a letter of 20 November 1963, she reaffirms the work's impact: "in the Tao of Painting—of which I never tire, permanent gifts, they have been, that I have for *all time.* Possessions that I carry with me in my mind—along with some incurable ignorances."[17]

Moore evidently went through *The Tao* more than once. Her intense reading is registered in a variety of forms in her own set of the work now housed in the Rosenbach Museum and Library: a note on the front endpaper of volume 1,[18] her characteristic marginal markings throughout both volumes, and her clippings of reviews and a notice of the book tucked in. Also inserted between its pages are clippings of reproduced Chinese paintings and calligraphy.[19] Her study led to her October 1957 lecture on "Tedium and Integrity." The typescript at the Rosenbach Museum and Library, despite its fragmented status, furnishes a record of Moore's passionate response to a useful work on Chinese aesthetic, and therefore promises to repay our scrutiny.

While we have no way of knowing the precise manner in which Moore opened her October 1957 lecture, we have her summary description in the foreword to *A Marianne Moore Reader:* "Of 'Tedium and Integrity' the first few pages are missing—summarized sufficiently by: manner for matter; shadow for substance; ego for rapture" (*MMR,* xiv). We have not missed too much, for her three sets of oppositions seem to serve as an introduction, and it is not until page 4 that she comes to her real point—homage to *The Tao:* "This whole theme—the thought of integrity—was suggested to me by THE TAO OF PAINTING."

Just as "tedium" is Moore's term for egotism, what the Buddhists call "ignorance," "integrity" is her expression for wholeness, a word chosen by her to sum up Sze's account of "Tao and the Tao" in chapter 1. It is unclear that she perceives the difficulty involved in any attempt to define the Chinese notion. Sze offers a variety of alternative terms for the Dao while stressing the notoriously slippery nature of the concept, quoting Laozi as saying: "The *Tao* that can be called the *Tao* is not the eternal *Tao*" (*The Tao,* 1:15). She mentions "*ch'i* [*qi*]," "*li*," "Great One," "Monad," "Primal Unity," and so on as words for portraying its dynamic force (1:6–7). None of these appears to have impressed Moore. In her attempt to interpret the Dao, she has singled out for quotation Sze's description of the Chinese character

道

(*dao*) as made up of "*ch'o* [*zu*], representing a foot taking a step, and *shou,* a head" (1:8). Her choice of the term "integrity" for the Dao is evidently based on this analysis. After dissecting the character into its two components, *shou* (head)

首   𦣻

and *zu* (foot)

辵   𤖊

Sze asserts, "the combination of *shou* (head) and *ch'o* [*zu*] (foot) symbolized the idea of wholeness, that is, spiritual growth. One aspect of the character *tao* thus represents an *inner* way, an integration of character with deep and complex psychological connotations (as to soul, mind, and emotions)" (1:8). Quoting Sze, Moore observes, "So we have the idea of wholeness of total harmony from head to foot. Step by step progress requires deliberateness, suggesting that . . . conduct is a thing of inner motivation" (see appendix).

Moore was no stranger to this kind of analysis. Before quoting Sze again, she refers to Chinese writing as "pictographic." She probably read Fenollosa's essay on "The Chinese Written Character" as early as 1920.

Her copy of Pound's *Instigations* with the essay, inscribed "Marianne Moore / St. Luke's Place/ 1920," is held in the Rosenbach Museum and Library. In the Rosenbach Moore Collection is also a copy of *Chinese: Wit, Wisdom and Written Characters* by Rose Quong, showing the pictographic elements of over a hundred Chinese characters, including the one for "man" as "standing upright on his two legs."[20] With books such as these she may well have tried, as Gaudier-Brzeska had tried, to figure out if she "'hadn't sense enough to see that *that* was a horse,' or a cow or a tree or whatever it might be" (*GB*, 46). However, not all Chinese characters can be analyzed in this manner, only a small number. Precisely because the Chinese character *dao* belongs to that splinter group can Sze depend on character analysis to treat its connotations in Chinese thought. Sze is most probably aware of the limits of her method of analysis. At least, she has applied it only to a few Chinese terms, and in doing so she never fails to refer to their early forms.

Sze's treatment of the term "Dao" proves intellectually defensible and effectively illuminating. Her description of the character *dao* as a combination of *shou* (head) and *zu* (foot) has appeal for Moore, for it crystallizes the central tenet of the Daoist aesthetic—the idea of wholeness, harmony, or "integrity" as Moore calls it. In Chinese thought, as Sze explains, the *shou-zu* polarity is likened to the polarities of Heaven and Earth, spirit and matter, soul and body—in short, the *Yin-Yang* of the Universe, suggesting unity of all polarities (*The Tao,* 1:9). This Daoist implication is duly stressed by Moore, who observes, citing Sze (1:93), "The *Tao* . . . [has] an identity of contraries which are not in the conflict but complementary opposites or two halves of a whole, as in the *Yin* and *Yang*—symbolized by the disc divided by an S-like curve" (see appendix).

Throughout Moore's career, unity or "integrity" is a concern central to her poetics. One purpose of her animal and landscape poems has been to discover and express a "oneness" of the human and natural worlds, or a "oneness" of spirit and matter. Her treatment of the jerboa, the basilisk, and the pangolin as creatures no less noble than humans really stems from a distrust of the Judeo-Christian belief that humans must "have dominion over the fish of the sea, and over the fowl of the air, and over the cattle, and over all the earth, and over every creeping thing that creepeth upon the earth."[21] It is in Chinese painting and poetry that Moore discovers a spirit akin to her own. For the Chinese, as she almost certainly recognizes, the individual functions in perfect harmony with landscape and animals. This Daoistic outlook is embodied in the design of the character *dao* as opposed to the design of the character *ren* (the individual). As Moore notes with apparent admiration, "Pictographically, man is but a pair of legs, whereas the Tao is an integration of body, legs, arms, and above all a head" (see appendix).

We can now see why Moore has chosen "integrity" as the term for the Dao. The English word, too, makes articulate both facets of the Daoist concept symbolized in the character *dao*—wholeness of all things (Heaven and Earth) and wholeness of character (the individual from head to foot). To make seen the value of the Dao as a mode of theorizing for art and poetry, Moore calls attention to Sze's remarks on two key aspects of Chinese painting—"the close relationship between painting and calligraphy" and "the traditional view that painting is not a profession but an extension of the art of living" (*The Tao,* 1:5). Moore's reading of the second aspect is not perfectly accurate. While Sze states that "most of the great masters first distinguished themselves as officials, scholars, or poets," adding that "some excelled in painting as well as in other fields" (1:5–6), Moore adduces only the additional idea. In observing that "A painter was likely to be an astronomer, a musician, perhaps a medical man," she probably had in mind her painter/poet friends. Despite her incomplete citation, Moore gets Sze's main point right. She makes clear that "In acquiring the education prescribed by the Tao of Painting, a painter underwent rigorous intellectual discipline which included intensive training of memory" (see appendix). Thus, in Chinese education ethic and aesthetic become one, and a theory of living becomes the basis of a complete theory of art and poetry. For Moore this second trait provides a useful perspective from which to appreciate the Dao of painting. In fact, it sets off a whole series of insights on her theme of "Tedium and Integrity." Her observation following a quotation from Sze is worth citing:

So authorship in China is integral to education, please note—not a separate proficiency to be acquired. (Rather humbling to those of us who devoted much time [to] incidental aspects of writing.) Chinese philosophy, Mme Mme [Mai-mai] Sze observes, might be said to be psychology—a development of the whole personality; and egotism—or what the Bhuddist [Buddhist] called ignorance—obscures a clear vision of the *Tao.* It is unusual, at least in my experience, to come on a book of verse which has not a tincture of sarcasm or grievance, a sense of injury personal or general, and I feel very strongly what Juan Ramon Jiménez said in referring to something else—to what is not poetry—"there is a profounder profundity" than obsession with self (see appendix).[22]

Two points made here demand clarification. First, not all Chinese philosophy is concerned with psychology. About this Sze asserts, "Most of Chinese philosophy might be said to be psychology, being concerned with the mind, emotions, and character—the development of the whole personality" (*The Tao*, 1:13–14). Second, the assumption that egotism (or "tedium") obscures vision is traceable to the Neo-Confucian thinker Wang Shouren (1472–1528), who considers "the mind of man" to be "Heaven." In *The Tao*, Sze quotes Wang as saying, "Every time we extend our intuitive knowledge, we clear away the obscurings, and when all of them are cleared away, our original nature is restored, and we again become part of this Heaven" (1:30).[23] The Chinese word for "selfishness" or "obscurings" is *siyu*, which Sze renders as "egotism," and the Sanskrit word for this motive is *avidyā*, which Sze renders as "ignorance" (1:31). That notion has great attraction for Moore. In it she seems to have found a way to account for the sublime detachment permeating all masterpieces of China. American poets, in her opinion, carry too much "tincture of sarcasm and grievance, a sense of injury personal or general." To rid themselves of all distracting thought and emotion—"egotism" or "ignorance" in the Daoist-Buddhist sense—they should take the advice of the Chinese philosopher Liezi (Lieh Tzu): "To a mind that is still, the whole universe surrenders" (*The Tao*, 1:18). This means that they should "still the heart" to "empty it of all distracting thought and emotion." As Sze explains, this exercise is absolutely necessary for artists because "'the emptiness' opens the way to a state of quiescence and receptivity, the ideal state in which to reflect the *Tao*" (1:17–18).

According to Cristanne Miller, Moore abandoned the Romantic role of a poet as "an unexamined egotis[t]" as early as her college days.[24] Later in her career, Miller also notes, this stance of Moore's was only to be consolidated. "Blessed Is the Man," a poem of 1956, for instance, "both manifests and praises a matter-of-fact, unegoistical mode of communication that is more likely to distance than draw a reader."[25] Moore's avowed objection to "egotism" underlies her attraction to the Daoist-Buddhist insistence on clearing away all *siyu* or obscurings. To imagine Moore's joy at sharing this insight with Chinese artists, one has only to read Sze's account of the eighteenth-century painter Shitao, who noted that "he had painted and written for many years, declaring his independence of orthodox methods, until one day he suddenly realized that the way he had thought his own was actually 'the *tao* of the ancients'" (*The Tao*, 1:5). The anecdote might have offered Moore a revelation: What she had been experimenting with poetry was, from the Chinese point of view, following the *Dao*.

In the remaining two pages of the lecture notes, Moore turns the attention to specific principles and elements of Chinese painting—"The Six Canons of Painting," "The Four Treasures: Brush, Ink, Inkstone, Paper," and "The Elements of a Picture." Of these, the "Six Canons" evidently made the strongest impression on Moore. In fact, it so overwhelmed her that when she referred to *The Tao* in the foreword to *A Marianne Moore Reader,* the only Chinese name given was Xie He (Hsieh Ho), the formulator of the Six Canons. Ironically, however, she confused him with the artist who painted the plum branch. She states incorrectly that "As antonym, integrity was suggested to me by a blossoming peach branch—a drawing by Hsieh Ho" (*MMR*, xiv). Xie He is famous not for the painting but for the Six Canons, to which every single book on Chinese art alludes as the most honored standards of Chinese art criticism. Binyon discusses them in *The Flight of the Dragon,* a book, according to Cynthia Stamy, Moore has read.[26] So does Hackney in *Guide-Posts.* If Binyon and Hackney's interpretations of the canons failed to impress Moore, Sze's elaboration surely brought them home.

Moore clearly agrees with Sze that the first canon, "spirit," or "*ch'i*" ["*qi*"], is "basic to all—control[s] the other five and applies to all kinds of painting." She does not expand on this perhaps because she dislikes repeating others. As for the other five canons she follows Sze and sets them forth as: "The brush is the means of creating structure"; "According to the object draw its form"; "According to the nature of the object apply color"; "Organize the composition with each element in its rightful place"; and "In copying, transmit the essence of the master's brush and methods" (see appendix).

Of these, Moore sensibly gives most attention to the fifth, which considers space as "the most important factor in harmonizing the elements of a picture." Moore's familiarity with avant-garde art and her obsessive interest in spatial form predict her appreciation of the Daoist position that "Space of any sort [is] . . . filled with meaning" (*The Tao*, 1:17). From the Daoist perspective, as Sze explains, empty space is synonymous with the Dao, or the *qi,* or the *Yin* as opposed to the *Yang* of painted objects. In her own poetry Moore had also experimented with attaching meaning to typographic spacing. As Moore almost certainly recognized, the beauty of *A Breath of Spring* lies in the perfect equilibrium created by the diagonal plum branch across a blank space that suggests approaching spring—in Williams's phrase, "a new world naked."[27] So much of *A Breath of Spring* depends on the blank space that to fill it with anything would spoil its effect. Further, as Moore explains, quoting *The Mustard Seed Garden Manual* (*Tao,* 2:21), one of the twelve faults in painting is "a crowded ill-arranged composition." "If a man had eyes all over his body," warns *The Manual,* "he would be a monstrosity. . . . A landscape with people and dwellings in it has life, but too many figures and houses give the effect of a market-place" (2:264). Moore admires the Chinese approach to space. She cites many more passages from *The Tao* that illustrate this aspect of the Dao of painting: "A hollow tree was not empty but filled with spirit"; "the space between the spokes of a wheel make the wheel of use, the inner space and not the pottery of a pitcher is its essential part and the space within four walls compose the usefulness of a room" (1:17). *A Breath of Spring,* with its underlying theory, might have prompted Moore to make a final revision of "Poetry," that is, to reduce it to the skeleton of a two-and-a-half-line poem and set it against a blank page, in a way, like the plum branch set against a blank universe.[28]

From the "Sixth Canon," Moore takes a sharp turn and tours back to the beginning, that is, the symbol of the Dao described by Sze as a circle whose "beginning (the head) and end (the foot) are the same . . . both unmoving and continually moving" (*The Tao,* 1:16). "Still life—*nature morte,*" as Moore observes citing Sze (1:86), "is contrary to the whole concept of Chinese painting. The Tao (a path) lies on the ground, is still, yet leans somewhere and so has movement; and we have, therefore, an identity of contraries which are not in conflict but complementary opposites or two halves of a whole, as in the *Yin* and *Yang*—symbolized by the disc divided by an S-like curve." Thus, Moore has brought to light the spirit of the Dao—its dual emphasis on passivity/activity, continuity/change, invisibility/visibility. This spirit is best embodied in the Chinese dragon, to which Moore, echoing Sze (1:81–83), refers as "a symbol of the power of Heaven," characterized by its movement—"slumbering in the deep or winging across the Heaven"—and by its change—capable of transforming from "a silkworm . . . so large as to fill the space of Heaven and Earth," simultaneously visible and invisible (see appendix). Unsurprisingly, the dragon is to be the central symbol of Moore's next book of verse, *O to Be a Dragon.*

PART 5

Late Modernism and the Orient

TWELVE

Moore and
O to Be a Dragon

TO SEE HOW *The Tao of Painting* has affected Moore's late aesthetic and poetry, one has only to reread *O to Be a Dragon*. Moore no doubt collects together these poems with *The Tao* in mind. She makes this plain in her letter of 18 April 1959 to Mai-mai Sze, whom she addresses as "angel to me and friend of the dragon-symbol": "Just please realize my gratitude, the fond thoughts you evoke—the celestial reveries for which you are responsible; my universe [is] enlarged and ever expanding by receiving from Mr. Barrett, the Tao OF PAINTING—the mustard-seed garden and above all Volume II."[1]

Five months later, upon receipt of an inscribed copy of *O to Be a Dragon*, Sze is evidently touched by Moore's remarkable tribute to her work. "I thank you very much indeed for your poems," she writes on 16 September 1959, "I thank you too for this extraordinary feeling of warmth you give me by your wonderful use of the dragon." What she observes next confirms not only their mutual respect but their shared preoccupation: "By curious coincidence, your finger pointing to 'an understanding heart' silently before your magical touch on the 'dragon' reaches me as I try to give form to a heap of material gathered on what the Chinese call *hsin t'ien* [*xin tian*] The heart's field. I cannot help feeling you've given me a powerful model to get on with it!"[2]

It is in the title poem that one hears Moore's most remarkable tribute to *The Tao*. The piece recalls Williams's lines—"Give me your face, Yang Kue Fei [Yang Guifei]! / your hands, your lips to drink!"—in "Portrait of the Author."[3] While both speakers articulate a desire to take on the Chinese power of transformation, Moore's alone has a mind like the Chinese. It is to *The Tao* that Moore owes her knowledge of the dragon, an origin from which to derive the power of the imagination. Her poem conceals a quotation from that book between two exclamations:

> my wish . . . O to be a dragon,
> a symbol of the power of Heaven—of silkworm
> size or immense; at times invisible.
> Felicitous phenomenon!   (*CPMM*, 177)

In the foreword to *A Marianne Moore Reader* she acknowledges her debt: "And the Tao led me to the dragon in the classification of primary symbols, 'symbol of the power of heaven'—changing at will to the size of a silkworm; or swelling to the totality of heaven and earth; at will invisible" (*MMR*, xiv).

In this collage of quotations and observations, rather than repeating *The Tao* verbatim, Moore condenses two separate statements from *The Tao* into one. In her account of the dragon, Sze begins by alluding to it as "a symbol of the power of Heaven" (*The Tao,* 1:81) and continues, two paragraphs later, to delineate it as "a symbol of change," in the words of seventh-century B.C. philosopher Guanzi, "at will reduced to the size of a silkworm, or swollen till it fills the space of Heaven and Earth" (1:82–83).[4] Going through Lu Ji's *Wen Fu* in translation (1951), Moore had been attracted to a passage about working "from the general to the particular."[5] Her quotation in "O to Be a Dragon," despite its brevity, recaptures Sze's alertness to this emphasis.

Sze's discussion is an example of what Moore in "Tell Me, Tell Me" calls the "Chinese / 'passion for the particular'" (*CPMM,* 231). Her reference to the dragon as "a symbol of the power of Heaven" steers directly to her characterization of the mythological creature as a composite figure, one having "the head of a camel, the eyes of a hare, the ears of a bull, the neck of a snake, the belly of a frog, scales like a fish, talons like an eagle, and paws like a tiger" (*The Tao,* 1:81).[6] Had Moore blended part of this description into "O to Be a Dragon," the reader would instantly think of "the nectarine-loving kylin / of pony appearance / . . . with antelope feet and no horn . . . enameled on porcelain"(*CPMM,* 30).

Similarly, Sze's remark on the dragon as a symbol of change leads to her detailed portrayal of it as a symbol of the *Yang* "dwelling in the sky, rivers, the sea, and wells," interacting with various elements of the *Yin.* From that elaboration Sze moves on to say, "The dragon is thus a symbol of the idea of the *Tao,* giving it substance and vividly illustrating

40. Chen Rong (active first half of 13th century), a section from *Nine Dragons,* 1244. Francis Gardner Curtis Fund, 17.1697. © 2000 Museum of Fine Arts, Boston. All Rights Reserved. (Courtesy, Museum of Fine Arts, Boston)

its main aspects" (*The Tao,* 1:83). It is not hard to imagine Moore's delight at reading this revealing statement with particular Chinese dragon pictures in mind.

One of such pictures would be "a dragon in the clouds, concealed but for a few claws" (*SLMM,* 197), which Moore saw in the Metropolitan Museum in 1923. In a way, all Chinese dragon pictures follow Chen Rong's *Nine Dragons* in the Museum of Fine Arts. Executed when the artist was in an intoxicated state of mind, as Wu Tung reports, the masterpiece brings into the open "mind-altering experiences and insights long associated with Daoist transcendental practices."[7] One captures such experiences and insights effortlessly in the middle section of the work, where the fifth dragon, a "youth," faces the sixth, his "grandfather" (fig. 40). What is represented is not only the meeting of the *Yang* and the *Yin,* but more importantly, the transformation of one into the other. Although Moore's poem does not include such details, by embracing a quotation within a quotation it unequivocally brings out the Daoist theme of change.

In "The Plumet Basilisk," Moore similarly celebrates qualities associated with the dragon such as transformation and invisibility. Early readers of the two dragon poems are apt to favor the longer attempt. While I agree that "The Plumet Basilisk" is a strong Moore poem, I also maintain that "O to Be a Dragon" has its own merit and is meant to be read together with the long dragon poem. As Bonnie Costello notes, the short poem is used by Moore "as an important counterpoint to the long poem."[8] In *O to Be a Dragon,* the short poem and the long poem alternate frequently to convey a general theme.

Cristanne Miller is justified in using "The Plumet Basilisk" to support her argument about "authority" in Moore. The long dragon poem affords her enough substance to show what tasks the Moore reader is challenged to fulfill: first "[i]dentifying the several references to myth and divinity within the poem," then "constructing from them an argument about Moore's purpose," and then "shar[ing] responsibility with Moore for its claims." This analysis leads to Miller's important conclusion: "Authority lies somewhere between the sources of Moore's information, her suggestive use of that material, and the reader's construction of an intellectual or moral argument from the poem's suggestions."[9]

It is not difficult to prove that "O to Be a Dragon" contains all the basic ingredients of "The Plumet Basilisk." We might use the short poem to expand Miller's argument. To interpret such a piece the reader is required to perform precisely the same tasks. Because in "O to Be a Dragon" Moore has restrained herself from indicating quotation and offering detailed description, the reader's task of "[i]dentifying . . . references to myth and divinity within the poem" gets more challenging. On the other hand, with less detailing, he or she is given greater freedom to make imaginative claims.

Restraint appears to be a prominent trait of Moore's late aesthetic. Its influence is traceable to *The Tao.* In her discussion of the dragon symbol, Sze pays due respect to its importance in Chinese art criticism: "In connection with the Taoist emphasis on *wu wei* (outer passivity/inner activity), there is an aspect of the dragon that should be mentioned, namely the power of restraint" (*The Tao,* 1:83). The idea was not new to Moore. For decades she had admired this quality in Chinese art and poetry. *The Tao* awakened her to its true meaning and possibilities. It encouraged her to rethink the value of her own ambiguity and reserve in some early experiments. That she republishes not one but three such pieces attests to her resolution to justify another resource in her aesthetic. These, along with the title poem, might be considered a manifesto.

"I May, I Might, I Must," a poem first published in 1909 under the title of "Progress,"[10] sustains its original message of confidence:

If you will tell me why the fen
appears impassable, I then
will tell you why I think that I
can get across it if I try.   (*CPMM*, 178)

Reprinted here after the title poem, the piece could also be interpreted as a dialogue between the speaker and the author of *The Tao*. As such, the "impassable fen" appears as an allusion to the Dao, and the repetition of "I," "you," "will tell," and "why" seems at once to stress challenge, self-assurance, and reserve.

With their "contextual codes" changed, to borrow a term from George Bornstein, "To a Chameleon" and "A Jelly-Fish" likewise take on new meanings.[11] Read here back to back, they are understood as instances in which the speaker manifests her ability to be a "dragon" and her ability to surmount the "impassable fen." The way she turns herself now into a chameleon, now into a jellyfish is comparable to the way a Chinese painter transforms himself or herself sometimes into a youthful, ascending dragon, and sometimes into an ancient, descending dragon. What Moore and Sze say in their correspondence will stand testament to this reading. Moore evidently has "To a Chameleon" and "A Jelly-Fish" in mind when she thanks Sze for "the celestial reveries for which [she is] responsible." Sze apparently hints at these same pieces when she congratulates Moore on her "wonderful use of the dragon."[12]

"To a Chameleon" has been rightly praised for its natural, accelerating rhythm, which Laurence Stapleton has pinned down in its last four words; for its "ironic ambiguity," which Linda Leavell explains at some length; and for its theme of continuous transformation, which Grace Schulman sees as conveyed in part by its use of the personal-impersonal and the negative-affirmative contrasts.[13] What is the force that integrates all these elements into one experience? Costello has provided a clue by noting that the chameleon here, like the dragon of "O to Be a Dragon," "is a 'symbol of the power of Heaven.'"[14] In plain terms, we might say further, the chameleon, like the dragon, is a symbol of the idea of the Dao, a force capable of fusing all the elements within and without the poem into a totality.

The poem was titled "You Are Like the Realistic Product of an Idealistic Search for Gold at the Foot of the Rainbow" in 1916. Moore, of course, saw it differently in 1959, when her new model was *The Tao*, discovering perhaps for the first time characteristics of the poem resembling those of the Chinese artists and poets. She would be amused

—indeed elated—to hear admiration for the same qualities from the perspective of *The Tao.* So, what Stapleton refers to as the "power to control, and to change tempo" is analogous to the Chinese painter's or poet's ability to blend spirit with matter by catching the rhythm of Heaven and Earth.[15] What Leavell stresses—the chameleon's domination, which makes "both artist and subject recede into mysteriousness"—calls to mind Chinese elusiveness in general and Chen Rong's *Nine Dragons* in particular.[16] In Chen Rong's dragons we witness precisely the same kind of mysteriousness that hides both painter and motif. Finally, what Schulman brings to light—the poem's striking correspondence between its transformation in form and its transformation in theme—seems emphatically to hint at the dragon being constant change.[17] That the poem is made up of an affirmative half and a negative half, a personal half and an impersonal half is similarly suggestive of the Dao,[18] in Sze's description, "The double action of the *Yin* and the *Yang,* on the one hand in conflict as opposites, on the other hand complementary as two halves of the whole" (*The Tao,* 1:93). The typographic pattern of the poem imitates not only "the winding shape of the chameleon," as Schulman notices,[19] but the winding shape of a dragon-turned-silkworm:

> Hid by the august foliage and fruit of the grape-vine
>   twine
>   your anatomy
>   round the pruned and polished stem,
>   Chameleon.
>   Fire laid upon
>   an emerald as long as
>   the Dark King's massy
>   one,
> could not snap the spectrum up for food as you have done.
>   (*CPMM,* 179)

"A Jelly-Fish" is just another one of "the celestial reveries for which [*The Tao* is] responsible."[20] Like the dragon and the chameleon, the jellyfish has invisibility, transformation, and constraint:

> Visible, invisible,
>   a fluctuating charm
> an amber-tinctured amethyst
>   inhabits it, your arm

approaches and it opens
   and it closes; you had meant
to catch it and it quivers;
   you abandon your intent.   (*CPMM,* 180)

As Costello reports, in 1909 the poem was meant to be a salutation to Longinus concealed in a portrayal of a sea creature Moore observed in her biology class.[21] By 1959, nonetheless, Moore had learned a new way of looking at the little piece. She had been told that invisibility and change reflected interaction between the *Yin* and *Yang,* and that what was beyond the eye was "nearer the limitless horizon, the infinity of the *Tao*" (*The Tao,* 1:94). When Wang Wei described "how layers of air, increasing with distance, obscured color, tone, and detail," she had been informed also, "he not only was observing changes in appearance but, by his description of air and atmosphere, was also noting the action of the Ch'i [*qi*] (Heaven's Breath)" (1:93).

All these might be useful insights, enabling Moore to rethink her 1909 "A Jelly-Fish." It should not be too difficult now to identify Daoist-like elements in this early experiment. Aside from invisibility and transformation, it has contrasts the Chinese would call *kai-he* ("open-together") and *qi-fu* ("rise-fall"), contrasts Sze regards as "descriptive of movement, of the *Yin* and *Yang*" (*The Tao,* 1:94). Restraint, yet another Daoist endorsed quality, is evident in the lines "You abandon / Your intent," although it is blurred by repetition. To bring this attribute into the open, Moore cut eight witless lines in the last section of the poem.[22]

I had in mind "A Jelly-Fish" (both versions) and "To a Chameleon" when recommending in chapter 4 Cristanne Miller's claim about Moore's "apparently impersonal and transparently personal" point of view.[23] I was looking back on the same little poems together with a group of longer ones from *Selected Poems* when at once admiring and challenging Leavell's speculation about the role modern art played in Moore's shifting point of view.[24] Here I would like to pause for a moment to clarify my notion of Moore's Orientalism in relation to claims made by Miller, Leavell, and other critics.

Moore indeed began by writing a poetry that asserts personal presence through a "non-'authorial,' abstract, shifting representation of identity or self."[25] The 1909 version of "A Jelly-Fish" and the 1916 version of "To a Chameleon" attest her early adoption of this stance. When she began, as Miller notes, her primary goal was to reject "both the romantic and the sentimental poetics."[26] She did not have any examples to follow. On the other hand, as she moved into the New York liter-ary/artistic community, she espied that in aesthetic she had more to share with visual artists than with poets. "Over here," she told Pound in early 1919, "it strikes me that there is more evidence of power among painters than among writers" (*SLMM*, 123). Leavell has done an im-pressive job in making this argument and in showing that modern art helped reinforce Moore's "non-'authorial,' abstract, shifting" point of view.[27] What I am suggesting is that while all this is valid, Chinese art provided her an additional model in which to perfect her idiosyncratic perspective.

Moore's interest in Chinese art is primarily an interest in Chinese animal pictures illustrating an approach that might be called "imagina-tive objectivism." In an account of this approach, Li Zehou sums up its characteristics as follows: "the realistic portrayal of images evoked by a scene or object when the general idea is grasped and the artist's feelings infuse his work"; the insistence on "absence of self"; the choice of "a many-pointed perspective"; and the allowance for "greater freedom of the imagination." About "absence of self" Li clarifies, "This does not mean the artist's own thoughts and feelings are truly absent, only that these have not been revealed directly."[28] Curiously enough, what he says of Chinese "imaginative objectivism" brings to mind Miller's char-acterization of Moore's idiosyncratic point of view: A Moore poem "is a work of art, a moral guide, every bit as much as it is a crea-ture scientifically observed and precisely rendered onto a page."[29] Each statement — Li's on "Chinese imaginative objectivism" and Miller's on Moore's "apparently impersonal and transparently personal" stance — describes the other's subject. Just as for Li a work of "imaginative ob-jectivism" is "a hallucination,"[30] so for Miller a Moore poem "is sleight of hand: Moore simultaneously asserts her objectivity and reveals it to be bogus."[31]

Perhaps it is not by accident that some of Moore's most radical ex-periments with her "apparently impersonal and transparently personal" aesthetic strategy occur in her poems with Chinese motifs, say, "The Plumet Basilisk," "The Buffalo," and "Nine Nectarines." Moore may well have been enchanted by the way Chinese motifs are visually presented, a way in which she discerns both the self and the other. In represent-ing these motifs she clearly attempts to follow the minds that have imagined them. If artworks such as "a dragon in the clouds," herd boys "mounted on water oxen,"[32] and a vase adorned with *qilin* have offered Moore examples in which to justify and extend her aesthetic, *The Tao* gives her a philosophy, a spirit with which to rethink her aesthetic and resurrect early experiments.

The Tao makes such a hit with Moore that as late as November 1963, in a letter to Sze, she refers to it as "permanent gifts . . . possessions that I carry with me in my mind—along with some incurable ignorances."[33] By "ignorances" she alludes at once to her imperfect understanding of *The Tao* and her incomplete suppression of egotism. In Sze's vocabulary, ignorance is synonymous with egotism, which "obscures a clear vision of the *Tao* (*The Tao*, 1:31).

Sze's notion of "emptying the heart of distractions, selfishness, and ignorance" (*The Tao*, 1:31) is attractive to Moore because it makes sense of what has been one of her own "biggest ideas," namely the rejection of the Romantic individualistic "ego." She is so enraptured by this discovery that between 1957 and 1963 she returns to the theme of "Tedium and Integrity" many times. In a 1958 review, she praises the American artist Robert Andrew Parker for having "depth and stature unvitiated by egotism" (*PrMM*, 502). In the 1961 foreword to *A Marianne Moore Reader,* she contrasts the Dao being a "oneness" with Western "egotism, synonymous with ignorance in Buddhist thinking" (*MMR*, xiv). And in a 1963 essay on "The Knife," she remarks on Daoist-Buddhist objection to egotism in one breath and quotes Confucius in the next: "In valor, there is small room for egotism. As Confucius says, 'If there be a knife of resentment in the heart, the mind fails to act with precision'" (*PrMM*, 568).[34] From Sze she has learned to overlook the distinction between Confucianism and Daoism/Buddhism. In *The Tao* the conception is introduced as a product of Wang Shouren's Neo-Confucianism meeting Daoism/Buddhism (*The Tao*, 1:30–31).

Moore's theme of "Tedium and Integrity" manifests itself in a variety of ways in *O to Be a Dragon.* In "O to Be a Dragon" and "I May, I Might, I Must," it is asserted without vivid embodiment. In "To a Chameleon" and "A Jelly-Fish," it is vividly embodied without assertion. And in "The Arctic Ox (or Goat)," it is both vividly embodied and explicitly asserted. The poem about the "musk ox" is like "To a Chameleon" and "A Jelly-Fish" in one way and unlike them in another. Like them, it infuses both the speaker and her subject with the spirit of integrity. Unlike them, it allows the speaker to affirm this spirit through comments.

"The Arctic Ox (or Goat)" is based on a 1958 *Atlantic Monthly* article, "Golden Fleece of the Arctic," by John J. Teal Jr. It calls to mind "The Buffalo" with material drawn from a heterogeneous mass of sources.[35]

The two poems, written in different periods, celebrate similar qualities in animals that appear related but actually are not: "The musk ox / has no musk and it is not an ox—" (*CPMM*, 193). In "The Buffalo," Moore's speaker contemplates the extinct Aurochs and other four classes of the *Bos* genus before giving the highest praise to the Indian buffalo. Unexpectedly, in "The Arctic Ox (or Goat)" the buffalo compares poorly with the "musk ox." The water buffalo is "neurasthenic—/ even murderous" (194), whereas the qiviut-producing (or wool-producing) mammal is serene, amiable, and bright. The poem, of course, offers particulars qualifying these attributes:

> They join you as you work;
> love jumping in and out of holes,
>   play in water with the children,
> learn fast, know their names
> will open gates and invent games.   (*CPMM*, 194)

More importantly, it inserts a comment: "Its great distinction / is not egocentric scent / but that it is intelligent" (193), which at once betrays the reason for bias and echoes the book's large theme.

It is clear that Moore, who rewrites John Teal's story, interprets the Arctic ox smelling of water as one without "egocentric scent." The spirit of this interpretation, a spirit derivable from *The Tao*, is found to dominate many other poems in *O to Be a Dragon*. If in "The Arctic Ox (or Goat)" it is embodied chiefly by the subject matter, in "Saint Nicholas" it is more acutely represented by the speaker's demeanor.

"Saint Nicholas" is supposedly a poem about Christmas wishes. All the things the speaker cares to have—a chameleon, a dress of qiviut, moonlight—are modest. And the manner in which she names them is humble. Costello perceives in this a tension between "desire and restraint," signaling the poem's real thesis. The speaker's humility, she argues, stems from her awareness that by possessing these things, "incarnation of spirit," she deprives them of not only freedom but the very power she admires.[36]

We ought to have noticed by now that in *O to Be a Dragon* Moore's "wonderful use of the dragon" occurs often in the least-expected places. This strategy contrasts sharply with overt exploitation of Chinese motifs in her earlier "Chinese poems." Only the late Moore will identify the dragon with the Arctic ox rather than the buffalo. Only the late Moore will infuse Daoist notions into a poem for Christmas. By withdrawing her attention from outward appearance and refocusing it on inner spirit, she has distinguished her late Orientalism from her early Orientalism and the Orientalism of most others.

Thus, "Combat Cultural," a poem about Russian ballet dance, might be read in part as about movement, a key aspect of the Dao incarnated in the dragon. For the Chinese, Moore has been told, the power of the dragon is derived from fusion of matter and spirit by catching the rhythm. In composing the poem she seems to be following the First Canon, turning adeptly from the "rhythmic vitality" of nature ("a laggard rook's high / speed at sunset") through that of dance ("drooping handkerchief / snapped like the crack of a whip") to that of wrestling ("with a jab, a kick, pinned to the wall").[37] The two dancers presented as "battlers, dressed identically—/ just one person" (*CPMM,* 200) are perhaps not just a sight recorded. It makes one think of the *Yin* and *Yang* as two halves of a whole. The gesture is claimed to be pointing to a moral: "[W]e must cement the parts of any / objective symbolic of *sagesse*" (200). It serves only to reinforce the theme of unity, wholeness, and integrity.

The theme of unity is evident also in "Leonardo da Vinci's," the last poem of *O to Be a Dragon.* In its own context, Moore's ekphrasis of da Vinci's unfinished painting, *Saint Jerome,* should of course be understood as celebration of unity between diversities as a Christian ideal. Nevertheless, in the context of the volume it might be interpreted as an additional tribute to wholeness in the Daoist sense. There are certainly details reminding one of the larger context. The lion being "made to carry wood and . . . not resist[ing]" (*CPMM,* 201), for instance, recalls the Arctic ox without "egocentric scent." The saint and his lion becoming "twinned; /. . . behav[ing] and also look[ing] alike" (201) echo the Russian dancers of "Combat Cultural." The poem's climax, moreover, contains a vital hint: "Pacific yet passionate—/ for if not both, how / could he be great?" (201). Its admiration for unity of virtue and ability might be read as alluding to *The Tao*'s emphasis on the unity of ethics and profession (*The Tao,* 1:5).

O to Be a Dragon therefore represents Moore's effort to view poetry as a way of attaining integrity, as Sze views painting as a way of attaining the Dao. Since the title poem suggests but by no means states this thesis, Moore finds it necessary to clarify it in the foreword to *A Marianne Moore Reader:*

As antonym, integrity was suggested to me by a blossoming peach branch—a drawing by Hsieh Ho—reproduced above a *New York*

Times Book Review notice of *The Mustard Seed Garden Manual of Painting* formulated about 500 A.D. — translated and edited by Miss Mai-mai Sze, published by the Bollingen Foundation in 1956 and as a Modern Library paperback in 1959. The plum branch led me to *The Tao of Painting,* of which "The Mustard Seed Garden" is a part, the (not "a") Tao being a way of life, a "oneness" that is tireless; whereas egotism, synonymous with ignorance in Buddhist thinking, is tedious. And the Tao led me to the dragon in the classification of primary symbols, "symbol of the power of heaven" — changing at will to the size of a silkworm; or swelling to the totality of heaven and earth; at will invisible, made personal by a friend at a party — an authority on gems, finance, painting, and music — who exclaimed obligingly as I concluded a digression on cranes, peaches, bats, and butterflies as symbols of long life and happiness, "O to be a dragon!" (The exclamation, lost sight of for a time, was appropriated as a title later.) (*MMR,* xiv–xv)

This is clearly meant to prepare the reader, who without alerting is apt to miss a preoccupation with China and with *The Tao.* For Moore, the unique importance of *The Tao* is its power at once to affirm and to intensify her aesthetic — her rejection of the Romantic ego, fusion of moral principles with art, and use of emptiness as form. If Moore's idiosyncratic modernist aesthetic triumphs in *Selected Poems* (1935), it gains a new vision, an underlying spirit for that aesthetic in *O to Be a Dragon* (1959). This spirit persists in *A Marianne Moore Reader* (1961), where "The Buffalo" and "Nine Nectarines," along with "The Steeple-Jack," head twenty-three poems from *Collected Poems* (1951) and where "Poetry" and "The Plumet Basilisk" are sacrificed to make room for the entire volume of *O to Be a Dragon.* To Moore, her poetry never appeared the same again after *The Tao.* Her outlook was revised, just as "Poetry" is revised in *Complete Poems* (1967), reduced to two and a half lines against a blank page, likely to remind us of her beloved plum branch against a blank space.

THIRTEEN

Nothingness and
Late Stevens

I HAVE SHOWN in previous chapters how Stevens introduced Chinese landscape along with Chan into American literary modernism, problematizing the boundaries between the Occident and the Orient, the verbal and the visual, the thing itself and the nothing. In this chapter I would like to augment this thesis by first tracing Stevens's return after the hiatus of 1924–30 to "The Snow Man," and then exploring how he brought his Chan-like meditative creativity to its acme in his final lyrics.

Various critics have recognized that Stevens's *Key West* poems, written shortly after the hiatus, show a tendency of going back to *Harmonium*. Harold Bloom, for instance, suggests that the singing girl at "The Idea of Order at Key West" (1934) parallels Hoon.[1] Helen Vendler remarks that "in its epigrammatic and elliptic form," "Like Decorations in a Nigger Cemetery" (1935) recalls "Thirteen Ways."[2] With regard to his restart, Stevens made a noteworthy statement in March 1933: "Writing again after a discontinuance seems to take one back to the beginning rather than to the point of discontinuance" (*L,* 265). By this he probably meant to suggest that his poetry was spontaneously going back to the most memorable moments of *Harmonium.*

Stevens made the above observation in answer to a request for poems from Morton Dauwen Zabel, assistant to Miss Monroe at *Poetry.* In the early 1930s Stevens had many such demands, few of which he satisfied. Zabel's invitation on behalf of *Poetry* was special, however. "Miss Monroe has always been so particularly friendly," he wrote, "that I should like to make a fresh effort for her" (*L,* 265). The fresh work he sent Zabel a year and eight months later (when Monroe was in Beijing) was "Decorations," whose fifty short stanzas call to mind "Thirteen Ways."[3]

For Walton Litz, quite a few stanzas in "Decorations," like those in "Thirteen Ways," "have a *haiku*-like structure, evolving around a concrete image."[4] For Monroe these stanzas were nevertheless more intimately associated with Chinese art. Her praise of the series, given in a letter she wrote after her return from Beijing, is reminiscent of Moore's 1924 eulogy of *Harmonium*'s resemblance to "the mind and the method of China": ". . . there is in Chinese art a most delicate combination of irony and humor and shy seriousness which one finds so often in your poetry, and now especially in these *Decorations*."[5]

There are a dozen or more stanzas in "Decorations" that could have prompted Monroe to link it to Chinese art, of which III and XXIV seem most revealing:

> It was when the trees were leafless first in November
> And their blackness became apparent, that one first
> Knew the eccentric to be the base of design.   (*CPWS,* 151)

> A bridge above the bright and blue of water
> And the same bridge when the river is frozen.
> Rich Tweedle-dum, poor Tweedle-dee.   (154)

The "delicate combination of irony and humor and shy seriousness" Monroe notices in "Decorations" is as evident in the winter landscapes discussed in chapter 5 as in *Bare Willows and Distant Mountains,* an autumn scene by Ma Yuan (fig. 41) in the Museum of Fine Arts, Boston, since 1914.[6] Serenity, barrenness, and stagnancy dominate all these landscapes. Yet one discerns in them life and constant movement—the "eccentric," or, in Bloom's phrase, "a figuration for 'mortal.'"[7] Stevens's stanzas have captured this irony with its dual emphasis on no movement/movement, the nothing/the thing itself. They have likewise captured the "shy seriousness" with which the Chinese painters treat their mysterious, common subjects.

It is true that Stevens may not have seen *White Heron, Winter Forest, Winter Riverscape,* or *Bare Willows.* But we know that for each such masterpiece are a hundred similar ones. Since Stevens acknowledged a connection between his interest in Oriental art and "Thirteen Ways," we can safely deduce that the sights and insights of this art had returned with the 1917 series to "Decorations." Compared with "Thirteen Ways," "Decorations" has taken a huge step forward. The earlier poem betrays a bias for the thing itself, whereas "Decorations" strikes a balance between the thing itself and the nothing. If the dual emphasis is not clear enough in III and XXIV, it surely is in VIII and XVII:

41. Ma Yuan (active before 1189–after 1225), *Bare Willows and Distant Mountains.*
Chinese and Japanese Special Fund, 14.61. © 2000 Museum of Fine Arts, Boston.
All Rights Reserved. (Courtesy, Museum of Fine Arts, Boston)

> Out of the spirit of the holy temples,
> Empty and grandiose, let us make hymns
> And sing them in secrecy as lovers do.   (*CPWS*, 151)

> The sun of Asia creeps above the horizon
> Into this haggard and tenuous air,
> A tiger lamed by nothingness and frost.   (153)

For Monroe what is most striking about XVII is obviously its irony
and humor, which she links to Chinese painting. For me on top of
irony and humor is a "lofty dryness" in this as well as other stanzas.
Vendler was perhaps the first critic to notice "the dryness of the poem."
"If we supply the missing links," she remarks, XXXVIII "might read:
'[Do not offer me] the album [of reproductions of paintings of sum-
mer] of Corot. [That] is premature [—to solace myself with art in the
absence of the reality it reproduces, since something of summer is still
left. Give me the album] a little later when the sky is black. [It is true
that the mists of autumn are around me, but they are tinged with the
gold of summer still, and] mist that is golden is not wholly mist.'" This

amplification, she insists, destroys "the dryness of the poem," its boiling concrete art ("The album of Corot") down to "mist, golden, wholly, mist" ("Mist that is golden is not wholly mist").[8]

"Lofty dryness," along with other essential qualities of Chan art,[9] keeps showing up in Stevens's poems between "The Man with the Blue Guitar" (1937) and "Notes toward a Supreme Fiction" (1942). In "The Poems of Our Climate" (1938), for instance, the speaker perceives "The day itself / . . . simplified: a bowl of white, / Cold, a cold porcelain, low and round, / With nothing more than the carnations there" (CPWS, 193). Again, in "The Man on the Dump" (1938), "the purifying change" (202) reduces the dump's diverse images to merely "The the" (203). The familiar theme of the thing itself becoming the nothing culminates in "The Latest Freed Man," yet another poem of 1938 to go into the 1942 volume, Parts of a World.[10]

Among Stevens's middle poems, "The Latest Freed Man" stands out as one of the most discussed. To cite two critical opinions, Joseph Carroll sees it as Stevens's proclamation of "extreme antidoctrinalism," whose "elaborate poetic rhetoric underlines the paradoxicality of describing that which supposedly transcends description."[11] B. J. Leggett maintains it to be a poem about "rejection of truth" that "itself takes the form of truth."[12] Despite dissimilarity in approach, both comments capture the poem's most distinctive attribute: its protagonist's predicament as to whether to speak or not to speak. To escape from doctrines and descriptions, the latest freed man must not speak. Nonetheless, to rejoice over his triumph in perceiving the thing itself and the nothing, he will speak.

The poem indeed begins with the latest freed man rising from bed at six beginning to speak to himself:

> "I suppose there is
> A doctrine to this landscape. Yet, having just
> Escaped from the truth, the morning is color and mist,
> Which is enough: the moment's rain and sea,
> The moment's sun (the strong man vaguely seen),
> Overtaking the doctrine of this landscape. Of him
> And of his works, I am sure. He bathes in the mist
> Like a man without a doctrine. The light he gives —
> It is how he gives his light. It is how he shines,
> Rising upon the doctors in their beds
> And on their beds. . . ."   (CPWS, 204–05)

What he said instead of showing him as a freed man rather shows him as a doctor prior to freedom from "the old descriptions of the world." Yes, he was tired of old doctrines and descriptions, and he was trying to escape from the truth. But for a brief moment at least, he still *supposed* there was "A doctrine to this landscape," and he still *imagined* the sun bathing "in the mist / Like a man without a doctrine." It was his mere gazing, his concentration on morning's "color and mist," that started up his change of consciousness.

The change of consciousness recalls "The Snow Man." As we recognized in chapter 5, the great poem of winter depicts a meditative experience in ways that match Buddhist attainment of enlightenment: first regarding a mountain as a mountain and a river as a river, then perceiving a mountain unlike a mountain and a river unlike a river, and finally beholding a mountain once more as a mountain and a river once more as a river. Is it possible that Stevens, spurred by a renewed interest in Chan Buddhism, was returning to the familiar vision? That is quite possible. First, the poet evidently reinvigorated a zeal for Chan in the Depression years. In 1935 he tried vigorously to get Mrs. Calhoun to send him a landscape painting. In 1937 he succeeded in obtaining a Buddha image through Leonard van Geyzel. Around that time, he presumably also dipped into a Buddhist text he had acquired, *The Dhammapada*, translated from Pali with an essay by Irving Babbitt (1936).[13] Second, Stevens's great poem of dawn manifestly goes back to his great poem of winter, echoing the Buddhist awakening through successive stages. If the first section of the 1938 poem portrays the latest freed man as one supposing the landscape with a doctrine, its second section presents him as "without a description of to be," thus signaling a change of consciousness:

> To have the ant of the self changed to an ox
> With its organic boomings, to be changed
> From a doctor into an ox, before standing up,
> To know that the change and that the ox-like struggle
> Come from the strength that is the strength of the sun,
> Whether it comes directly or from the sun.

And before the poem concludes, one seems to hear, to quote Stevens in another context, "words . . . spoken as if there [were] no [words]" (*CPWS*, 358): ". . . everything bulging and blazing and big in itself, / The blue of the rug, the portrait of Vidal, / *Qui fait fi des joliesses banales,* the chairs" (*CPWS*, 205). The vision is Chan-like because it is nonjudgmental and nonverbal. "The blue of the rug" is just "The blue of the rug"; "the portrait of Vidal" just "the portrait of Vidal"; "the chairs" just "the chairs"—in short, "The the the" with no definition, no evaluation, no emotion.

In considering "The Latest Freed Man," MacLeod's suggestion that "the simply furnished bedroom" reveals the "Dutch aspect of [Stevens's] sensibility" cannot be disregarded.[14] Desiring to escape into a private world, Stevens would no doubt find much satisfaction in the domestic scenes of seventeenth-century Dutch painting. The still lifes of the Hollandish School he idolized might indeed have inspired the poem's plain setting. Nevertheless, they alone could not have stimulated its vision that unites the thing itself and the nothing.

In the 1940s Stevens's interest in writing "domestic" poems continued. It is fascinating that its very best example, "The House Was Quiet and the World Was Calm," opens in a fashion that once more recalls both Dutch still life and Chinese landscape:[15]

> The house was quiet and the world was calm.
> The reader became the book; and summer night
>
> Was like the conscious being of the book.
> The house was quiet and the world was calm.

As the poem continues and approaches its end, however, we realize that the epistemology behind it goes far beyond what is generally held to be Occidental:

> The words were spoken as if there was no book,
> Except that the reader leaned above the page,
>
> Wanted to lean, wanted much most to be
> The scholar to whom his book is true, to whom
>
> The summer night is like a perfection of thought.
> The house was quiet because it had to be.
>
> The quiet was part of the meaning, part of the mind:
> The access of perfection to the page.
>
> And the world was calm. The truth in a calm world,
> In which there is no other meaning, itself
>
> Is calm, itself is summer and night, itself
> Is the reader leaning late and reading there.   (CPWS, 358–59)

The book is a trope of knowledge, while the quiet house and the calm summer night are tropes of meditation. With this understanding, Stevens's musings on book, reader, house, and night bring to mind passages from *The Dhammapada* in Babbitt's translation. Note chapter 25 ("The Monk"), sections 372–373:

> Without knowledge there is no meditation, without meditation there is no knowledge: he who has both knowledge and meditation is near unto Nirvāna.

> A monk who with tranquil mind has entered his empty house feels a more than earthly delight when he gains a clear perception of the Law.

Note chapter 7 ("The Venerable [Arhat]"), section 96:

> His thought is quiet, quiet are his words and deed, when he has obtained freedom by true knowledge, when he has become a quiet man.

And also chapter 8 ("The Thousands"), section 100:

> Even though a speech be composed of a thousand words, but words without sense, one word of sense is better, which if a man hears he becomes quiet.[16]

"The House Was Quiet," we might say, triumphs over both the Buddhist insights and the way they are expressed, what Babbitt characterizes as "damnable iteration."[17] For Stevens as for Buddhists, forms are born in emptiness. Indeed, chapter 25, section 369 of *The Dhammapada* instructs: "O monk, bale out this boat! If emptied it will go quickly."[18] Stevens echoes the figuration without having to repeat the word "empty." Apparently his reader in the quiet house must empty the self to become the book. The book must empty its words to become the summer night. And the summer night must empty all its particulars to merge with the book and the reader.

What then are we to make of Stevens's "calm world"? A year earlier, in 1944, he wrote the long poem "Esthétique du Mal," whose section XII seems to have offered a clue. The aesthete sees the world as divided into the peopled and the unpeopled. To escape from both he creates a third world. The calm world the "reader" envisions cannot be "the peopled world," in which "there is, / Besides the people, his knowledge of them." Nor can it be "the unpeopled world," in which "there is his knowledge of himself." It can only be the third world, "In which no one peers, in which the will makes no / Demands" (*CPWS*, 323). Commenting on "Esthétique du Mal," sections XII–XIII, Bevis notices a connection to a single line in Stevens's journal for 14 May 1909: "'Sakamuni [Śākyamuni] — all evil resides in the individual will to live' (*SP*, 221)."[19] True, the gap of thirty-five years may discourage this link. But the notion of a world without will and pain (evil) is similarly expressed in *The Dhammapada*, chapter 9, "Evil," and chapter 10, "Punishment."[20] Further, Stevens still had his copy of *Buddhism in China* at his elbow. With his 1919 notation, "The Awakened 83," he could easily go back to the passage that describes how Śākyamuni retires from the world of "suffering" via a stage of "absence of light" into "the great awakened state of 'perfect light.'"[21] It is reasonable to suppose, therefore, that Stevens's "calm world" has its origin in Buddhism.

For many, Stevens's interest in the Orient faded in the 1950s. A statement he made in 1953 seems to support this view: "I hate orientalism." To know what the poet actually meant by this remark, however, we must look into the context in which he pronounced it. This assertion Stevens made on 19 August 1953 to Paule Vidal with regard to the French artist Roger Bezombes (b. 1913): "I lost a great deal of my interest in Bezombes when I read the brochure which you were kind enough to send me. I hate orientalism" (*L*, 796). A week later, it is important to note, the poet confided to Barbara Church why he had changed his mind about Bezombes:[22] "No Bezombes after all. Miss Vidal sent me a brochure about him which he had given her which gave me a painful chill. He is an orientalist and he has ideas about painting from a universal point of view. By this I mean that he thinks that a painting should be neither eastern nor western, but a conglomeration of both, a kind of syncretism. I can only say that I detest orientalism: the sort of thing that Fromentin did, which is the specific thing, although I like it well enough the way Matisse does it" (*L*, 797). So what Stevens abhorred was the idealistic thematic Orientalism of a Eugène Fromentin, what Said would call "a European invention" of the Orient.[23] This abhorrence clearly had nothing to do with Far Eastern culture.

By 1953 Stevens had befriended Peter Lee. His vigorous correspondence with the Korean poet is sufficient proof of his sustained interest in the Far East. Lee's gifts to Stevens — two large scrolls from Korea — no doubt rekindled an old passion in him. But with or without Lee, Stevens's meditative creativity was to shine in his final phase.

Stevens's poem "The Rock" (1950) and those afterward, in fact, consist principally of meditations upon the thing itself and nothing. This tendency is revealed in titles: "Final Soliloquy of the Interior Paramour"; "To an Old Philosopher in Rome"; "The Poem That Took the Place of a Mountain"; "Looking across the Fields and Watching the Birds Fly"; "The World as Meditation"; "The Dove in Spring"; and, of course, the powerful lyric on the last page of *The Collected Poems*, "Not Ideas about the Thing but the Thing Itself."

Robert Tompkins is no doubt justified in singling out the title poem of *The Rock* as a fine example of late Stevens's "illimitable insight," which closely parallels those of Buddhism: "[T]his poem marks the point of greatest tension in Stevens' thought. Here the being of time imagines itself as *evolving* toward a spiritualization or cure which, if true, must destroy not only its own current self-image but the very basis of that image, time, the apparent opposition by an inhuman other —the 'not yet.'" This concept might be amended by saying that the poem's equilibrium between life and illusion, "the houses of mothers" and their "rigid emptiness," "The words spoken" and "nothingness" (*CPWS*, 525–26) results in a progress toward suppression of both self and other, a motif that, according to Tompkins, cannot be interpreted without reference to "the notions of emptiness (sunyata) and suchness (tathata), which lie at the heart of Mahayana [Buddhist] thought."[24] The concept (nothing/the thing itself) attributed to Buddhism is also helpful in uncovering the meaning of "cure," a key word of the poem:

> It is not enough to cover the rock with leaves.
> We must be cured of it by a cure of the ground
> Or a cure of ourselves, that is equal to a cure
>
> Of the ground, a cure beyond forgetfulness.   (*CPWS*, 526)

For J. Hillis Miller "a cure / Of the ground" signifies both "scour[ing] it clean" and "making it solid."[25] For me it suggests at once "emptying it" and "filling it up." Following Miller, the two meanings of "cure" deconstruct one another, whereas following Buddhism they join each other, becoming one.

"The Course of a Particular" (1951), more so than "The Rock," presents Stevens's Chan-like insistence on the unity of the thing itself and nothing. The "particular" refers to the "cry" of leaves, while the course is the movement toward its being through persistent purging. The "cry" of the leaves reverberates throughout the poem. The thing itself rises, not "despite every Stevensian rejection of it as pathetic fallacy," as Bloom claims,[26] but *because of* every Stevensian rejection of it as "not yet" so. This continuous negating or purging culminates in the final two tercets, where the thing itself combines the nothing and "a busy cry, concerning someone else" is metamorphosed into one that "concerns no one at all":

> The leaves cry. It is not a cry of divine attention,
> Nor the smoke-drift of puffed-out heroes, nor human cry.
> It is the cry of leaves that do not transcend themselves,
>
> In the absence of fantasia, without meaning more
> Than they are in the final finding of the ear, in the thing
> Itself, until, at last, the cry concerns no one at all.   (*OP*, 123–24)

George Lensing sensibly identifies a certain genesis in "The Snow Man."[27] The ur-poem's abstraction here has given way to a series of concrete denials and assertions, which signal a marriage of the thing itself and the nothing. To some readers this marriage is hardly thinkable. Yet, in the East, as D. T. Suzuki notes, all schools of Buddhism teach, "*śūnyatā* ("emptiness") is *tathatā* ("suchness"), and *tathatā* is *śūnyatā*."[28] Thus a Chinese reader impulsively senses the thing itself and the nothing in the Tang poet Bo Juyi's references to "the mountains" and "the Nine Roads": "A thousand coaches, ten thousand horsemen pass down the Nine Roads; / Turns his head and looks at the mountains,—not one man!"[29] Similarly, the Japanese reader perceives both nothingness and suchness in "water-sound" in Bashō's famous haiku: "Old pond—/ and a frog-jump-in / water-sound."[30]

Surprisingly, in "The Course of a Particular" the trope for the thing itself/the nothing is also a particular sound. Was Stevens thinking of Bashō? Had he acquired certain Chan qualities from the Japanese haiku? That is possible.[31] But again, we must remember the poet's stress on art's impact. Indeed, from Chan art one can learn as much, if not more, about the attainment of the thing itself/the nothing through meditation. An example showing art's power of conveying the spirit of Chan is *Luohan in Meditation Attended by a Serpent,* a masterpiece on display in the MFA, during and after Stevens's Cambridge years (fig. 17). The painting illustrates the very moment a Luohan perceives the thing itself in meditative nothingness. The suchness in the "cry" of waves cannot be attained without his denial of sight. The Luohan has shunned all distractions. The stirring of the serpent in front of him and the "cry" of the leaves by his side, for instance, are not reflected in his halo.

Similarly relevant to Stevens's recurrent motif of nothingness is Bunsei's *Landscape* (fig. 23), another Boston masterpiece to which Stevens had access. We might see the painting as an example of "pictorial self-reference," focusing on the relation between the perceiver and the perceived.[32] From the Western standpoint, the figure in the picture cannot be the painter/perceiver, because his face is turned away from that scene. Nonetheless, from the Chan standpoint, the painter/perceiver absolutely needs this "turning away" ("emptying out") to achieve the thing itself/the nothing of the scene. The "turning away," like the denying of sight in the Luohan painting, precisely distinguishes a work as a Chan masterpiece. Further, one may wonder why the figure is positioned under a roof. My answer is that such a positioning may lead us to imagine him at once as the painter and as the collector of the painting. This interpretation is based on the Daoist view that art can "speak" on nature's behalf. Guo Xi, a spokesman of this theory, maintains that an artist's business is to enable those who wish to "enjoy a life amidst the luxuries of nature" but "are debarred from indulging in such pleasures" to "behold the grandeur of nature without stepping out of their houses."[33]

Stevens had long been fascinated by Guo Xi's essay on "The Noble Features of the Forest and the Stream," which expressed once and for all that outlook. It is amazing that four decades after his discovery of Guo Xi, the Song art critic's sentiment resurfaces in "The Poem That Took the Place of a Mountain" (1952):

There it was, word for word,
The poem that took the place of a mountain.

He breathed its oxygen,
Even when the book lay turned in the dust of his table.

It reminded him how he had needed
A place to go to in his own direction,

How he had recomposed the pines,
Shifted the rocks and picked his way among clouds,

For the outlook that would be right,
Where he would be complete in an unexplained completion:

The exact rock where his inexactnesses
Would discover, at last, the view toward which they had edged,

    Where he could lie and, gazing down at the sea,
    Recognize his unique and solitary home.   *(CPWS,* 512)

That is the mode of Guo Xi, whose painting took the place of mountains, streams, clouds, rocks, and pines. Bunsei's *Landscape,* one of the thousands of pictures in Guo Xi's tradition, shows that a scene affects its viewer/perceiver even when his face is turned away from it. Similarly, as Daniel Schwarz remarks, Stevens's poem affects its reader, "Even when he is not reading it."[34] Stevens is once more returning to "The Snow Man," whose character, like a Chan meditator, perceives not with his eyes but with his ears, not with his ears but with his mind, not with his mind but with an achieved state of no-mind.

    Late Stevens was a far more brilliant and complex poet than the Stevens of "The Snow Man," however. A. Walton Litz, with the acutest eye for stylistic changes, attests that the impersonality of "The Snow Man" is not as rigid as that of "The Course of a Particular."[35] An intense impersonal stance, though vital, is not in my view Stevens's greatest achievement in the meditative mode. In his final years, I would argue, Stevens was able to enact within the limited space of a short lyric something like a debate between meditative sublimity and imaginative sublimity. This double representation, a greater success than intensified impersonality or sharpened clarity, is nowhere more evident than in "Not Ideas about the Thing but the Thing Itself." The poem opens remarkably with a man's meditative experience:

    At the earliest ending of winter,
    In March, a scrawny cry from outside
    Seemed like a sound in his mind.

    He knew that he heard it,
    A bird's cry, at daylight or before,
    In the early March wind.

Stevens's earlier meditative poems present vivid imaginative moments only to be dismissed and replaced by suchness/nothingness. By contrast, "Not Ideas about the Thing," despite its declaration of a bias for the thing itself in the title, concludes with a beautiful epiphany that is not the thing itself but ideas about the thing:

    That scrawny cry—It was
    A chorister whose c preceded the choir.
    It was part of the colossal sun,

Surrounded by its choral rings,
Still far away. It was like
A new knowledge of reality. (*CPWS*, 534)

Bevis aptly suggests "The last line leads back to the title, the title to the
first line, the first line to the last."[36] This way one can avoid catching
an ironical tone. In the poem's opening and middle sections, the man's
perception has transformed through a series of denials ("No longer";
"It was not") from an idea about the thing ("a scrawny cry from outside / Seemed like a sound in his mind") to the thing itself ("A bird's
cry, at daylight or before"). Why does Stevens choose not to close at
the end of the fourth tercet? Why must he go on to offer the beautiful
epiphany? Does he desire to express a greater yearning for imaginative
sublimity? If so, he ought to have named the poem differently. What
he wants to show, I think, is the ephemeral nature of the thing itself.
That is to say, he wants to demonstrate how easily one can lose what
has been gained. Bevis drives this point home when he comments that
"The plot of the poem, from the Buddhist and from Stevens' point of
view, is based on the tragedy of desire: to love the other is to lose it by
making it oneself."[37]

With a sudden swerve from meditation to imagination, "Not Ideas
about the Thing but the Thing Itself" marks a giant leap forward in
Stevens's appreciation of Chan Buddhism. Near the end of his career,
Stevens in fact was able to present double representation in a variety of
ways. For example, "A Clear Day and No Memories," the poet's ultimate
vision, opens with extraordinary elements of the imagination:

No soldiers in the scenery,
No thoughts of people now dead,
As they were fifty years ago:
Young and living in a live air,
Young and walking in the sunshine,
Bending in blue dresses to touch something—
Today the mind is not part of the weather.

We are not to be distracted by the negatives—"No Memories"; "No soldiers"; "No thoughts." They are unlike those in, say, "The Latest Freed
Man," where the hero dismisses not splendid memories but abstract
ideas. One may want to call them litotes. However, this possibility is
questioned first by the line "Today the mind is not part of the weather,"
and then by further negations in the second half of the poem:

Today the air is clear of everything.
It has no knowledge except of nothingness
And it flows over us without meanings,
As if none of us had ever been here before
And are not now: in this shallow spectacle,
This invisible activity, this sense.   (*OP*, 138–39)

Is it uncharacteristic of Chan, one wonders, to recall splendid memories prior to the attainment of the thing itself/nothing? Not really. Chan meditation seldom begins with denial of abstract ideas. More often it starts with denial of concrete thoughts. The Luohan painting in the MFA as a Chan masterpiece elects to present the "unnoticed" serpent and leaves in the foreground. In Bashō's haiku, enlightenment or *satori* resides in the contrast between the old pond and the sudden splash of water caused by a frog leaping in. Similarly, the thing itself in "A Clear Day and No Memories" is made only fiercer following the speaker's rejection of spontaneous, dazzling memories.

Critics who are quick to notice a chilling tone in "A Clear Day and No Memories" seem slow in recognizing a strong sense of elation in theme. It is worth noting that in a letter to Peter Lee written four months before he died, Stevens found it necessary to allude, in a personal way, to his final vision that unites joy and desolation: "[T]he rabbits are definitely out of their holes for the season; the robins are back; the doves have returned from Korea and some of them sit on our chimney before sunrise and tell each other how happy they are in the most melancholy tones. Robins and doves are both early risers and are connoisseurs of daylight before the actual presence of the sun coarsens it" (*L,* 879). The robins and doves are tropes for Stevens himself and the young Korean poet. As "early risers" they recall "A Clear Day," "Not Ideas," and "The Dove in Spring." It seems that Stevens had a sense that he owed much of his final lyrics' sensibility to the Orient, and it is logical that he felt comfortable sharing his insight with someone from Korea.

FOURTEEN

The Chinese in
Rock-Drill
and *Thrones*

REVIEWING *The Letters of Ezra Pound,* edited by D. D. Paige in 1951, Wyndham Lewis reminded us of Vorticism by using "The Rock Drill" as the heading.[1] When Pound followed Lewis's example and affixed to his eleven Washington Cantos the title of Jacob Epstein's Vorticist masterpiece,[2] he similarly acknowledged the genesis of his poetics. After all, it was in 1914–15, in the heyday of Vorticism, that Pound first learned about "the force of Chinese ideographs."[3] It was in 1918–19, under the impact of Vorticism, that he began experimenting with what was to grow into the "ideogrammic method."[4] Nonetheless, it was after four decades of trial that Pound was finally able to validate the procedure associated with the Chinese script by exploiting a long series of Chinese characters.

It is true that the Middle Cantos contain a large number of characters. Not counting 信 (*xin*) in Canto 34, which was added in 1956, the earliest introduced characters in *The Cantos* are 正名 (*zheng ming*), placed at the end of Canto 51. These are followed by a total of forty-three characters in the China Cantos, with one preceding the group, one in Canto 52, fourteen in Canto 53, one in Canto 54, thirteen in Canto 55, nine in Canto 56, one in Canto 57, two in Canto 60, and one in Canto 61. Their effects, nevertheless, are decidedly superficial when compared with those of the characters found in *Rock-Drill* and in *Thrones.* Take the first *Rock-Drill* Canto (Canto 85), for example. It alone has 104 characters running from the beginning to the end. The second *Rock-Drill* Canto (Canto 86) has thirty-seven characters. Where the characters in the Middle Cantos add an odd look to Pound's poetry controlled by English, those in *Rock-Drill* and in *Thrones* serve not only to alter its look but also to affect the way it is read.

Critics have long recognized the visual attractiveness of the characters in the Late Cantos. William Cookson has regarded such "ideograms" as "an important means of creating the general effect of radiance."[5] Jerome McGann, who sees "bibliographic codes" or physical features of a text as significant constituent of meanings, has emphasized that under their influence "Looking and reading converge as reciprocal functions."[6] Put together, these two observations point to what I believe to be the most notable characteristics of the Chinese in *Rock-Drill* and *Thrones:* its faculty to suggest the aura of a Confucian text and its force of guiding our eyes to look and read in several directions. A careful examination of the opening passage of Canto 85 will illuminate what I mean:

LING[2]

Our dynasty came in because of a great sensibility.

All there by the time of I Yin

All roots by the time of I Yin.

Galileo Index'd 1616,

Wellington's peace after Vaterloo

chih[3]

a gnomon,
Our science is from the watching of shadows;
That Queen Bess translated Ovid,
        Cleopatra wrote of the currency,
Versus who scatter old records
        ignoring the hsien[2] form

(*C*, 563)

Readers who are familiar with the topography of the characters in the Middle Cantos and the Pisan Cantos will at once notice several major changes.[7] First, unlike those in the earlier cantos that are hand-drawn, mostly by Dorothy and occasionally by Ezra himself, the characters here are reproduced from standard Chinese scripts.[8] Second, unlike those in the earlier cantos that are printed basically in one size, the characters here are in three sizes and two calligraphic styles (the Song style for the small type and the regular-script style for the larger types).[9] Third, unlike those in earlier cantos that are placed everywhere, the characters here occupy a central position, comprising an outstanding subtext to be looked at or read from top to bottom.

Canto 85, according to Pound's footnote, "is a somewhat detailed confirmation of Kung's view that the basic principles of government are found in the Shu [*Shu jing*], the History Classic" (*C,* 579). Comparison reveals that *Rock-Drill's* small characters match those in Séraphin Couvreur's and James Legge's bilingual editions of *Shu jing,* whereas its larger ones match those of the Tang dynasty Stone-Classics printed *en face* in Pound's edition of *Confucius.*[10] What difference do these specially chosen characters make to Pound's new cantos? They do not simply make Chinese more elegant to look at; in a fashion similar to that of the Stone-Classics, they bring us nearer to the Confucian world. This statement is based on Martin Heidegger. For him, van Gogh's painting "spoke [*Dieses hat gesprochen*]," because "In the vicinity of the work we were suddenly somewhere else than we usually tend to be."[11] Pound has not presented Confucius in the original. But by using a series of characters that correspond to those of standard Confucian texts, he has preserved at least a part of their magic appeal. This is what I mean by "suggesting the aura of a Confucian text." Massimo Bacigalupo testifies to my assumption when he asserts: "Cantos 85–86 usher in *RD* with an extreme instance of Pound's captivation with the word transmitted, with the textual source . . . which in turn captivates the reader precisely as a textual object."[12]

Commenting on Louis Zukofsky's "Starglow," Marjorie Perloff has claimed that "we can read the poem, not only from left to right, but from top to bottom and vice versa, creating new relationships between word units."[13] Many will already have noticed, perhaps, that her remark can be used to describe Pound's *Rock-Drill* Cantos with equal legitimacy. Certainly, we can read the above passage, a typical page from a *Rock-Drill* canto, in several directions. Let us suppose that we begin by surveying the characters from top to bottom. As soon as our eyes hit the large character 靈, they will glance from right to left to see its transliteration LING² and then from left to right to regard its shape. If we continue to read the lines in English—"Our dynasty came in because of a great sensibility"—from left to right, our eyes are likely to glance up first to catch the juxtaposition between "a great sensibility" and 靈, and then from left to right to compare "I Yin" with the characters for "I Yin." Of course, we can read the passage in other ways. But whatever direction we take, our reading will be "more spacious, less linear,"[14] because one or another character is there to compel us to look while we read.

McGann is precise when he states that "the Chinese characters are an index of the kind of attention all scripted forms demand, even—and perhaps most crucially—those forms which are most familiar to us, such as the forms of our own languages."[15] Graphed in a doubly increased, calligraphic type, the character 靈 no doubt draws a lot of attention first to itself. Some may discern rain falling on the open mouths of dancers. Subsequently, in Canto 104, Pound will pictographically annotate 靈 as "The small breasts snow-soft over tripod / under the cloud / the three voices" (C, 760). Here, however, he simply glosses it as "a great sensibility." The reader is therefore not encouraged to focus on the character's formation. Instead, he or she is guided to look for the word's practical meaning in the contexts of Galileo's curiosity about moon shadows, Wellington's peace talk after Waterloo, Queen Elizabeth's familiarity with Ovid, and Cleopatra's interest in the currency. With the character 靈 and its gloss "great sensibility" in mind, one will estimate these figures in a new light. Placed together, these personages will in turn make the social implications of 靈 /sensibility more concrete.

This is a superb instance of Pound's "ideogrammic method." The piling together of figures from diverse cultures and historical periods reminds one of the "Troy-ANAXIFORMINGES-Aurunculeia-Cadmus" bit in Canto 4 (C, 13). While both juxtapositions are comparable to the "rose–cherry–rust–flamingo" formula, and are therefore linked to Pound's Fenollosan approach, the 1955 instance alone is accompanied by a Chinese ideogram. The 靈 (ling²) character, recurring four times in Cantos 85 and one more time in Canto 86, is culled from Couvreur's or Legge's bilingual edition of Shu jing, Zhou shu 14, where the Duke of Zhou addresses the Shang beaten troops: 今惟我周王丕靈 承帝事.[16] Pound has turned this into "Our dynasty came in because of a great sensibility." He is very Confucian to trace the roots of Zhou's sensibility back six hundred years to the Shang founder, whose minister Yi Yin's admonition to the heir is given in both Couvreur's and Legge's versions of *Shang shu 4*. Pound is also very Confucian to juxtapose Yi Yin with Galileo, Wellington, Queen Elizabeth, and Cleopatra. Wellington's peace talk, in particular, exemplifies a key Confucian sensibility, 止 (*zhi*) or "know[ing] when to stop."

"*There is no more important technical term in the Confucian philosophy than this chih (3),*" declared Pound in reference to a passage in *The Analects* (*Con*, 232). It seems that he did not recognize *zhi*'s place in the Confucian canon until he was in the U.S. Army Disciplinary Training Center (DTC) outside Pisa. In 1945 he copied the phrase 黃鳥止 (*huang niao zhi*) from Legge's bilingual edition of *The Great Learning* into his draft for Canto 79 (*C*, 507). It survived his editors' unauthorized omission of fifty-odd sets of Chinese characters for the Pisan sequence.[17] In *Rock-Drill*, Pound used 止 (*zhi*) five times, twice in Canto 85, twice in Canto 87, and one more time in Canto 93. The 1956 printing of *The Cantos*, by New Directions, gave him an opportunity to add yet another 止 (*zhi*) to Canto 52. In the opening passage of Canto 85, however, he glosses 止 (*zhi*) as "a gnomon," alluding at once to the sensibility of Galileo's theory and that of primitive Chinese science.

I am tempted to endorse Pound's interpretation of the Chinese characters from the *Shu jing* when suddenly he undermines himself. By the end of the passage, he directs our eyes to "the hsien[2] form 賢," a composite phonogram whose top, a phonetic, is not supposed to be visually analyzed. When he was in St. Elizabeths Hospital in Washington, D.C., Pound heard complaints about his approach to Chinese. Cheadle offers an account of how he benefited most from Willis Hawley and Achilles Fang.[18] To repeat only a few details, in the winter of 1946–47, Pound received from Hawley a copy of *Mathews' Chinese-English Dictionary*,[19] with recommendation for its phonetic organization. In the early 1950s, while making drafts for *Rock-Drill*, he discussed Confucian terms such as 止 (*zhi*) and 敬 (*jing*) with the more scholarly Fang.[20] Throughout this period, he listened to both experts' objections to treating phonetics in characters as ideographs. As a result of this interaction, *Rock-Drill* is somewhat curbed in the kind of pictographic rendering that abounds in *The Analects*. This is not to say, however, that Pound has given up his Fenollosan approach. His choice of 賢, a rarely used, archaic form for "virtue," over 賢, the form picked by Couvreur and Legge, should confirm his continued commitment to Fenollosa.[21] Obviously, he sees its phonetic top as consisting of 臣 ("subject") and 忠 ("loyal"), the analysis of which is out of the question with the form found in Couvreur or Legge or the Tang stone text.

Pound's enthusiasm for Chinese sound in *Rock-Drill* is genuine, though. Having noticed some inconsistency in Pound's romanization, Fang offered to make corrections.[22] Pound would not let him. He had taken counsel with both Couvreur and Legge. The romanization systems are signs to track down his sources. Thus, there is little ground for the argument that *Rock-Drill*'s opening with Wade spelling is relied exclusively on Couvreur's Chinese-French text. On the other hand, the two pages reproduced in figure 42 cannot be based on Legge, for they are filled with Courvreur's transliterations.

Courvreur and Legge both follow *Shu jing*'s chronology of the Xia, Shang, and Zhou. To compress all this material into one canto, Pound must find a focal point. What he has chosen is the Duke of Zhou's epoch-making address to the Shang officers at Zhou's new capital, Luo Yi. From this speech, *Duoshi*, or "*O nombreux officiers*," he can easily go back to earlier moments in history when Shang rulers prospered because of 靈 /a great sensibility. After each flashback recurs the statement "Our dynasty came in because of a great sensibility" and the character 靈 with increased rhetorical force.

When we reach the passage reproduced below (fig. 42), we are literally overwhelmed by Chinese and other foreign words. In his footnote to Canto 85, Pound asks the reader not to be daunted by his ideograms: "Meaning of the ideograms is usually given in the English text" (*C,* 579). A look at the two pages confirms the truth of his words. As the character 貳 representing "*pou éul cheu / pu erh*⁴" has its English equivalent "The arrow has not two points" affixed to its upper left,[23] so the character 邑 standing for Luo Yi, the site of the address, is set side by side with the title of the address, "*O nombreux officiers.*" These are followed by the names of three Shang rulers: 太戊 T'AI MEOU 1637–1562 [B.C.], 武丁 OU TING 1324–1265 [B.C.], and TSOU KIA, who "reigned 33 years." What early Shang rulers abided by appears to have been an oral tradition, "惟正之供 *wei tcheng tcheu koung,*" or "naught above just contribution" (*C,* 577).[24] This ancient paradigm leads to a notion pivotal to Pound's late Confucianism, *jiao* in Chinese and "Sagetrieb" in the Poundian vocabulary. "明 *míng ngò tsiun* 俊" or "train the fit men" is just another way of saying it.[25]

Ira Nadel calls Pound's characters in *The Cantos* a device of "Visualizing history."[26] In visualizing the histories of ancient Shang and Zhou,

Pound devotes particular attention to key Confucian standards by presenting related words in large, calligraphically inscribed types. Who can ignore, for instance, the aural effects of the characters 靈 (*ling*) and 教 (*jiao*) in Canto 85? One figures strikingly at the opening, and the other, aside from its first occurrence in the above passage, stands out emphatically at the close (*C, 579*).

If there is a thematic core in *Rock-Drill* and in *Thrones,* it is the dichotomy of 靈 sensibility/教 Sagetrieb. Its spirit pervades these decads even where the characters 靈 and 教 are absent. Such are the cases with the third and fourth *Thrones* Cantos (Cantos 98 and 99) based on F. W. Baller's bilingual edition of *The Sacred Edict.* Slim as it appears, Baller's book contains three versions of Kangxi's "Sacred Edict" (*Shengyu,* 1670): an amplified version by Yongzheng (*Wenli,* 1724), a colloquial rendering of Yongzheng's version by Shanxi salt commissioner Wang Youpu, and an English version of the colloquial rendering by Baller. Two efforts involved—Yongzheng's to expand his father's tenets in a simple, literary style, and Wang's to render Yongzheng's version into "popular speech"—fascinated Pound. Both are exceptional examples of "mak[ing] it new," examples of Confucian sensibility/Sagetrieb.

I have denoted that the characters 靈 / 教 are missing in Cantos 98 and 99. By this I do not imply to say that these cantos contain no words, Chinese or Poundian English, that convey the message of 靈 / 教. Canto 98, in fact, opens with "新 hsin¹ / Make it new" (*C,* 704), which at once brings to mind the sensibility/Sagetrieb of the "make-it-new" Shang founder Chengtang. What's more, in Canto 98 the word "Sagetrieb" occurs twice: "thought built on Sagetrieb" (706) and "Thought is built out of Sagetrieb" (710). In Canto 99, in place of "Sagetrieb" are references to "tuan¹ / cheng⁴ / the teacher's job" (719) and to "That job . . . / To trace out and to bind together / From sonship . . . to clan" (715).

The centrality of Sagetrieb in Pound's work of the 1950s is indisputable. During a 1954 visit to Pound at St. Elizabeths, David Gordon witnessed him pencil 教 on the half-title page of his 1948 *Cantos.* In both 孝 (*xiao*) ("filial piety") and the later chosen form for Sagetrieb 教 (*jiao*) ("teach"), according to Gordon, Pound saw "an old man" handing something down to "a child" or, conversely, "a child" receiving something from "an old man." [27] Although Cantos 98 and 99 offer no pictographic analysis, they involve a series of texts that exemplify such relationships. Yongzheng received an edict from his father, Kangxi,

不   p'i

The arrow has not two points

貳   pou éul cheu
     pu erh⁴

"O nombreux officiers

Imperator ait.

邑

Iterum dico

太   T'AI MEOU   1637
戊   1562

武   OU TING   1324
丁   1265

cognovit aerumnas

TSOU KIA reigned 33 years

惟   wei

576

42. Ezra Pound, *The Cantos of Ezra Pound* (New York: New Directions, 1998), pages 576–77. (Courtesy, New Directions Publishing Corporation, New York)

正   tcheng

之   tcheu

XV: 11   供   koung

naught above just contribution

invicem docentes   胥   siu   M.2835

hsü, in the first tone
kiaó. chiao,[1-4]

that is Sagetrieb   教

時   chêu

我   ngò

We flop if we cannot maintain the awareness   XVI.4
Diuturna cogites   10
respect the awareness and
            train the fit men.

明 mìng ngò tsiun 俊   XVI.20

        chün[4]   1727. Mat.

577

and transmitted his interpretation of it to Wang, who in turn transmitted his colloquial rendering of the version to Baller. Each recipient/interpreter added something new to what he received. So Sagetrieb has a deep implication: A worthy disciple should be a creative interpreter.

Accordingly, Cantos 98 and 99 are Pound's attempt to represent at once the triply rewritten "Sacred Edict" and the essence of Sagetrieb. Surely he is committed to the "make-it-new" principle. Meanwhile, he is also doing his best to preserve the attribute of each precursor. Of the four, he apparently prizes Yongzheng and Wang most, one for his exposition and the other for his idiom.

Not surprisingly, the salt commissioner's name appears five times in Canto 98, twice in characters and three times in transliterations: "Until in Shensi, Ouang, the Commissioner Iu-p'uh / volgar' eloquio 又樸" (*C*, 706); "*Ouang-iu-p'uh* 王又 / on the edict of K'ang-hsi / in volgar' eloquio taking the sense down to the people" (708); "Despite Mathews this Wang was a stylist" (710). Pound's fascination with Wang is evident: "our debt here is to Baller / and to *volgar' eloquio*" (710). By "*volgar' eloquio*" he alludes to Wang, who allows him to perceive perhaps for the first time the musical force of spoken Chinese. Yes, I do mean to say spoken Chinese. Even in a written text, native users of Chinese can identify Wang's language as an old-fashioned Mandarin speech. Did Pound hear Wang's sentences read aloud by one of his Chinese-speaking visitors?[28] At any rate, in Cantos 98 and 99 he displays a tremendous effort to recapture Wang's colloquial mode, and it is in this effort that we witness his belated enthusiasm for Chinese sound.

Clearly, Pound has recognized Wang's preference for two-character words and multicharacter phrases. By reproducing a large number of such expressions in Cantos 98 and 99, he brings out an essential quality of modern Chinese. Yes, it is true that we have 正名 (*zheng ming*) and 新日日新 (*xin ri ri xin*) in the Middle Cantos (*C*, 252 and 265, for example) and 惟正之供 (*wei zheng zhi gong*) in *Rock-Drill* (576–77). But it is in *Thrones* where multicharacter expressions overshadow single characters for the first time. To verify this impression, we need only to take a glance at Canto 98. Halfway through the text, we notice, "太 t'ai⁴ / 平 p'ing²" and "風 tso feng suh" leading to "en¹ 恩 ch'ing² 情" and "i⁴ 義 / ch'i⁴ 氣" (709–10). Next, one observes "敬 reverence / order 孝" and "正 cheng/ 經 king" followed by "cheng 正 / king 經" and "[孔] Kung's porch 門 mên³" (711).

Most Chinese words in Canto 98 are represented by both characters

and their transliterations. While the tone symbols are not a new con-
trivance, they are used here for additional purposes. Of course, they still
operate to distinguish homophones with different tones. For instance,
hua⁴ tou² is 話頭 meaning "thread of discourse" or "tongue words" (708)
rather than *hua² tou²* 滑頭 meaning "artful." Similarly, *yi⁴ qi* is 義氣
meaning "graceful" (710) rather than *yi¹ qi³* 一起 meaning "together"
or *yi² qi⁴* 遺棄 meaning "abandon." Nonetheless, in *Thrones,* it seems,
Pound designates the tones not so much for differentiating meaning as
for signaling Chinese cadence. After all, the music of *hua⁴ tou²* is evident in a glide from one tone to another ("falling"-"rising"). So is that
of *en¹ qing²* ("flat"-"rising").

Pound's effort to juxtapose Chinese speech with English speech culminates in Canto 99. At first glance, we may get the impression that it
does not have as much Chinese as Canto 98. This is because with four
exceptions all the Chinese words in that canto are transliterated. If one
tries to put them back into characters, one will get over 160 of them![29]
Even Canto 85 does not have so many. Where Canto 98 takes advantage of two-character words in modern Chinese, Canto 99 enables us
to hear for the first time in *The Cantos* some lively expressions of the
Chinese villagers. "Despite Mathews this Wang was a stylist. / Uen-li
will not help you talk to them," affirms Pound (*C*, 710). Wang's phrases
are so vivacious that Pound sometimes cannot resist translating them
word for word into English: "Nor scrape iron off the point of a needle"
(716) for *zhenjian shang xue tie*, for instance.[30] More frequently, he just
sets them side by side with his English: "pu / k'o / hsin . . . do not
believe 'em" (721).[31]

Canto 99 is one of Pound's most lyrical cantos. Some of its musical
effects are derivable from the coupling of Chinese cadence and American English cadence. Pound obviously takes delight in bringing over
Chinese alliteration:

chih²⁻⁵ ma   set out hemp
chung³ mi'en² cotton
            t'ung² all together.

It seems that he enjoys the musical effect so much that after a few lines
he tries alliteration across tongues:

fei (four), waste time, flounder in business,
The organization is functional
and to maintain a liquidity . . .   (*C*, 716)

And at the midpoint of the canto he handles this technique effortlessly: "che yang ti jen / a low-flow and a liu² flow / a rice dog-head pai lui for ruin" (724).[32]

True, Chinese sound is beyond this book's central thesis, but the Chinese character is not. Without looking into Pound's phonetic as well as pictographic use of the character, readers would get an incomplete picture of his understanding of Chinese. If Pound has previously ignored Chinese phonetics, he is making amends for his neglect by overeulogizing it in Canto 99. *Ming* used to be the "sun" and "moon" combined to suggest "radiance." Here it is no more than a sound repeated with other sounds, Chinese and English, to make music and sense:

2 incarnations in every home　佛
　　　　　huo⁴⁻⁵ fu²⁻⁵
and you go up hill to seek wooden ones.
Kuang
Kuang
Ming　　　　　　　　　　　　Saith Khaty
Ming

　　　　　　　tien
　　　　　　　t'ang²
　　　　　　　hsin¹
　　　　　　　li³⁻⁵
Confucians observe the weather,
　　　　　hear thunder,
　　　　　seek to include.　　　　　　　　　(C, 722)[33]

In Canto 99, Pound shows his passionate rejection of a prolonged indifference to *melopoeia* in Chinese. From this, nonetheless, we still cannot conclude that by the late 1950s Pound had come to grips with the place of Chinese sound. Certainly we do not get a lot of pictographic renderings of Chinese in *Thrones*. But the few instances of such analyses in Cantos 98 and 99 are proof of his unchanged ardor for seeing phonetics in Chinese as pictographic significants. For him 青 (*qing*) in 情 (*qing*) is forever "the colour of nature" (C, 709) rather than merely a sound symbol, and 㬎 (*xian*) in 顯 (*xian*) is always "the silk cords of the sunlight" (714) rather than just *xian*.

The homely language of Cantos 98 and 99 reminds one of Wang Youpu. The viewpoint represented, however, is that of Kangxi and Yongzheng. Kangxi identified sixteen ethic points to make certain that his people remained controllable. In the second year of his reign, Yong-zheng republished his father's "Edict" with detailed commentary, commissioning officials such as Wang to introduce it in simple language to villagers. All this Pound acknowledges in Canto 98: "Iong-ching republished the edict / But the salt-commisioner took it down to the people / who, in Baller's view, speak in quotations; / think in quotations" (*C,* 710).

In interpreting Yongzheng and Kangxi through Wang and Baller, however, Pound dilates only on themes appealing to him. First of these comes the seventh clause on "Heresy and Orthodoxy." Pound is supposedly returning to the China Cantos and to his assault on "taozers" and "hochangs." He *is* returning to the China Cantos, but there is no more "Foe's, that is / goddam bhuddists [buddhists]" (*C,* 284). He is not attempting to reinforce his indiscriminate attack on Daoists and Buddhists. Rather, he is trying to clarify his intent, which is to deride corrupt institutionalization of religion.

The primary source of Pound's China Cantos is de Mailla's *Histoire,* a French translation of an early-eighteenth-century updated edition of the prestigious "Comprehensive Mirror." [34] According to John Nolde, de Mailla arrived in Beijing probably in the 1720s and his manuscript was sent to France in installments in the early 1730s. [35] So, *Histoire* was a product of the era of the reissued "Sacred Edict" (1724). Despite their contemporaneity, the two texts display differences not to be overlooked. Where de Mailla fails to illuminate whom the Neo-Confucian historians mean by "heretics," Yongzheng makes it decisively clear. In the mid-1950s Pound learned something new about Chinese modes of thought. One of the books that helped him was Baller's *The Sacred Edict.* Indeed, to rewrite it afforded him an occasion to make some amends.

To many readers Pound appears ironic after presenting negative pictures of "Buddhists" and "Daoists" to offer lines such as "Manners are from earth and from water / They arise out of hills and streams" (*C,* 718). Pound is no more ironic than Yongzheng. We have been slow in recognizing the real target of his—or Yongzheng's—charges. This is the way the assault begins in Canto 98:

> "and that Buddha abandoned such splendours,
>   is it likely!" said Yong Tching . . .
> "Who has seen Taoist priests fly up in broad daylight?

This is how it carries on:

"Is the Bhud likely to return for these harridans?
    having had his palace with court yards
and a dragon verandah, plus a feng-ko
presumably furnished with phoenix
and he *ch'id* 'em or *shed* 'em
    棄   捨   (*C,* 707)

Evidently, the raid is not directed toward the Buddha, or Laozi and Zhuangzi. Instead, it is aimed at those who took advantage of their names. Pound, of course, is following Yongzheng, whose exposition, in Wang's version, is represented at greater length in Canto 99:

As to building temples for the benefit of contractors
    or images for the benefit of the gilders,
The incense market will benefit
    from your wives' red and green dresses
As they run about mid riff-raff
    acquiring merit by comedy
    or by tragedy after fool vows.   (*C,* 723)

Once told that Yongzheng was a learned Chan Buddhist devotee, we shall look at his seemingly contradictory beliefs differently. The ninth-century Chan master Yixuan urged: "If you see the Buddha on the road, kill him."[36] Yongzheng's similar scorn of false religious commentaries and practices appears to have stemmed from the accepted Chan disbelief in symbols. According to Jonathan Spence, Yongzheng spent as much time on Buddhist meditation as Kangxi did on hunting. During his reign, he "authorized a Buddhist press to print sutras—passages from Buddhist scripture." Moreover, he "met regularly in his Peking palace with a fourteen-person Chan study group, consisting of the five brothers he still trusted, select senior officials, one Daoist, and five Buddhist monks."[37] Pound is not likely to have known all this. Nevertheless, he did manage to bring across some of the Manchu ruler's Chan sense: his disgust with religious symbols and his passion for climate and scenery.

The last point leads to the Edict's ninth clause, "Manners and Customs," which Pound touches upon more than lightly. In Canto 98 he at once presents and visually defines the characters for "manners and customs": "Earth and water dye the wind in your valley / tso feng 風 tso feng suh" (*C,* 709). In Canto 99 he goes on to cite a quotation of Yongzheng's from a Han Confucian scholar with Daoist leanings:[38]

The sages of Han had a saying:
>   Manners are from earth and from water
>   They arise out of hills and streams
>   The spirit of air is of the country
>   Men's manners cannot be one
>   (same, identical)
Kung said: are classic of heaven,
They bind thru the earth
>   and flow
With recurrence,
>   action, humanitas, equity   (C, 718)

This passage is followed by Pound's variations on the Edict's tenth tenet, "PEN YEH 本業," which he connects first to "$\tau \acute{\epsilon} \chi \nu \eta$" (C, 707), then to "ne ultra crepidam" (712), and finally to "the family profession" (717), "a developed skill from persistence" (718).

The Edict's interest in these ethical points, from respect for elders to charges against religious follies to good manners and customs to "PEN YEH," as Peter Makin has rightly commented, is "for the sake of stability solely."[39] During the first decades of Kangxi's reign, there was an apparent lack of support from the Han Chinese. The Edict was one of the measures Kangxi took to strengthen his political authority. As for Yongzheng, he had an additional reason for upholding the Edict. Kangxi died without publicly naming an heir.[40] It was Yongzheng who announced to the Qing court that he was the dying Kangxi's chosen successor. Thereafter, in the thirteen years of his rule (1723–35), Yongzheng worried about accusations that he was a usurper. The message of the Edict, spread to the grassroots level, helped maintain a national stability he strongly desired.

In her review of the evolution of Pound's Confucianism, Cheadle identifies three periods: an early period, characterized by his emphasis on a "respect for individual variety" and a concern for social order; a middle period, characterized by his "'totalitarian' and Fascist application"; and a late period, characterized by his attention to the importance of verbal precision.[41] Certainly, Pound's Confucianism in *Rock-Drill* and in *Thrones* is less political and more metaphysical. Cheadle has provided a convincing account of Pound's underlying comparison of Mussolini/Fascism and Confucianism in the Middle Cantos.[42] Hardly any such comparison is detected in the Late Cantos. This does not imply that the late Chinese cantos are apolitical. Pound's sources, the *Shu jing* and the *Shengyu,* were composed, edited, and handed down from generation to generation for political ends. In incorporating these texts into his modernist epic, Pound has kept intact their politically instructive tones:

Our dynasty came in because of a great sensibility.

All there by the time of I Yin   伊

All roots by the time of I Yin.   尹   (*C,* 563)

One village in order,
          one valley will reach the four seas.

CHÊN, *yo el Rey,* wish you to think of this EDICT.   (729)

His goal can be no other than "using Confucius to civilize the Western world."

Can Confucianism keep Western society from corruption? Anyone who doubts this need only ask another question: Did Confucianism keep Chinese society from corruption? Hugh Gordon Porteous, a British sinologist, warned as early as 1939 that Confucius was not all-powerful. He quoted Han Feizi, the third-century B.C. legalist, as saying, "ten honest gents to every hundred offices, therefore 90 crooks in office; no system of govt. however nice on paper will ever work until you solve that conundrum."[43] Evidently Pound paid no heed to Porteous. Nor did he, in the 1950s, pay heed to Baller, who wrote: "The Sacred Edict well exemplifies both the strength and weakness of mere morality. There is high thinking, but the outcome is low living. These moral maxims have no life-giving power in them."[44]

It is ironic that Pound promoted Confucianism at a time when the Chinese were beginning to recognize its shortcomings. Confucianism played a positive role in shaping the Chinese culture and the Chinese character, but too often in Chinese history the ruling classes exploited it to serve their private interests. In 1919, and again in 1949, in their search for a modern nation, the Chinese people rose to break from Confucianism, which formed the foundation of the feudal bureaucracy. They rose to break from the very Confucian codes Pound was preaching. Didn't Pound become doubtful about Confucianism in his last years? Maybe he did after 1960.[45] Didn't he criticize Confucianism in

Thrones? His criticism sounds very absurd. He was sorry that the Manchu rule did not endure long enough: "And Byzance lasted longer than Manchu / because of an (%) interest-rate" (*C,* 710).

I began this study by stressing the persuasive power of the graphic and plastic arts. For Pound, Moore, and Stevens, the increasing number of Chinese ink paintings, bronzes, porcelains, and calligraphic objects transferred to England and America functioned powerfully. These objects—more than any Western commentaries—brought to light an aesthetic that at once verified and challenged modernist sensibilities. They afforded the poets not only a robust creative resource but also ways of redefining their evolving poetics. Nonetheless, it must be pointed out that like their verbal counterparts these art objects from China tended to mislead as well as enlighten, make visible as well as hide. What's more, they reflected reality only from the standpoint of a specific historical period, a specific political-economic institution, and a specific class. How much did Pound, Moore, and Stevens learn about China from art and literature, then? Did they ever question the limitations of such sources? Most probably they did. Or in their late years they would not have been so inspired by and devoted to friendships with people from the Far East, notably, Achilles Fang, Peter Lee, and Mai-mai Sze. Orientalism is after all a shifting process. Had they been given chances, the three modernist poets would all have been glad to visit China. In 1968, during an interview for an Italian documentary, Pound expressed his regret for not having been to China. When asked, "Is this a disappointment for you, not to have seen China, which inspired you so much?" he replied, "Yes, I have always wanted to see China. It's awfully late now, but who knows?" (*P&P,* 10: 317).

Appendix

Moore's Typescript for "Tedium and Integrity," pp. 4–7, RML-
MMC, II: 06: 12. (Courtesy of Marianne Craig Moore; courtesy,
Rosenbach Museum and Library, Philadelphia)

. . . This whole theme—the thought of integrity—was suggested to
me by THE TAO OF PAINTING, with a translation of THE MUS-
TARD SEED GARDEN MANUAL OF PAINTING 1679–1701, by Miss
Mme Mme [Mai-mai] Sze; published by the Bollingen Foundation,
1956. Hsieh Ho [Xie He] whose Six Canons of Painting were formulated about A.D. 500 said, "The terms ancient and modern have no
meaning in art." I indeed felt that art is timeless when I saw in the Book
Review section of The New York Times last spring, the reproduction
of a plum branch by Tsou [Zou] Fu-lei, XIV century—a blossoming
branch entitled A Breath of Spring. (Sometimes, I am tempted to add,
when one breaks open a plum, one gets a fragrance of the blossom).
    Tao means way or path. There is a Tao and there is The Tao, as Miss
Mme Mme [Mai-mai] Sze explains. In Chinese writing, which is pictographic as you know, The Tao is portrayed as a foot taking a step (ch'o
[zu]) and a head (shou). So we have the idea of wholeness of total harmony from head to foot. Step by step progress requires deliberateness,
suggesting that meditation is basic to living, to all that we do, and that
conduct is a thing of inner motivation. Pictographically, man is but a
pair of legs, whereas the Tao is an integration of body, legs, arms, and
above all a head. China's concept of The Tao as the center of the circle,
the creative principle, the golden mean, is one of the oldest in Chinese thought, shared by all schools. The Tao is the mark. The soul is the

arrow. Indeed Lieh Tzu [Liezi] said, "To the mind that is still the whole universe surrenders."

It is not known in what period the idea of Yin and Yang originated, but as early as the XI century [B.C.] they were mentioned as the two primal forces. The Yang, the Male Principle—symbolized by the right foot—was identified with sun, light, action, positiveness; and Yin, the Female Principle, with the moon, darkness and quiescence.

There are two important features of Chinese painting.

1. The close relationship between painting and calligraphy. Writing Chinese characters developed a fine sense of proportion—prominent in every aspect of Chinese life. Confucius regarded a sense of fitness as one of the Five Cardinal Virtues.

2. The view that painting is not a profession but an extension of the art of living. Usually therefore, painting was an expression of maturity. A painter was likely to be an astronomer, a musician, perhaps a medical man. In acquiring the education prescribed by the Tao of Painting, a painter underwent rigorous intellectual discipline which included intensive training of memory. So authorship in China is integral to education, please note—not a separate proficiency to be acquired. (Rather humbling to those of us who devoted much time [to] incidental aspects of writing.) Chinese philosophy, Mme Mme [Mai-mai] Sze observes, might be said to be psychology—a development of the whole personality; and egotism—or what the Bhuddist [Buddhist] called ignorance—obscures a clear vision of the *Tao*. It is unusual, at least in my experience, to come on a book of verse which has not a tincture of sarcasm or grievance, a sense of injury personal or general, and I feel very strongly what Juan Ramón Jiménez said in referring to something else—to what is not poetry—"there is a profounder profundity" than obsession with self.

Painting should be a fusion of that which pertains to Heaven—the spirit—and of matter, which pertains to Earth, as effected by the painter's insight and skill. The search for a rational explanation of nature and the universe encourage a tendency to classification—almost a disease as noted by Miss Mme Mme [Mai-mai] Sze, when carried to an extreme; and in China Six Canons of Painting were formulated, as has been said, about A.D. 500 by Hsieh Ho [Xie He]. Of these the first—basic to all—controlled the other five and applies to all kinds of painting was spirit. The word ch'i [*qi*]—in the Cantonese version pronounced *hay,* is almost like exhaling a breath, cognate in meaning to *pneuma* and the word *spiritus*.

2. The Second Canon says "The brush is the means of creating structure." The ideal takes form. The spiritual aspect has tangible expression, and while one result of the tendency by Sung [Song] academicians to stress faithful representation, was to hamper spontaneity, a happy result was the superb paintings of insects, flowers, animals, and birds. In Volume II of the Manual where methods are illustrated, we have bud and buds beginning to open, thick leaves that withstand winter, plants with thorns and furry leaves, grasshoppers, large grasshoppers, crickets, beetles and the praying mantis; small birds fighting while [flying], a bird bathing and a bird shaking off water.

3. According to the object draw its form.

4. According to the nature of the object apply color.

5. "Organize the composition with each element in its rightful place." One is reminded here of Hsieh Ho's [Xie He] statement: "Accidents impair and time transforms but it is we who choose." In Volume II, in which methods are illustrated, one has "tiled structures at several levels, at a distance," (nests of very beautiful drawings), walls, bridges, temples, a lean-to of beanstalks. "If a man had eyes all over his body," the Manual says, "his body would be a monstrosity. . . . A landscape with people and dwellings in it has life, but too many figures and houses give the effect of a market-place." Perhaps the most important factor in harmonizing the elements of a picture is space, Miss Mme Mme [Mai-mai] Sze feels: "the most original contribution of Chinese painting, the most exhilarating." "Space of any kind was regarded as filled with meaning—in fact was synonymous with the *Tao*. A hollow tree was not empty but filled with spirit. The spaces between the spokes of a wheel make the wheel, and inner space, not the pottery of the pitcher, is its essential part," it is not a set of walls but "the space in a room that is its usefulness." One of the Twelve Faults was "a crowded ill-arranged composition"; or "water with no indication of its source."

6. In copying, transmit the essence of the master's brush and methods. Chinese thinking abounds in symbolism and the circle as a concept of wholeness is surely one of great fascination. Everything must be in proper relation to the center. A circle's beginning (its head), and end (or foot) are the same, unmoving and continually moving and still life—*nature morte*—is contrary to the whole concept of Chinese painting. The *Tao* (a path) lies on the ground, is still, yet leans somewhere and so has movement; and we have, therefore, an identity of contraries which are not in conflict but complementary opposites or two halves of a whole, as in the *Yin* and *Yang*—symbolized by the disc divided by

an S-like curve. It is not known in what period the idea of *Yin* and *Yang* originated, but as early as the XI century [B.C.] they were mentioned as the primal forces. The *Yang,* the Male Principle identified pictographically with the right foot—was identified as well, with sun, light, action, positiveness; and *Yin,* the Female Principle, with the moon, darkness, and quiescence.

The Chinese dragon is a symbol of the power of Heaven, a main characteristic being constant movement—slumbering in the deep or winging across the Heaven. At will it could change and be the size of a silkworm or swell so large as to fill the space of Heaven and Earth, and so represents totality. It had also the gift of invisibility. A second type of symbol pertains to flowers, birds, and animals—the phoenix, the tortoise, the unicorn, the crane, the pine, the peach, being motifs for long life, and the bamboo, a symbol of elegance.

So complete is the Manual that the brush, the ink, inkstone, and paper (or silk)—the Four Treasures—are minutely discussed. In making the brush into one end of the hollow bamboo holder, a tuft of hair or fur is inserted and fixed with a little glue. As for glues, the much-esteemed Tang-o [Dong'e] glue was made by boiling donkey-hides in Tang [Dong] River water, which contained special minerals. Other good glues were made from deer horns or fish skin. The jet blackness and sheen of a certain ink made from pine-soot, also depend on the preparation. "To dull the ink, pulverized oyster-shells or powdered jade were added although jade was put in principally as a gesture of respect to the ink." "Old ink sticks and cakes have a unique fragrance, often heightened by adding musk, camphor, or pomegranate-bark." "Old ink is treated like a vintage wine." "Not only can great variety of tone be produced from one stick, but several kinds are often used in one painting, since ink often blended with color, enriched the venerable air of trees and rocks," the Element of the mysterious, the dark and fertile dignity hovering over hillock and pool."

"The aim of the entire Manual is to develop the painter's spiritual resources." "There is an old saying": (quoted in this Preface to the Shanghai Edition (1887) of the Manual) "that those who are skilled in painting will live long because life created through the sweep of the brush can strengthen life itself, both being of the spirit—the *ch'i* [*qi*]."

"To achieve trueness and naturalness is to be in harmony with the *Tao*—the equival of an act of worship." "Natural spontaneous brushwork is like the flight of a bird." "The function of brush and ink is to make visible the invisible."

Notes

PREFACE

1. See, for example, William Bevis, *Mind of Winter: Wallace Stevens, Meditation, and Literature* (Pittsburgh: Univ. of Pittsburgh Press, 1988); Zhaoming Qian, *Orientalism and Modernism: The Legacy of China in Pound and Williams* (Durham, N.C.: Duke Univ. Press, 1995); Robert Kern, *Orientalism, Modernism, and the American Poem* (Cambridge: Cambridge Univ. Press, 1996); Mary Paterson Cheadle, *Ezra Pound's Confucian Translations* (Ann Arbor: Univ. of Michigan Press, 1997); Cynthia Stamy, *Marianne Moore and China: Orientalism and a Writing of America* (New York: Oxford Univ. Press, 1999); Zhaoming Qian, ed., *Ezra Pound and China* (Ann Arbor: Univ. of Michigan Press, 2003).

2. The Moore-Stevens-Pound link is noted by Celeste Goodridge in *Hints and Disguises: Marianne Moore and Her Contemporaries* (Iowa City: Univ. of Iowa Press, 1989), 9, where she argues that "[Moore's] deepest alliances were with Stevens and Pound, and not, as most have suggested, with Williams and Eliot."

3. W. J. T. Mitchell, *Picture Theory: Essays on Verbal and Visual Representation* (Chicago: Univ. of Chicago Press, 1994), 160. For my discussion, see 47. Wendy Steiner, *Pictures of Romance: Form against Context in Painting and Literature* (Chicago: Univ. of Chicago Press, 1988), 7–42. For my discussion, see 131, 133.

4. Marjorie Perloff, *21st-Century Modernism: The "New" Poetics* (Oxford: Blackwell Publishers, 2002), 3.

5. The term is taken from W. J. T. Mitchell, who discusses "an instrument of cultural power" in his *Landscape and Power* (Chicago: Univ. of Chicago Press, 1994), 1–2.

6. Stevens to Earl Miner, 30 November 1950, UCLA, Special Collections, 821:1: "While I know about haiku, or hokku, I have never studied them and certainly I did not have them in mind when I wrote THIRTEEN WAYS ETC. I have been more interested in Japanese prints although I have never collected them."

7. See Mitchell, *Picture Theory*, 151–52.

8. See Pound, "Lawrence [*sic*] Binyon," *Blast* 2 (July 1915): 85–86; reprinted in *P&P*, 2:99. See also Binyon, *The Flight of the Dragon: An Essay on the Theory and Prac-

tice of Art in China and Japan Based on Original Sources (1911; reprint, London: Murray, 1959), hereafter *Flight*.

9. See, in particular, Stevens to Barbara Church, 27 August 1953, in *L*, 797, where he criticizes the French painter Bezombes's Orientalism.

10. See Edward Said, *Orientalism* (New York: Random House, 1978), 1–28, especially 3. In Said's most radical definition, Orientalism is "a Western style for dominating, restructuring, and having authority over the Orient." For broader understandings of Orientalism, see Said, "Orientalism Reconsidered," in Said, *Reflections on Exile and Other Essays* (Cambridge: Harvard Univ. Press, 2000), 198–215; Homi K. Bhabha, "Difference, Discrimination, and the Discourse of Colonialism," in *The Politics of Theory*, ed. Francis Barker et al. (Colchester, U.K.: Univ. of Essex, 1983), 194–211, especially 199–201; Lisa Lowe, *Critical Terrains: French and British Orientalism* (Ithaca, N.Y.: Cornell Univ. Press, 1992), 4–5; Zhang Longxi, *Mighty Opposites: From Dichotomies to Differences in the Comparative Study of China* (Stanford, Calif.: Stanford Univ. Press, 1998), 188–96; Malini Johar Schueller, *U.S. Orientalisms: Race, Nation, and Gender in Literature, 1790–1890* (Ann Arbor: Univ. of Michigan Press, 1998), ix–x.

11. Charles Altieri, *Painterly Abstraction in Modernist American Poetry: The Contemporaneity of Modernism* (1989; reprint, University Park: Pennsylvania State Univ. Press, 1995), 9.

ONE. Pound and Chinese Art in the "British Museum Era"

1. Geoffrey H. Hartman, *The Fatal Question of Culture* (New York: Columbia Univ. Press, 1997), 61. On Pound and modern art, see Altieri, *Painterly Abstraction,* 283–320; Peter Nicholls, *Modernisms: A Literary Guide* (Berkeley and Los Angles: Univ. of California Press, 1995), 167–79; Reed Way Dasenbrock, "Pound and the Visual Arts," in *The Cambridge Companion to Ezra Pound,* ed. Ira B. Nadel (New York: Cambridge Univ. Press, 1999), 224–35.

2. Binyon acknowledges his indebtedness to H. A. Giles, *An Introduction to the History of Chinese Pictorial Art* (1905; reprint, London: Quaritch, 1918); Friedrich Hirth, *Scraps from a Collector's Note-book* (New York: Stechert, 1905). Neither has the breadth of Binyon's *Painting in the Far East: An Introduction to the History of Pictorial Art in Asia Especially China and Japan* (London: Arnold, 1908), hereafter *Painting.*

3. Dasenbrock, "Pound and the Visual Arts," 226–27. On Roger Fry's two Post-impressionist shows, see Frances Spalding, *Roger Fry: Art and Life* (Berkeley and Los Angelos: Univ. of California Press, 1980), 131–41, 153–63.

4. James J. Wilhelm, *The American Roots of Ezra Pound* (New York: Garland, 1985), 68.

5. On China in the centennial exhibition held in Philadelphia, May–November 1876, see Benjamin March, *China and Japan in Our Museums* (New York: American Council Institute of Pacific Relations, 1929), 20–21, 86. See also Wilhelm, *American Roots,* 67.

6. For a brief history of Chinese art in the University of Pennsylvania Museum, see Dilys Pegler Winegrad, *Through Time, Across Continents: A Hundred Years of Archaeology and Anthropology at the University Museum* (Philadelphia: University Museum, 1993), 60–68.

7. Ibid., 69.

8. Pound was at Penn in 1901–3 and 1905–7. His dorm on the east of Memorial Tower Arch (1901–3) was only a five-minute walk from the museum. See Emily Mitchell Wallace, "Youthful Days and Costly Hours," in Daniel Hoffman, ed., *Ezra Pound & William Carlos Williams: The University of Pennsylvania Conference Papers* (Philadelphia: Univ. of Pennsylvania Press, 1983), 14–58, especially 18. For a catalogue of the Buddhist Temple, see Maxwell Sommerville, *The Buddhist Temple in the Free Museum of Science and Art* (Philadelphia: Univ. of Pennsylvania, 1904).

9. Pound is cited as stating, "and my gt aunt's third husband / received in ms / from a friend / the 49th canto—," in Mary de Rachewiltz, *I Cantos* (Milan: Mondadori, 1985), 1536. My thanks to Richard Taylor for bringing my attention to this citation.

10. Binyon, who entered the British Museum in 1893, was transferred from the Department of Printed Books to the Department of Prints and Drawings in 1895. See Binyon, *Catalogue of English Drawings in the British Museum,* 4 vols. (London: British Museum, 1898–1907); *William Blake,* vol. 1 (London: Methuen & Co., 1906).

11. On Japonisme and Western art, see two surveys: Siegfried Wichmann, *Japonisme: The Japanese Influence on Western Art Since 1859* (London: Thames and Hudson, 1999); and in the U.S. context, Julia Meech and Gabriel P. Weisberg, *Japonisme Comes to America: The Japanese Impact on the Graphic Arts 1876–1925* (New York: Harry Abrams, 1990). See also Earl Miner, *The Japanese Tradition in British and American Literature* (Princeton, N.J.: Princeton Univ. Press, 1958), 66–96.

12. Pound states in "The Renaissance" (1914), reprinted in *LE,* 215: "The last century rediscovered the middle ages. It is possible that this century may find a new Greece in China."

13. See Binyon, *Guide to an Exhibition of Chinese and Japanese Paintings* (London: British Museum, 1910), hereafter *Guide.*

14. See Sidney Colvin, *Guide to an Exhibition of Chinese and Japanese Paintings* (London: British Museum, 1888).

15. Sidney Colvin, "Department of Prints and Drawings Report Respecting Offers for Purchase, 27 March 1903," BMCA.

16. Ibid.

17. See, for example, Wang Bomin et al., *Zhongguo meishu tongshi* (A history of the fine art of China) (Jinan: Shandong jiaoyu, 1987), 1:60; Wen C. Fong, *Beyond Representation: Chinese Painting and Calligraphy, 8th–14th Century* (New Haven, Conn.: Yale Univ. Press, 1992), 24; Jessica Rawson, *The British Museum Book of Chinese Art* (London: Thames and Hudson, 1993), 104.

18. See Roderick Whitfield and Anne Farrer, *Caves of the Thousand Buddhas: Chinese Art from the Silk Route* (New York: Braziller, 1993), 15.

19. According to Whitfield and Farrer, *Caves of the Thousand Buddhas,* 15, "Stein was allowed to remove scrolls and other material in return for contributions toward the renovation of the temples and the improvement of lodging facilities for visiting pilgrims." See also Marc Aurel Stein, *Serindia: Detailed Report of Explorations in Central Asia and Westernmost China* (1921; reprint, Delhi: Banarsidass, 1980), 2:791–830.

20. The Indian government and the British Museum jointly financed Stein's second expedition (1906–9). The antiquities taken were divided between the British Museum and the Museum of Central Asian Antiquities in New Delhi.

21. According to Whitfield and Farrer, *Caves of the Thousand Buddhas,* 9, the antiquities gathered by Paul Pelliot of France are housed in the Musée Guimet and the Bibliothèque Nationale, Paris; those by Oldenbourg of Russia are in the State Hermitage, Leningrad; those by Otani of Japan are in the Tokyo National Museum, the National Museum of Korea, and at Lushun in China.

22. Guillaume Apollinaire, "Chinese Art: Chinese Raphaels and Rembrandts," in *Apollinaire on Art: Essays and Reviews 1902–1918,* ed. LeRoy C. Breunig (New York: Viking, 1972), 127–29.

23. Ibid., 127–28.

24. On 8 March 1909, Stein gave an account of his explorations to the Royal Geographical Society. See *Times* (London), 9 March 1909, 11. According to Whitfield and Farrer, *Caves of the Thousand Buddhas,* 15, "the bundles acquired by Stein at Dunhuang arrived in London at the National History Museum, South Kensington, in January 1909 and were transferred to the basement of the British Museum in Bloomsbury in August of that year."

25. YCAL-PP, 59:2660.

26. Ezra Pound to Homer Pound, 11 February 1909, YCAL-PP, 59:2659.

27. In a letter to Binyon, 6 March 1934, in *SLEP,* 255, Pound writes: "'Slowness is beauty,' which struck me as very odd in 1908 (when I certainly did not believe it) and has stayed with me ever since."

28. Ernest Fenollosa, *Epochs of Chinese and Japanese Art: An Outline History of East Asiatic Design,* 2 vols. (London: Heinemann, 1912) includes five illustrations from the British Museum. In the foreword to *Epochs,* 1:vi, Mary Fenollosa acknowledges her indebtedness to Binyon.

29. See my *Orientalism and Modernism,* 56–64.

30. Fenollosa went on many lecture tours between 1901 and 1906. In 1903, for example, he gave a course of lectures on "Landscape Poetry and Painting in Medieval China." For the lecture notes, see YCAL-PP, 101:4250–102:4254.

31. Compare Carroll F. Terrell, "The Na-Khi Documents I," *Paideuma* 3.1 (1974): 95; and Woon-ping Chin Holaday, "Pound and Binyon: China via the British Museum," *Paideuma* 6.3 (1977): 29.

32. "Mr. L. Binyon on Chinese Art," *Times* (London), 23 January 1912, 6.

33. Donald Hall, "Ezra Pound," in *Writers at Work: The Paris Review Interviews,* 2nd series, intro. Van Wyck Brooks (New York: Viking, 1963), 47.

34. Olga Rudge on 26 August 1972: "[H]e dreamt: 'of Mrs. Binyon . . . it was said that Queen Victoria had helped her with the twins. . . .' Later in conversation E. said that their birth was announced in London papers as 'To Mr & Mrs Laurence Binyon, twins, prematurely.'(They were born when E. just got to London.)" See "I Ching Notebook: Apr. 72–Nov. 72," YCAL-RP, 93:2490.

35. "Chinese and Japanese Paintings," *Times* (London), 20 June 1910, 8.

36. The Annual Report for 1912, BMCA, shows that the exhibition was removed in April 1912. However, Binyon's 1913 revised *Painting,* 277n, indicates that some

Dunhuang images remained in the British Museum Asiatic Saloon until later than 1913.

37. Pound's drawing of 1899, "The Way Poundie Felt," YCAL-PP, 59:2647, includes an image of a dragon in the Western style. For a reproduction of Dorothy Pound's drawing of a Chinese dragon, see my *Orientalism and Modernism*, 10 (fig. 1).

38. Holaday, "Pound and Binyon," 34–35. On Pound and Guanyin, see Britton Gildersleeve, "'Enigma' at the Heart of Paradise: Buddhism, Kuanon, and the Feminine Ideogram in *The Cantos*," in my *Ezra Pound and China*. For *Standing Guanyin*, see my *Orientalism and Modernism*, 15 (fig. 7).

39. Dorothy Pound's 1901 notebook is in Omar Pound's collection. See *L/DP*, 118.

40. According to Cheadle, *Pound's Confucian Translations*, 222–23, while Dorothy Pound drew "most of the Chinese words through *The Cantos* into the 'Pisan Cantos,'" Willis Hawley supplied "most of the characters for 'Rock-Drill,' 'Thrones,' and 'Drafts and Fragments.'"

41. The Visitors Book, vol. 22, BMPDA.

42. Ezra Pound to Isabel Pound, 11 January 1913, YCAL-PP, 60:2671: "Binyon is back wailing that the Fuller collection (chinese & Jap. art) in Detroit is better than anything they'll ever get here. He ought to know."

43. The Visitors Book, vols. 22 and 23, BMPDA.

44. YCAL-PP, 60:2670.

45. See my *Orientalism and Modernism*, 10–11 (figs. 1–4).

46. Lionel Cust, "A Museum of Oriental Art," *Burlington Magazine* 20.108 (March 1912): 344: "One need only walk down Bond Street and S. James's Street to become aware how assertive in the market have become the wares of the Far East in ceramics and textiles, even in painting and sculpture."

47. The loss of Wadsworth's *Khaki* is mentioned in Richard Cork, *Vorticism and Abstract Art in the First Machine Age* (Los Angeles: Univ. of California Press, 1976), 2:360.

48. Wadsworth's *New Delight* is reproduced in Cork, *Vorticism and Abstract Art*, 2:359.

49. Compare Ezra Pound to Homer Pound, 5 December 1913, YCAL-PP, 60:2672: "If you get Fenollosa's 'Epochs of Chinese and Japanese Art', you'll get some idea of what his work means, & of his unique opportunity."

50. In an essay in *The Great Bronze Age of China*, ed. Wen Fong (New York: Metropolitan Museum of Art, 1980), 35–36, K. C. Chang observes that "the characteristic feature of the Chinese Bronze Age is that the use of that metal was inseparable from ritual and from war." For a recent survey of bronze in ancient China, see Wu Hung, *Monumentality in Early Chinese Art and Architecture* (Stanford, Calif.: Stanford Univ. Press, 1995), 64–72.

51. The bronze drum (fig. 7) entered the British Museum in 1903. The Shanghai Museum keeps similar bronze drums. A note says that theirs, unearthed in Southwest China, were "used in rituals, battles, large gatherings, and burial ceremonies; also served as storage containers and musical instruments."

52. Shang-Zhou bronze objects in the shape of human figures with creatures can

also be found in the Cernuschi Museum, Paris; the Sumitomo Collection, Kyoto; and the Freer Gallery of Art, Washington. See Jessica Rawson, *Chinese Bronzes: Art and Ritual* (London: British Museum, 1987), 71.

TWO. Chinese Art Arrives in America

1. A biographical sketch of Okakura Kakuzō can be found in Jan Fontein, "A Brief History of the Collections," in *Selected Masterpieces of Asian Art: Museum of Fine Arts, Boston* (Boston: Museum of Fine Arts, 1992), 10–11.

2. Quoted in Fontein, "Brief History," 6.

3. The William Sturgis Bigelow Collection and the Fenollosa-Weld Collection both include Chinese paintings. See Wu Tung, *Tales from the Land of Dragons: 1,000 Years of Chinese Painting* (Boston: Museum of Fine Arts, 1997), 171–77 (nos. 48–62), 185 (no. 77), 209 (no. 108), 210 (no. 110), 212 (no. 112), 214 (no. 116), 217 (no. 120), 219 (no. 124), 220 (no. 125), 232 (no. 148).

4. For a biographical sketch of Hayasaki Kōkichi, see Fontein, "Brief History," 10.

5. Ibid, 10.

6. Visits to collections of Far Eastern art in Boston, Detroit, Chicago, and New York are mentioned in Laurence Binyon to Frederick Kenyon, 24 November 1912, BMCA.

7. The handscroll *The Nymph of the Luo River* and the handscroll *Clearing Autumn Skies over Mountains and Valleys* entered the Freer Collection in 1914 and 1916, respectively.

8. Ezra Pound to Homer Pound, 11 January 1913, YCAL-PP, 60:2671.

9. Rapid growth of the Metropolitan Museum Department of Far Eastern Art began in 1914 when S. C. Bosch Reitz was appointed the first curator. See March, *China and Japan in Our Museums*, 80.

10. See "The Subtle Pictorial Art of the Chinese as Shown in the Exquisite Porcelains Brought to America," *New York Times*, 4 April 1909, 6.

11. None of Mi Fu's (1052–1107) original paintings are known to survive. Some of the works formerly attributed to him have been reattributed to his son, Mi Youren (1074–1153).

12. See note 10.

13. Ibid.

14. Ibid.

15. Ibid.

16. George S. Lensing, *Wallace Stevens: A Poet's Growth* (Baton Rouge: Louisiana State Univ. Press, 1986), 87.

17. Robert Buttel, *Wallace Stevens: The Making of Harmonium* (Princeton, N.J.: Princeton Univ. Press), 156. A blunder by Stevens while copying the lists into his journal has led Buttel to assume in *Wallace Stevens*, 70, that "Colors" was inspired by Japanese prints. Compare *L*, 137, and *SP*, 222.

18. Joan Richardson, *Wallace Stevens: The Early Years, 1879–1923* (New York: Morrow, 1988), 337.

19. Arthur Ficke later dispersed his collection of Japanese prints through auction. See Meech and Weisberg, *Japonisme Comes to America*, 165–68.

20. See James Kraft, ed., *The Works of Witter Bynner: Prose Pieces* (New York: Farrar, Straus, Giroux, 1979), 103–13.

21. James Kraft, ed., *The Works of Witter Bynner: Selected Letters* (New York: Farrar, Straus, Giroux, 1981), 163–64.

22. Holly Stevens notes in *L,* 241: "[O]n October 18, 1923, he and his wife sailed from New York on a fifteen-day cruise to California by way of Havana and the Panama Canal, returning overland through New Mexico." Their visit to Bynner in Santa Fe is mentioned in Stevens to Louise Seaman Bechtel, 25 August 1944, in *L,* 471.

23. For an account of Bynner's pink abode, see Bynner to Annie Louise Wellington, 3 October 1924, in Kraft, *The Works of Witter Bynner: Selected Letters,* 111–13.

24. Lucy Monroe Calhoun, sister of Harriet Monroe, sent Stevens various items from Beijing in fall 1922. See *L,* 229–31.

25. In 1920 Bynner was elected president of the Poetry Society of America. Stevens at that point "had given up moving with the New York 'artistic crowd.'" See Richardson, *Wallace Stevens,* 339, 519.

26. Fenollosa visited the Astor Library in late 1900. For his notes taken there on "Nov. 28, '00," see "Chinese Intercourse," vol. 2, YCAL-PP, 99:4216.

27. Okakura Kakuzō, *The Ideals of the East, with Special Reference to the Art of Japan* (London: Murray, 1903), 156, 160.

28. See also *L,* 137–38. The eighth subject, "Evening Snow," is left out in Binyon's *Painting* (1908), 133. In a 1913 revised edition, the omission is corrected.

29. For an earlier version of Wang Anshi's poem, see H. A. Giles, *Gems of Chinese Literature* (1884; reprint, London: Quaritch, 1926), 1:392. Stevens would later acquire Giles's *Gems* (1926). The set is held in the Huntington Library.

30. The MFA Japanese Department, formed in 1890, was renamed Department of Chinese and Japanese Art in 1903. Early editions of *Handbook of the Museum of Fine Arts* (1906: 164–65; 1915: 300) recommend two sets of Chinese works: the ten Buddhist pieces purchased through Fenollosa and the sixteen Buddhist pieces in the Bigelow Collection, indicating that examples were on view.

31. See, for example, "Prince Kung's Collection of Bronzes and Jades at American Art Galleries," *New York Times,* 23 February 1913, sec. 4, 7.

32. On Stevens and the Armory Show, see Glen MacLeod, *Wallace Stevens and Modern Art: From the Armory Show to Abstract Expressionism* (New Haven, Conn.: Yale Univ. Press, 1993), 3, 5–7.

33. According to Richardson, *Wallace Stevens,* 402, Stevens possibly read Stieglitz's *Camera Work,* August 1912 and June 1913, with Gertrude Stein's verbal portraits of Matisse and Picasso.

34. In *Epochs,* 2:12–19, Fenollosa provides extracts from a translation of this treatise by Japanese scholars. For a more recent English version, see Susan Bush and Shih Hsio-yen, eds., *Early Chinese Texts on Painting* (Cambridge: Harvard Univ. Press, 1986), 150–54.

35. On Guo Xi, see Wen Fong et al., *Images of the Mind: Selections from the Edward L. Elliott Family and John B. Elliott Collections of Chinese Calligraphy and Painting at the Art Museum, Princeton University* (Princeton, N.J.: Art Museum, 1984), 47–51.

36. HL-WAS, 1926.

37. Ibid.

38. James Longenbach, *Wallace Stevens: The Plain Sense of Things* (Oxford: Oxford Univ. Press, 1991), 36.

39. Quoted in Moore, "'New' Poetry Since 1912" (1926), reprinted in *PrMM,* 120–21.

40. Bryn Mawr 1908–9 class lists, BMA.

41. Course description from the Bryn Mawr 1908–9 catalogue, BMA.

42. Ibid.

43. Cyrus H. Gordon, *The Pennsylvania Tradition of Semitics: A Century of Near Eastern Biblical Studies at the University of Pennsylvania* (Atlanta: Scholars Press, 1986), 10.

44. George A. Barton (1859–1942), Professor of Semitic Languages at the University of Pennsylvania, 1922–32.

45. Bryn Mawr 1908–9 class lists, BMA.

46. Marianne Moore to her family, 28 March 1909, RML-MMC, VI: 15a: 04.

47. Ibid.

48. Ibid.

49. "A Talisman," *The Lantern* (Bryn Mawr) 20 (spring 1912): 61; reprinted in *BMM,* 171.

50. See, for example, Cornelius Vermeule, *Cameo and Intaglio: Engraved Gems from the Sommerville Collection* (Philadelphia: Univ. of Pennsylvania, 1956), 3 (nos. 16, 20).

51. The minutes of an April 1911 meeting of the Board of the Museum Managers, UPMA, suggest that the Glyptic Collection remained on view along with the Buddhist images until later than April 1911. Within the Glyptic Collection were Near Eastern, Egyptian, classical, postclassical, Asian, Maori, and Mexican gems, amulets, talismans, and seals. The items numbered over four thousand, of which about three hundred were Near Eastern and over one hundred Asian. See Maxwell Sommerville, *Engraved Gems* (Philadelphia: Biddle, 1901) with forty-four illustrations, including one of a Chinese cameo.

52. For a summary of George Barton's career, see Morris Jasrow Jr., "George Aaron Barton: An Appreciation," *Bryn Mawr Alumnae Quarterly,* November 1919, 132–36.

53. Among George Barton's early scholarly works are *Some Contracts of the Persian Period from the KH Collection of the University of Pennsylvania* (Chicago: Univ. of Chicago Press, 1900), *The Roots of Christian Teaching as Found in the Old Testament* (Philadelphia: Winston, 1902), *A Year's Wandering in Bible Lands* (Philadelphia: Ferris and Leach, 1904), and *A Critical and Exegetical Commentary on the Book of Ecclesiastes* (New York: Scribner, 1908).

54. George Barton, *The Religions of the World* (Chicago: Univ. of Chicago Press, 1917), 202–03.

55. Ibid., 219.

56. See ibid., 390–91: "Outline of a Book to be Written by the Student": "Chapter 24: 1) The Animism of the Chinese; 2) Ancestor-Worship in China; 3) The State Religion of China; 4) Confucius and His System; 5) Mencius and the State Religion. Chapter 25: 1) The Taoism of Lao-tze [Laozi]; 2) The Taoism of Kwang-tze [Guanzi];

3) The Degeneracy of Taoism; 4) The Introduction of Buddhism into China; 5) The History and Character of Chinese Buddhism; 6) Popular Religion in China."

57. See Mary Norcross to Marianne Moore, 19 January 1908, RML-MMC, VI: 14: 02. I wish to thank Patricia Willis and Linda Leavell for bringing the letter to my attention.

58. See Anthony Griffiths and Reginald Williams, *The Department of Prints and Drawings in the British Museum: User's Guide* (London: British Museum, 1987), 3.

59. "Chinese and Japanese Paintings," *Times* (London), 20 June 1910, 8.

60. Ibid.

61. Linda Leavell, *Marianne Moore and the Visual Arts* (Baton Rouge: Louisiana State Univ. Press, 1995), 10.

62. Marianne Moore to John Warner Moore, 30 July 1911, in *Marianne Moore Newsletter* 6 (spring/fall 1982): 22. Mrs. Moore's letters of 27, 29, and 31 July 1911, while indicating separate tours of the British Museum, provide no details.

63. Apollinaire, "Chinese Art," 128.

64. See note 62.

65. Annette Cottrell, ed., *Dragons* (Boston: Museum of Fine Arts, 1962); Robert Treat Paine Jr., ed., *Animals in Paintings from Asia* (Boston: Museum of Fine Arts, 1956; reprint, 1965).

66. Winegrad, *Through Time,* 61–63.

67. For Sheeler's photograph of the 1916 Chinese art show, see Winegrad, *Through Time,* 63. For Sheeler's photographs of modern art in the Arensberg apartment, see MacLeod, *Stevens and Modern Art,* 12–15.

68. Howard Mansfield (1849–1938) served as both trustee and treasurer of the Metropolitan Museum of Art and acted as its de facto curator of Far Eastern art until 1914.

69. See "Fine Examples of Early Chinese Painting: Art at Home and Abroad," *New York Times,* 5 March 1916, sec. 6, 14.

70. Ibid.

71. Ibid.

72. See "A Collection of Antique Chinese Objects," *New York Times,* 9 March 1918, 12; "An Exhibition of Ancient Paintings by the Chinese," *New York Times,* 21 March 1918, 12; "Chinese Art Sale Brings $9,116," *New York Times,* 31 March 1918, sec. 1, 15.

73. See "Old Chinese Paintings," *New York Times,* 9 April 1918, 10; "New Installations of Chinese Ceramics: Art at Home and Abroad," *New York Times,* 18 August 1918, sec. 6, 14.

74. See "November Exhibitions in Great Variety: Art at Home and Abroad," *New York Times,* 17 November 1918, sec. 4, 4; "Old Kakemonos on View," *New York Times,* 14 December 1918, 9.

75. See "November Exhibition in Great Variety," *New York Times,* 17 November 1918, sec. 4, 4. The review covers both the exhibition of Chinese portraits and potteries at the Montross Gallery and the exhibition of American modernist paintings at the Bourgeois Galleries. It speaks of American modernists' "attempt to reconcile the civilizations of the East and the West by using the modern Western tradition in rendering Eastern subjects."

76. Richardson, *Wallace Stevens,* 454.

77. Yve-Alain Bois speaks of Picasso transforming "his painting into a kind of writing," in Bois and Rosalind E. Krauss, *Formless: A User's Guide* (New York: Zone Books, 1997), 27. See also Yve-Alain Bois, "The Semiology of Cubism," in *Picasso and Braque: A Symposium,* ed. William Rubin and Lynn Zelevansky (New York: Museum of Modern Art, 1992), 169–208, particularly 186–87.

78. Stevens read a different version of Guo Xi's dictum in an August 1911 newspaper.

79. Earl Miner, *The Japanese Tradition in British and American Literature* (Princeton, N.J.: Princeton Univ. Press, 1958), 194.

80. Jeanne Heuving, *Omissions Are Not Accidents: Gender in the Art of Marianne Moore* (Detroit: Wayne State Univ. Press, 1992), 83.

81. William Carlos Williams, *Selected Essays of William Carlos Williams* (New York: New Directions, 1952), 30–31.

82. See "Chinese Paintings Shown in Museum," *New York Times,* 10 March 1923, 12.

83. According to Stamy, *Moore and China,* 136, Moore's library holds *Metropolitan Museum of Art Bulletin* (Dec. 1919) entitled "The Treasure of Luhan [Luohan]," Bourgeois Gallery pamphlet for an exhibition of early Chinese paintings and sculptures (Nov.-Dec. 1922), and many other books and catalogues on Chinese art.

84. Marianne Moore to family, 28 March 1909, RML-MMC, VI: 15a: 04.

85. On the Arts and Crafts movement, see Leavell, *Moore and the Visual Arts,* 15–16, 138–39.

86. Bernard Engel, *Marianne Moore* (Boston: Twayne, 1989), 4.

87. Similarly, in a 1933 review, reprinted in *PrMM,* 292, Moore identifies "An element of the Chinese taste" in Emily Dickinson's "choiceness."

88. Arthur Waley, *An Introduction to the Study of Chinese Painting* (New York: Grove, 1923), 242.

THREE. Pound and Pictures of Confucian Ideals

1. Ezra Pound to Homer Pound, 22 September 1915, YCAL-PP, 60:2678.

2. On Pound's familiarity with Allen Upward's "Sayings of K'ung the Master" in *The New Freewoman,* November and December 1913, see Philip Grover, preface to his *Ezra Pound: The London Years, 1908–1920* (New York: AMS Press, 1978). Although Pound received Fenollosa's notebooks in December 1913, he did not give attention to the Chinese poetry notes until November 1914.

3. Mitchell, *Picture Theory,* 2, 159–60.

4. Zhang Hua (A.D. 232–300), poet and court official. His 334-character tract is also entitled the *Admonitions of the Instructress to Court Ladies (Nushi jian).*

5. Ban Zhao (ca. A.D. 49–ca. 120), sister of the Han historian Ban Gu (A.D. 32–92). After Ban Gu's death she put together his unfinished *History of Han.* Because of her great learning, Emperor He of Han (r. A.D. 89–105) made her tutor of his empress and palace ladies.

6. Lady Feng, a concubine of Emperor Yuan of Han (r. 48–33 B.C.), became grand empress dowager during the reign of her grandson, Emperor Ai (6–2 B.C.).

7. See Bush and Shih, *Early Chinese Texts,* 20, 33–34.

8. Walter Benjamin, "The Work of Art in the Age of Mechanical Reproduction," in *Illuminations,* ed. Hannah Arendt, trans. Harry Zohn (New York: Schocken, 1968), 238.

9. Martin Heidegger, "The Origin of the Work of Art," in *Poetry, Language, Thought,* trans. Albert Hofstadter (New York: Harper and Row, 1971), 68. Gianni Vattimo, "Art and Oscillation," in *The Transparent Society,* trans. David Webb (Baltimore: Johns Hopkins Univ. Press, 1992), 51.

10. See note 7.

11. J. Hillis Miller, *Illustration* (Cambridge: Harvard Univ. Press, 1992), 27.

12. Arthur Waley, in *Study of Chinese Painting,* 50, renders the passage as "Lady Pan refuses to ride with the Emperor Ch'eng (32–5 B.C.) in his litter, 'lest she should distract his thoughts from affairs of state.'"

13. According to Binyon, *Guide,* 14–15, the other four surviving panels of the *Admonitions* are: "The mutability of fortune"; "A sage reproving a lady of the harem"; "A lady seated in meditation"; and "Two ladies of the harem and the instructress."

14. See my *Orientalism and Modernism,* 23–25.

15. H. A. Giles, *A History of Chinese Literature* (New York: Appleton, 1901), 100.

16. Ban Jieyu, sometime favorite of Emperor Cheng of Han (r. 32–36 B.C.), was the great-aunt of Ban Zhao, the historian and palace tutor.

17. For H. A. Giles's version, see Giles, *History of Chinese Literature,* 101.

18. Wai-lim Yip, *Ezra Pound's Cathay* (Princeton, N.J.: Princeton Univ. Press, 1969), 93.

19. Qian, *Orientalism and Modernism,* 85.

20. Quoted in ibid., 69.

21. For a reproduction of the illustration for "Taking Leave of a Friend" from *Tang shi san bai shou* (Three hundred poems of the Tang) (Dalian: Dalian, 1992), see my *Orientalism and Modernism,* 70 (fig. 14).

22. For a reproduction of Zhu Bang's *The Forbidden City,* see ibid., 11 (fig. 4).

23. Martin C. Powers, *Art and Political Expression in Early China* (New Haven, Conn.: Yale Univ. Press, 1991), 43, 188.

24. Wu Hung identifies further traits of the genre (what he terms "feminine space") in *The Double Screen: Medium and Representation in Chinese Painting* (Chicago: Univ. of Chicago Press, 1996), 211–12: "In each case not only is a woman presented as the subject of the male gaze, but she belongs to (and dissolves into) a feminized landscape, in which flowers and plants reflect her radiance and luxury, and mirrors and screens reveal her loneliness and sorrow."

25. Hugh Kenner, *The Pound Era* (Berkeley and Los Angeles: Univ. of California Press, 1971), 194.

26. Ibid., 193.

27. For a transcript of Fenollosa's notes for the untitled poem, see ibid., 193.

28. Rey Chow, *Primitive Passion: Visuality, Sexuality, Ethnography and Contemporary Chinese Cinema* (New York: Columbia Univ. Press, 1995), 68.

29. Qian, *Orientalism and Modernism,* 76–82.

30. For a transcript of Fenollosa's notes for "The River-Merchant's Wife," see

Sanehide Kodama, *American Poetry and Japanese Culture* (Hamden: Archon Books, 1984), 80–84. For the Chinese text and a word-for-word translation by Wai-lim Yip, see my *Orientalism and Modernism,* 78–79.

31. Ronald Bush, "Pound and Li Po: What Becomes a Man," in *Ezra Pound among Poets,* ed. George Bornstein (Chicago: Univ. of Chicago Press, 1985), 35–62; here 42.

32. Fenollosa renders the last four lines as: "If you be coming down as far as the Three Narrows sooner or later, / Please let me know by writing / For I will go out to meet, not saying that the way be far. / And will directly come to Chofusha." See Kodama, *American Poetry and Japanese Culture,* 84.

33. See note 31.

34. Pound was evidently reading M. G. Pauthier, *Doctrine de Confucius: Les quatre livres de philosophie morale et politique de la Chine* (1852; reprint, Paris: Librairie Garnier Frères, 1910) in 1915–16. Two lines in "Three Cantos," in *P,* 233, echo Pauthier, 75, and anticipate Canto 13, in *C,* 59.

35. Carroll F. Terrell gives credit to David Gordon for locating the lines Pound relied on. See Terrell, *A Companion to the Cantos of Ezra Pound* (Berkeley and Los Angeles: Univ. of California, 1980), 60.

36. See ibid., 61, 64.

37. Cheadle, *Pound's Confucian Translations,* 16.

38. Ibid., 20.

39. See Pauthier, *Les quatre livres,* 142 ("Le Lun-Yu" 11.25); cf. Pound, *Con,* 243.

40. Cheadle, *Pound's Confucian Translations,* 21.

41. The line echoes Pauthier, *Les quatre livres,* 75 ("Le Lun-Yu" 1.2.): "*La piété filiale, la déférence fraternelle, dont nous avons parlé, ne sont-elles pas le principe fondamental de l'humanité ou de la bienveillance universelle pour les hommes?*" However, "order" is not mentioned; cf. Pound, *Con,* 195.

42. Where Pauthier's Tseu-lou states, "*je pourrais faire en sorte que le peuple de ce royaume reprit un courage viril,*" Pound has him say, "I would put the defences in order." Where Pauthier's Khieu responds, "*soit préposé à son administration, en moins de trois ans je pourrais faire en sorte que le peuple eût le suffisant,*" he has him reply, "I would put it in better order than this is." Where Pauthier's Tchi observes, "*Lorsque se font les cérémonies du temple des ancêtres, et qu'ont lieu de grandes assemblées publiques, revêtu de ma robe d'azur et des autres vêtements propres à un tel lieu et à de telles cérémonies, je voudrais y prendre part en qualité d'humble fonctionnaire,*" he has him remark, "With order in the observances." See Pauthier, *Les quatre livres,* 140–41; Pound, *C,* 58; cf. Pound, *Con,* 242.

43. For the Chinese text, see Pound, *Con,* 28, 30.

44. *Ta Hio* (Seattle: Univ. of Washington Book Store, 1928) was based on Pauthier, *Les quatre livres,* 1–26.

45. According to Cheadle, *Pound's Confucian Translations,* 59, *The Great Digest* and *The Unwobbling Pivot* were "based on the Chinese texts and on two 'cribs': Pauthier's translation in part but primarily the nineteenth-century English translations of James Legge."

46. See John Nolde, *Blossoms from the East: The China Cantos of Ezra Pound* (Orono: National Poetry Foundation, 1983), 25–27.

47. See ibid., 106.

48. Ibid., 122.

49. For de Mailla's French version of the tale and an English translation, see ibid.

50. Ibid.

51. Compare *Ta Hio,* 8, where the Confucian concern for verbal precision is absent: "those who desired this rectitude of spirit, tried first to make their intentions pure and sincere; those who desired to render their intentions pure and sincere, attempted first to perfect their moral intelligence; the making as perfect as possible, that is, the giving fullest scope to the moral intelligence (or the acquaintance with morals) consists in penetrating and getting to the bottom of the principles (motivations) of actions."

FOUR. The Eternal Dao

1. See Cynthia Stamy, *Moore and China,* 31, 41.

2. On Gu Kaizhi's attachment to "transmitting spirit beyond likeness," see Li Zehou, *The Path of Beauty: A Study of Chinese Aesthetics,* trans. Gong Lizeng (New York: Oxford Univ. Press, 1994), 93–94.

3. Nan Huaijin, *Zhongguo daojiao fazhan shilue* (A history of Daoism in China) (Shanghai: Fudan Univ. Press, 1996), 1. Nan traces the Dao to the prehistoric culture of the Yellow Emperor, ca. 4000 B.C.

4. Kenner states in *Pound Era,* 456, that the term "Dao" is mentioned "some 80 times in the *Analects.*"

5. Man-ho Kwok, Martin Palmer, and Jay Ramsay, trans., *Illustrated Tao Te Ching* (New York: Barnes and Noble, 1993), 27.

6. Wu Tung, *Tales,* 13.

7. For Su Shi (1037–1101), a Song thinker and poet, art is a means of achieving the Dao. On the influence of this notion, see Wen Fong, *Beyond Representation,* 122.

8. The British Museum keeps two scenes from Yunqiao Zhuren's *Eight Views,* the other being the "Snowy Evening" (fig. 5).

9. See Jean Hagstrum, *The Sister Arts: The Tradition of Literary Pictorialism and English Poetry from Dryden to Gray* (Chicago: Univ. of Chicago Press), 10, 58. On the "twin sister arts," see Qian Zhongshu, *Zhongguo shi yu zhongguo hua* (Chinese poetry and Chinese painting), in *Qian Zhongshu lunxue wenxuan,* ed. Shu Zhan (Guangzhou: Huacheng, 1990), 6:5.

10. Qian Zhongshu, *Zhongguo shi yu zhongguo hua,* 6:5.

11. Su Shi: "When one savors Wang Wei's poems, there are paintings in them; / When one looks at Wang Wei's pictures, there are poems." See Bush and Shih, *Early Chinese Texts,* 203.

12. See Binyon, *Painting,* 75–76.

13. Long handscrolls are unrolled from right to left to reveal an arm's length at a time. On how to view a long handscroll painting, see Wu Hung, *Double Screen,* 57–59.

14. For English versions of "Wangchuan Villa" and "Farm Field Pleasure," see Pauline Yu, *The Poetry of Wang Wei: New Translations and Commentary* (Bloomington: Indiana Univ. Press, 1980), 197–99, 201–05.

15. YCAL-PP, 99:4220.

16. Quoted in my *Orientalism and Modernism,* 174.

17. The third of "Nine Poems," in *Little Review* 5.7 (November 1918): 2.

18. The term "observing things in terms of things" (*yi wu guan wu*) is taken from Shao Yong (1011–77), who argues in "On the Observation of Things" (*Guan wu pian*) that things should be observed "in the light of their own Principle" rather than "with the eye." "Forgetting self" is also taken from Shao Yong's *Guan wu pian*. According to Shao, to attain a state in which, to quote Laozi, "he does nothing, yet there is nothing that is not done," one must "forget self" and "give free play to other creatures." See Fung Yu-lan, *A History of Chinese Philosophy*, trans. Derk Bodde (Princeton, N.J.: Princeton Univ. Press, 1952–53), 2:466, 467.

19. Kenner, *Pound Era*, 456.

20. Moore to Pound, 9 January 1919, in *SLMM*, 123: "I have no Greek, unless a love for it may be taken as a knowledge of it and I have not read very voraciously in French; I do not know [René] Ghil and [Jules] Laforgue and know of no tangible French influence on my work."

21. Quoted in Patricia Willis, *Marianne Moore: Vision into Verse* (Philadelphia: Rosenbach Museum and Library, 1987), 34.

22. "Chinese and Japanese Paintings," *Times* (London), 20 June 1910, 8.

23. "The World of Art," *New York Times*, 11 March 1923, sec. 4, 12.

24. *The New York Times* photograph, "Water Buffalo from Eastern Asia" (24 April 1932), is reproduced in Willis, *Marianne Moore*, 53. The Met Annual Report indicates that the exhibition was held from 9 March through 22 April 1923.

25. Andrew M. Lakritz, *Modernism and the Other in Stevens, Frost, and Moore* (Gainseville: Univ. Press of Florida, 1996), 123–24.

26. Leavell, *Moore and the Visual Arts*, 155.

27. Ibid., according to Leavell, "Black Earth" can be read either as "about Philip Melanchthon, the Reformation leader" or as about "a literal elephant."

28. "Landscape Poetry and Painting in Medieval China," YCAL-PP, 101: 4250–102: 4254. Omar Pound confirmed on 25 November 1999 that the additional autographed copy in PP, 102:4254 "is DP's hand."

29. Giles, *History of Chinese Literature*, 63. Compare Burton Watson, trans., *Chuang Tzu: Basic Writings* (New York: Columbia Univ. Press, 1996), 45.

30. For Fenollosa's notes for Li Bo's "No. 9 of Ancient Airs," see "Rihaku" notebook, vol. 2, YCAL-PP, 101:4236.

31. Frank Kermode, ed., *Selected Prose of T. S. Eliot* (New York: Farrar, Straus, Giroux, 1975), 40.

32. Sanford Schwartz, *The Matrix of Modernism: Pound, Eliot, and Early Twentieth-Century Thought* (Princeton, N.J.: Princeton Univ. Press, 1985), 67.

33. See Heuving, *Omissions*, 31; Cristanne Miller, *Marianne Moore: Questions of Authority* (Cambridge: Harvard Univ. Press, 1995), 28. For Heuving, Moore's speakers "are not concerned with constructing an identity through others, but rather with encountering the otherness of others." For Miller, Moore's poetry is "both personal and impersonal," "apparently impersonal and transparently personal."

34. Yu, *Poetry of Wang Wei*, 26.

35. Qian, *Orientalism and Modernism*, 84–85.

36. C. Miller, *Marianne Moore*, 34.

37. Ibid., 34–35; Leavell, 73–74.

38. C. Miller, *Marianne Moore*, 35.

39. John Gould Fletcher, *Life Is My Song: The Autobiography of John Gould Fletcher* (New York: Farrar and Rinehart, 1937), 79.

40. On the "Southern School of Landscape," see Qian Zhongshu, *Zhongguo shi yu zhongguo hua*, 6:7–13.

41. See Wen Fong, *Beyond Representation*, 58; Binyon, *Painting*, 75.

42. Du Mu's poem on Wang Wei echoes an episode from Zhuangzi. When asked how he was able to cut up an ox with marvelous skill, Cook Ding relied: "When I first began cutting up oxen, all I could see was the ox itself. After three years I no longer saw the whole ox. And now—now I go at it by spirit and don't look with my eyes." See Watson, *Chuang Tzu*, 46–47.

43. Notebook 1250/2 (1916–21), RML-MMC, VII: 02: 02, shows that preparatory work on "The Jerboa" and "The Buffalo" began in 1920. See also Laurence Stapleton, *Marianne Moore: The Poet's Advance* (Princeton, N.J.: Princeton Univ. Press, 1978), 69, 75.

44. On Pound's effort to translate Wang Wei, see my *Orientalism and Modernism*, 100–05.

45. Christine Froula, *To Write Paradise: Style and Error in Pound's Cantos* (New Haven, Conn.: Yale Univ. Press, 1984), 40–41.

46. Qian, *Orientalism and Modernism*, 97–109.

47. Kenner, *Pound Era*, 456.

48. Reed Way Dasenbrock, *The Literary Vorticism of Ezra Pound and Wyndham Lewis: Towards the Condition of Painting* (Baltimore: Johns Hopkins Univ. Press, 1985), 220.

49. Li Zehou, *Path of Beauty*, 49.

50. Wen Fong, *Beyond Representation*, 40, 75.

51. Kenner, *Pound Era*, 456.

52. Ibid., 284.

53. Wen Fong, *Beyond Representation*, 363.

54. Binyon in *Painting*, 57, refers to philosophical Daoism as "the pure authentic doctrine of [Laozi]," and occult Daoism as "that popular cult which is chiefly associated with magic rites and exorcisms, and especially with the chimerical pursuit of the elixir of immortality." "Mr. Okakura has proposed the name Laoism," he also notes, "as a conveniently distinctive title for the yet uncorrupted teaching of Lao Tzŭ [Laozi]."

55. Quoted in William McNaughton, "A Report on the 16th Biennial International Conference on Ezra Pound, Brantôme, France: 18–22 July, 1995," *Paideuma* 27.1 (1998), 130. For an account of McNaughton's visits to St. Elizabeths, see McNaughton, "Pound, a Brief Memoir: 'Chi Lavora, Ora," *Paideuma* 3.3 (1974), 319.

FIVE. Stevens and Chan Art

1. Robert Aitken, "Wallace Stevens and Zen," *Wallace Stevens Journal* 6 (fall 1982): 69–73; Robert Tompkins, "Stevens and Zen: The Boundless Reality of the Imagination," *Wallace Stevens Journal* 9 (spring 1985): 26–39.

2. On the problematic origin of Chan, see Bernard Faure, *The Rhetoric of Immediacy: A Cultural Critique of Chan/Zen Buddhism* (Princeton, N.J.: Princeton Univ.

Press, 1991), 12–31, especially 28. For Faure, "the Chan tradition is a fictional remembering of origins, that is, an active forgetting of the fact that there never was any pure origin."

3. See chapter 6, note 4.

4. Fenollosa made his first trip to Japan in 1878 for an appointment as Professor of Political Economy and Philosophy at the Tokyo Imperial University. Bigelow traveled to Japan in 1882, where he stayed until 1889. See Fontein, "Brief History," 8–10.

5. Both Fenollosa and Bigelow studied Tendai Buddhism in Japan in the mid-1880s and both became Buddhists of the Tendai sect before their return to America. See Lawrence W. Chisolm, *Fenollosa: The Far East and American Culture* (New Haven, Conn.: Yale Univ. Press, 1963), 106–11.

6. According to *Epochs*, 1:xviii, Fenollosa sold his collection to Charles Goddard Weld in 1886 "under the condition that it was to remain permanently in the Boston Museum of Fine Arts, and have the name Fenollosa attached to it." The Fenollosa-Weld Collection and the Bigelow Collection entered the MFA in 1889 though they were not accessioned until 1911.

7. Bevis states in *Mind of Winter*, 188: "Harvard's first Asian studies course had been initiated by Professor Charles C. Everett in 1891: 'Comparative History of Religions, particularly the Vedic Religion, the Hindu philosophies, Buddhism, Mazdaism, and the Chinese Religions.'"

8. For a list of the exhibitions organized by Fenollosa in 1892–95, see Chisolm, *Fenollosa*, 91–93.

9. See Ernest Fenollosa, *A Special Exhibition of Ancient Chinese Buddhist Paintings, Lent by the Temple Daitokuji of Kioko, Japan* (Boston: Alfred Mudge and Son, 1894). For commentaries on and reproductions of the ten Buddhist paintings acquired by the MFA, see Wu Tung, *Tales*, 160–67.

10. Quoted in Fontein, "Brief History," 9.

11. Kojiro Tomita notes that the set "was taken to Japan in the thirteenth century and was deposited at the temple Jufukuji at Kamakura. Subsequently it was transferred to Sōun-ji in Hakone. . . . Again the set was removed . . . in 1590 to Kyoto. . . . Later the paintings became the property of Daitokuji in the same city." See Wu Tung, *Tales*, 160.

12. For reproductions of the two Buddhist paintings acquired by Charles Freer, see Wen C. Fong, *The Lohans and a Bridge to Heaven* (Washington, D.C.: Smithsonian Institution, 1958), 61–62.

13. See chapter 2, note 30.

14. Bernard Faure, "The Buddhist Icon and the Modern Gaze," *Critical Inquiry* 24.3 (1998): 768–813; here 812.

15. Daisetsu T. Suzuki, *Zen and Japanese Culture* (1959; reprint, Princeton, N.J.: Princeton Univ. Press, 1970), 6.

16. Fenollosa, *Special Exhibition*, 17–18.

17. Wu Tung, *Tales*, 165. Wu Tung's account is based on a 1341 text by Monk Nianchang, *Fozu tongzai, juan* 9.

18. Bevis, *Mind of Winter*, 104. On Middle Way Buddhism, see ibid., 60. Middle Way Buddhism gave rise to Chan.

19. Ibid., 209.

20. Ibid., 12.

21. Ibid., 178. As I was finalizing this text, Bevis's new essay came to my attention. See Bevis, "Stevens, Buddhism, and the Meditative Mind," *The Wallace Stevens Journal* 25.2 (fall 2001), 148–63, especially 148, where he acknowledges that "Wallace Stevens' relation to Buddhism raises questions not only of his knowledge of Eastern culture, derived mostly from books and prints, but more importantly of consciousness."

22. Fenollosa, *Special Exhibition*, 7–8. According to the *Handbook of Museum of Fine Arts* (1911), 351–52, the 1894 catalogue remained obtainable "by inquiry at the door" in 1911.

23. John Gould Fletcher, "The Secret of Far Eastern Painting," January 1917; reprinted in *Selected Essays of John Gould Fletcher*, ed. Lucas Carpenter (Fayetteville: Univ. of Arkansas Press, 1989), 221–28; here 222. In an article of 1945 reprinted in *Selected Essays*, 57, Fletcher states: "I had been familiar with some of the great products of Chinese pictorial and sculptural art since the days when I, as an undergraduate at Harvard [1902–7], had first walked into the Oriental Wing of the Boston Museum of Fine Arts, and had looked at the treasures magnificently displayed there."

24. Bevis, *Mind of Winter*, 178.

25. Arthur Waley, *Zen Buddhism and Its Relation to Art* (London: Luzac, 1922); Daisetsu Suzuki, *Essays in Zen Buddhism*, 3 vols. (1926–34; reprint, London: Rider, 1953).

26. Chan art is discussed in Fenollosa, *Epochs*, 2:1–110. Among its illustrations are Liang Kai, *Śākyamuni;* Muqi, *Luohan with a Snake;* and two episodes from Zhou Jichang and Lin Tinggui, *One Hundred Luohans.* Stevens could have read *Epochs* in New York in 1912–16.

27. Okakura, *Ideals of the East*, 160–61, 164.

28. The newspaper clipping enclosed in Stevens's letter of 20 August 1911 to his wife (HL-WAS, 1926).

29. Stevens to Miner, 30 November 1950, UCLA, Special Collections, 821:1.

30. See Buttel, *Wallace Stevens*, 64–74; A. Walton Litz, *Introspective Voyager: The Poetic Development of Wallace Stevens* (New York: Oxford Univ. Press, 1972), 14–20.

31. Miner, *Japanese Tradition*, 194.

32. Wendy Steiner, *The Colors of Rhetoric: Problems in the Relation between Modern Literature and Painting* (Chicago: Univ. of Chicago Press, 1982), 180.

33. Hisamatsu Shin'ichi, *Zen and the Fine Arts*, trans. Gishin Tokiwa (Tokyo: Kodansha, 1971), 30; hereafter *Zen.*

34. *White Heron, Winter Forest,* and *Winter Riverscape* entered the MFA in 1889, 1914, and 1917, respectively. See Wu Tung, *Tales*, 257, 155, 222. By 1915, according to the *Handbook of Museum of Fine Arts* (1915), front endpaper, 274, 298, the MFA had opened two galleries for its limited number of Chinese paintings. In addition, new arrivals would first go to a gallery where "Objects recently acquired in all the departments are shown."

35. Litz, *Introspective Voyager*, 65.

36. Helen Vendler, *On Extended Wings: Wallace Stevens' Longer Poems* (Cambridge: Harvard Univ. Press, 1969), 75.

37. Suzuki states in *Zen and Japanese Culture*, 28: "All these emanate from one central perception of the truth of Zen, which is 'the One in the Many and the Many

in the One,' or better, 'the One remaining as one in the Many individually and collectively.'"

38. Bevis, *Mind of Winter,* 62–63.

39. Quoted in ibid., 62.

40. This parallel has been noted by Harold Bloom in *Wallace Stevens: The Poems of Our Climate* (Ithaca, N.Y.: Cornell Univ. Press, 1976), 61.

41. Aitken, "Wallace Stevens and Zen," 72.

42. Ibid., Aitken states: Stevens is "one of the very few great poets who will be a source of endless inspiration for future generations of Western Zen teachers."

43. Samuel Beal, *Buddhism in China* (London: Society for Promoting Christian Knowledge, 1884), 199.

44. Ibid., 215.

45. Ibid., 82–83.

46. Quoted in Peter Brazeau, *Parts of a World: Wallace Stevens Remembered* (New York: Random House, 1983), 137.

SIX. Stevens's "Six Significant Landscapes"

1. Mitchell, *Picture Theory,* 166. On ekphrasis, see also Marray Krieger, *Ekphrasis: The Illusion of the Natural Sign* (Baltimore: Johns Hopkins Univ. Press, 1992); James Heffernan, *Museum of Words: The Poetics of Ekphrasis from Homer to Ashbery* (Chicago: Univ. of Chicago Press, 1993); Wendy Steiner, *Colors of Rhetoric,* 41–43.

2. Mitchell, *Picture Theory,* 156.

3. Litz, *Introspective Voyager,* 39–40.

4. Following the fall of the (Northern) Song capital, Kaifeng, to the Jin, Emperor Huizong's ninth son, Prince Kang, fled south and reestablished the Song court at Hangzhou in South China, proclaiming himself Emperor Gaozong (r. 1127–62). The new regime, the Southern Song, lasted until 1279, when it was annexed by the Mongols.

5. Li Zehou, *Path of Beauty,* 192. Mitchell's claim in *Landscape and Power,* 9, that landscape as an independent genre of painting "flourished most notably at the height of Chinese imperial power" becomes questionable in the face of this historical evidence.

6. On the "Ma-Xia school" of painting, see Li Zehou, *Path of Beauty,* 191–94; Wu Tung, *Tales,* 32–33.

7. Suzuki, *Zen and Japanese Culture,* 22.

8. Man-ho Kwok et al., *Illustrated Tao Te Ching,* 41, 93.

9. See Richard M. Barnhart, *Along the Border of Heaven: Sung and Yuan Paintings from the C. C. Wang Family Collection* (New York: Metropolitan Museum of Art, 1983), 82.

10. For the *Sixteen Luohans* in the Bigelow Collection, see Wu Tung, *Tales,* 170–77. The *Sixteen Luohans* and the ten Buddhist pieces purchased through Fenollosa are referred to as the backbone of the MFA Chinese art in the 1906 and 1915 editions of *Handbook of the Museum of Fine Arts,* 164–65; 300. *The Luohan Fanaposi* is reproduced in the 1915 *Handbook.*

11. The attribution to Huizong is questionable. Compare Ma Yuan's *Scholar View-*

ing the Moon in the Mokichi Okada Association Museum, Japan, reproduced in Kei Suzuki, *Comprehensive Illustrated Catalog of Chinese Paintings* (Tokyo: Univ. of Tokyo Press, 1982), 3:349 (JM 28–003).

12. Fenollosa states in *Epochs*, 2:44, that Xia Gui "quotes [these] as a poem especially liked by a painter."

13. Man-ho Kwok et al., *Illustrated Tao Te Ching*, 37.

14. According to the Met archival records, this handscroll was purchased from V. G. Simhovitch of New York in 1923. For a review of an exhibition of the Simhovitch Collection, see "An Exhibition of Ancient Paintings by the Chinese," *New York Times*, 21 March 1918, 12.

15. A "memory-picture," according to Heffernan, *Museum of Words*, 98, refers to "a place at which—if not in which—the poet has stored idealized images of sea and sky."

16. *Scholar with Attendants under a Tree* (Denman Waldo Ross Collection 08.61) is reproduced in Wu Tung, *Tales*, 252. *Landscape* by Bunsei is reproduced in the 1906 *Handbook of the Museum of Fine Arts*, 173.

17. In his 1917 article, reprinted in *Selected Essays*, 226, Fletcher states: "When Ma Yuan in one of his landscapes gives us a fisherman's hut, a few sprays of bamboo, and the outlines of immense distant mountains, the subject matters very little, the treatment becomes everything."

18. Xia Gui's *Landscape* and Tan Song's *Landscape in the Style of Guo Xi* are reproduced in Kei Suzuki, *Comprehensive Illustrated Catalog*, 1:19 (A 1–101), 12 (A 1–049).

19. *Pines and Rocky Peaks* in the collection of Yanosuke Iwasaki, Tokyo, is reproduced in Binyon, *Painting*, 130.

20. For Wang Anshi's original poem, *Ye zhi* (On night duty), see *Linchuan ji* (Works of Linchuan [Wang Anshi]) (Taibei: Zhonghua shuju, 1970), 2:31. See also chapter 2, note 29.

21. Litz, *Introspective Voyager*, 30.

22. Bevis, *Mind of Winter*, 7, 240.

SEVEN. Moore and Ming-Qing Porcelain

1. See Richmond Lattimore, trans., *The Iliad of Homer* (Chicago: Univ. of Chicago Press, 1951), 388–91 (Book 18, lines 478–607).

2. Mitchell, *Picture Theory*, 178.

3. On the circular quality of ekphrasis, see Leo Spitzer, *Essays on English and American Literature*, ed. Anna Hatcher (Princeton, N.J.: Princeton Univ. Press, 1962), 73.

4. Heffernan, *Museum of Words*, 19.

5. Krieger, *Ekphrasis*, 18.

6. Heffernan, *Museum of Words*, 109.

7. Stapleton, *Marianne Moore*, 77.

8. For accounts of the Jingdezhen imperial factory, see Michel Beurdeley and Guy Raindre, *Qing Porcelain: Famille Verte, Famille Rose 1644–1912*, trans. Charlotte Chesney (New York: Rizzoli, 1987), 30–40; Jean McClure Mudge, *Chinese Export Porcelain: For the American Trade 1785–1835* (Newark: Univ. of Delaware Press, 1981), 67–78.

9. In 1611 Shah Abbas the Great of Persia presented to the dynastic shrine at Ardebil 1,162 Chinese porcelain pieces, of which "805 remain today." See John Pope, *Chinese Porcelains from the Ardebil Shrine* (London: Bernet, 1981), 8–10, 49.

10. Plate 90 in Pope, *Chinese Porcelains* (Ardebil 29.150). Other objects with the peach illustrated in Pope include plates 40 (29.62) and 52 (29.479).

11. Plate 99 in Pope, *Chinese Porcelains* (Ardebil 29.423, 29.424). Other objects with the *qilin* illustrated in Pope include plates 26 (29.522), 71 (29.137), 73 (29.142), 89 (29.314), 117 (29.764).

12. In 1780 Zang Yingxuan was appointed director of the Jingdezhen imperial factory. The appointment gave an impetus to porcelain production. See Lu Minghua, *Qing chu Jingdezhen ciqi gaishu* (Early Qing Jingdezhen porcelain) in *Qingdai ciqi jianshang* (A study of Qing porcelain), ed. Qian Zhengzong (Shanghai: Shanghai kexue jishu, 1995), 14–15.

13. According to Beurdeley and Raindre, *Qing Porcelain,* 86, 112, Yongzheng "regularly sent antique ceramics to Jingdezhen in order to have them copied," and Qianlong wrote instructions and comments on reports from Jingdezhen.

14. Plates 107, 016 in Qian Zhengzong, *Qingdai ciqi jianshang.* Other objects with the peach illustrated in Qian include plates 039, 062, 075, 201, 248, 289. Other objects with the *qilin* illustrated in Qian include plates 007, 058, 261.

15. Wu Cheng'en, *The Journey to the West,* trans. Anthony Yu (Chicago: Univ. of Chicago Press, 1977), 1:133–44.

16. See Arthur Waley, trans., *The Book of Songs* (1937; reprint, New York: Grove, 1996), 12n; Benjamin Britten, *Songs from the Chinese,* Op 58 (1958), no. 6 "Dance Song." My thanks to Daniel Albright for drawing the second item to my attention. According to *Zuo zhuan* (Records of Lu and its neighboring states), in the fourteenth year of Duke Ai of Lu (481 B.C.), Prince Sun's charioteer caught a beast with a single horn and mistook it for a bad omen. Confucius came and identified the *qilin.* See Gao Heng, ed., *Shi jing jinzhu* (Annotated Shi jing) (Shanghai: Guji, 1980), 1–2, 13–15.

17. Sima Qian, *Records of the Historian,* trans. Yang Hsien-yi and Gladys Yang (Hong Kong: Commercial Press, 1974), 14.

18. On Kangxi's wooing of the Confucian scholar, see Jonathan D. Spence, *The Search for Modern China* (New York: W. W. Norton, 1990), 58–64.

19. Theoretically only the oval peach symbolizes longevity. However, in painting the peach, Chinese artists tend to overlook distinctions between the oval peach (*pan tao*) and the nectarine (*you tao*). The image Moore saw may have appeared like the nectarine.

20. Three stanzas and seven lines are deleted from the version "Nine Nectarines and Other Porcelain" in *SPMM,* 30.

21. On Yongzheng and *famille-rose,* see Beurdeley and Raindre, *Qing Porcelain,* 90–91.

22. Lu Minghua, *Jingdezhen ciqi,* 90.

23. Ian Jack, *Keats and the Mirror of Art* (Oxford: Oxford Univ. Press, 1967), 217–19.

24. On Mei Lanfang's tour, see J. Brooks Atkinson, "China's Idol Actor Reveals His Art," *New York Times,* 17 February 1930, 18.

25. Notebook 1250/6 (1930–1943), RML-MMC, VII: 02: 02, 18–20, 102.

26. According to Stapleton, *Marianne Moore,* 77, Moore learned of de Candolle's claim about the peach's Chinese origin from the *Encyclopedia Britannica* (Cambridge: Cambridge Univ. Press, 1910), vol. 21. Her endnotes indicate that she had also drawn on Alphonse de Candolle, *Origin of Cultivated Plants* (New York: Appleton, 1886), 221–22; Frank Davis, "A Page for Collectors: The Unnatural History of China: The Lions of Buddha," *Illustrated London News,* 7 March 1931, 384.

27. Engel, *Marianne Moore,* 36.

28. See, for example, entry for the *qilin* in the *Cihai* dictionary (Shanghai: Cishu, 1979), 2065.

29. In Frank Davis's description, those engaging animals are "in various shades of green, aubergine, and yellow."

30. Donald Hall, *Marianne Moore: The Cage and the Animal* (New York: Pegasus, 1970), 92.

31. Heffernan, *Museum of Words,* 154.

32. Prior to *Pictures from Breughel* (1962), Williams wrote two other poems about pictures by Breughel: "The Dance" (1942), in *The Collected Poems of William Carlos Williams,* ed. Christopher MacGowan (New York: New Directions, 1988), 2:58–59, and *Adoration of the Magi* (1958), in *Paterson,* ed. Christopher MacGowan (New York: New Directions, 1992), 223–25.

33. The omitted passage refers to "Hunts and domestic scenes . . . / in France," an English "officer / in jack-boots seated in a / bosquet"; and a series of other European motifs. See *SPMM,* 30–31.

34. In Davis's description, the *qilin* "has the body of a stag, with a single horn, the tail of a cow, horse's hoofs, a yellow belly, and hair of five colours, and is, *moreover, a paragon of virtue*" (italics added).

EIGHT. Pound's Seven Lakes Canto

1. The "screen book" from the U.S. is acknowledged in Ezra Pound to Isabel Pound, 1 March 1928, YCAL-PP, 61:2695.

2. On Pound's "screen book," see Sanehide Kodama, "The Seven Lakes Canto" (first published under the title "The Eight Scenes of Sho-sho" in *Paideuma* [1977] 6.2), in his *American Poetry and Japanese Culture,* 105–20.

3. Kodama, *American Poetry and Japanese Culture,* 115.

4. Daniel D. Pearlman, *The Barb of Time: On the Unity of Ezra Pound's Cantos* (New York: Oxford Univ. Press, 1969), 310–11 (appendix B).

5. For a typescript of an oral translation of the eight Chinese poems, see Ezra Pound to Homer Pound, 30 July of [1928], YCAL-PP, 61:2696. The typescript on three separate leaves is reproduced in Hugh Kenner, "More on the Seven Lakes Canto," *Paideuma* 2.1 (spring 1973): 43–44; hereafter Kenner, "More." On the order of the poems, see Richard Taylor, "Canto XLIX, Futurism, and the Fourth Dimension," *Neohelicon* (Budapest) 20.1 (1993): 339–40.

6. Ezra Pound to Isabel Pound, 1 March 1928; Ezra Pound to Homer Pound, 30 May 1928, 1 August 1928, 1 September [1928]; YCAL-PP, 61:2695–2696. See also Ezra Pound to Glenn Hughes, 17 May 1928, YCAL-PP, 23:1014. A biographical sketch of Miss Zeng Baosun is provided in Angela Jung Palandri, "The 'Seven Lakes Canto' Revisited," *Paideuma* 3.1 (1974): 51–54.

7. For Miss Zeng's "paraphrases," see Kenner, "More," 43–44; Taylor, "Canto XLIX," 354–55. See also note 5 above.

8. Mitchell, *Picture Theory*, 160.

9. See Hans H. Frankel, "Poetry and Painting: Chinese and Western Views of Their Convertibility," *Comparative Literature* 9.4 (fall 1957): 289–91; Qian Zhongshu, *Zhongguo shi yu zhongguo hua*, 6:5–7.

10. A. Philip McMahon, trans., *Treatise on Painting* by Leonardo da Vinci (Princeton, N.J.: Princeton Univ. Press, 1956), 1:17. Compare Su Shi's lines, "Tu Fu's [Du Fu's] writings are pictures without forms, / Han Kan's paintings, unspoken poems," in Bush and Shih, *Early Chinese Texts*, 203.

11. For the original poems, see Su Shi, *Dongpo qiji* (Works of Dongpo [Su Shi]) (Taibei: Zhonghua shuju, 1970), 4: *Dongpo xuji, juan 2, 6.*

12. See Shen Kuo, *Mengxi bitan [jiaozheng]* (Mengxi jottings, with amendations), ed., Yang Jialuo (Taibei: Shijie shuju, 1961), 1: 549–50.

13. This account, based on "a local history for the [Hunan] province," is taken from Alfreda Murck, "Eight Views of the Hsiao and Hsiang Rivers by Wang Hong," in Wen Fong et al., *Images of the Mind*, 216.

14. For translations of Huihong's eight poems, see Murck, "Eight Views," 224–32. For Huihong's original poems, see Huihong, *Shimen wenzi chan* (Shimen Chan words), in *Jingyin wenyuan ge siku quanshu* (Siku complete works) (Taibei: Shangwu, 1986), vol. 1116:239–40.

15. For Huizong's inscription on his own copy of the eight views, see Zhang Cheng, *Hualu guangyi* (Record of painting, supplement), in *Yishu congbian* (Selected works on art), ed. Yang Jialuo (Taibei: Shijie shuju, 1975), 10:174.

16. Ma Yuan's eight views are mentioned in Zhu Derun, *Cunfuzhai ji* (Cunfuzhai anthology), reprinted in *Peiwenzhai shu hua pu* (Peiwenzhai guide to painting and calligraphy), ed. Wang Yuanqi et al. (Taibei: Xinxing shuju, 1972), *juan 84, 18.*

17. Wang Hong's eight views are reproduced in Murck, "Eight Views," 225–34.

18. The Idemitsu Museum of Arts, Tokyo, owns Yujian's "Mountain Town" and Muqi's "Wild Geese." The Nezu Institute of Fine Arts, Tokyo, houses Muqi's "Fishing Village." The Hatakeyama Collection, Tokyo, keeps Muqi's "Evening Bell." The Tokugawa Museum, Nagoya, preserves Yujian's "Sailboats Returning" and Muqi's "Autumn Moon." For reproductions of Muqi's four scenes, see Hisamatsu, *Zen*, 174–77 (plates 67–70).

19. Daitoku-ji, Kyoto, holds Soami's eight views. For reproductions of his "Autumn Moon," "Mountain Town," "Snowy Evening," and "Sailboats Returning," see Hisamatsu, *Zen*, 202–05.

20. Nos. 128–34 (last two scenes both numbered 134) and nos. 153–56 (each number including two scenes) in the British Museum 1910–12 exhibition. See Binyon, *Guide*, 37–38, 40.

21. YCAL-PP, 61:2695.

22. Mitchell, *Picture Theory*, 157.

23. See Kenner, "More," 43; Taylor, "Canto XLIX," 354. Where Taylor's version incorporates Pound's revisions, Kenner's does not.

24. Kodama, *American Poetry and Japanese Culture*, 107.

25. The eight Chinese poems are written out in three calligraphic styles: "Night Rain," "Autumn Moon," and "Evening Bell" in regular script (*kai shu*); "Sailboats Returning," "Snowy Evening," and "Wild Geese" in running script (*xing shu*); "Mountain Town" and "Fishing Village" in seal script (*zhuan shu*).

26. Kodama, *American Poetry and Japanese Culture,* 113.

27. Kenner, "More," 44.

28. See Kenner, "More," 43; Taylor, "Canto XLIX," 354.

29. See Kenner, "More," 44; Taylor, "Canto XLIX," 354.

30. Ibid.

31. Steiner, *Pictures of Romance,* 13.

32. In Yujian's masterpiece one witnesses three partially concealed masts in the background. For a reproduction, see Kei Suzuki, *Comprehensive Illustrated Catalog,* 3:284 (JM 15–008).

33. Steiner, *Pictures of Romance,* 17–22, 36–37.

34. Ibid., 36.

35. Wu Hung, *Double Screen,* 59.

36. For an excellent description of Pound's "screen book," see Taylor, "Canto XLIX," 340.

37. I am grateful to Mary de Rachewiltz for providing slides (by Richard Taylor) of the eight paintings and photographs of the sixteen manuscript poems.

38. For transcripts of the poems in Chinese and Japanese accompanied by English versions, see Kodama, *American Poetry and Japanese Culture,* 108–12.

39. See Kenner, "More," 44; Taylor, "Canto XLIX," 355.

40. The "hint" is in the "paraphrase": "Bullrushes have burst into snow-tops / The birds stop to preen their feathers." See Kenner, "More," 44; Taylor, "Canto XLIX," 355.

41. The Nerchinsk Treaty, 1689. In 1684, 1689, 1699, 1703, 1705, and 1707, Kangxi made six "Southern Tours." He saw "hill lakes" not in the Xiao-Xiang region but in Suzhou and Hangzhou in the Yangtze delta. On Kangxi's "Southern Tours," see Jonathan D. Spence, *Ts'ao Yin and the K'ang-hsi Emperor* (New Haven, Conn.: Yale Univ. Press, 1966), 124–34.

42. The passage (dated 12 September 1901) can be found in Fenollosa, "Mori's Lectures on the History of Chinese Poetry," YCAL-PP, 100:4226.

43. According to Taylor, "Canto XLIX," 344, "TenShi is taken here for a place name, but is in fact a compounding of two separate Japanese words which mean Son of God." As in the thirteenth century the Grand Canal was extended to Beijing in the North and Hangzhou in the South, it is historically correct to substitute TenShi (the seat of the Son of Heaven) for Kaifeng.

44. For transcripts of the two ancient songs, see Kenner, "More," 45–46. See also Kenner, *Pound Era,* 222.

45. My account of the tale is based on Yuan Ke, *Zhongguo shenhua chuanshuo* (Chinese mythology) (Beijing: Zhongguo wenyi, 1984), 1:272.

46. Compare Fenollosa, "Early Chinese Poetry: Kutsugen (Ka-Gi): tr. by Ariga," YCAL-PP, 99:4221: "God lingers in his dwelling place and comes not to us, who can so long stop at the little isle in the middle of the river and wait for you? Please come

soon." For a better version of the song, see David Hawkes, trans., *The Songs of the South: An Ancient Chinese Anthology of Poems by Qu Yuan and Other Poets* (Harmondsworth, U.K.: Penguin, 1985), 106–07.

47. Heffernan, *Museum of Words,* 139.

NINE. Pound, Fenollosa, and *The Chinese Written Character*

1. The genesis of "Three Cantos" is given by Ronald Bush in *The Genesis of Ezra Pound's Cantos* (Princeton, N.J.: Princeton Univ. Press, 1976), 24, where he shows them to have been "planned and written" in 1914–15.

2. Said, *Orientalism,* 3. A case of "left Orientalism" in English poetry would be Shelley's "The Revolt of Islam."

3. Kenner, *Pound Era,* 173.

4. Korin's *Wave Screen* in the Museum of Fine Arts, Boston, is reproduced in Binyon, *Painting,* 206.

5. Achilles Fang to Noel Stock, 20 July 1955, in University of Texas at Austin, Harry Ransom Humanities Research Center, Pound Collection.

6. Wen Fong et al., *Images of the Mind,* 74.

7. Holland Cotter, "Writing on the Wall, and on the Soul," *New York Times,* 15 September 2000, B25, B29.

8. See Xu Shen (A.D. 30–124), *Shuowen jiezi* (The explication of graphs and analysis of characters), (reprint, Taibei: Zhonghua shuju, 1975), 2: *juan* 15, i, 2–3. For a stimulating discussion, see Haun Saussy, *Great Walls of Discourse and Other Adventures in Cultural China* (Cambridge: Harvard Univ. Press, 2001), 35–74, especially 38–39, 66–67.

9. James J. Y. Liu, *The Art of Chinese Poetry* (Chicago: Univ. of Chicago Press, 1962), 5. Liu has overlooked a fifth category, "Simple Phonogram." Where *lai* 來 for "wheat" is a Simple Ideogram, *lai* 來 for "come" is a Simple Phonogram. In traditional Chinese etymology, *lai* for "come" is treated as *jiajie* ("borrowing").

10. Ibid., 4–5. "Archaic" is Bernhard Karlgren's term for the script and phonetics of the Western Zhou (eleventh to sixth centuries B.C.). See Karlgren, *Grammata Serica: Script and Phonetics in Chinese and Sino-Japanese* (Stockholm: Museum of Far Eastern Antiquities, 1940), 3.

11. Ernest Fenollosa, *The Chinese Written Character as a Medium for Poetry,* ed. Ezra Pound (1936; reprint, San Francisco: City Lights Books, 1968), 8; hereafter *Character.*

12. The radical 木 may also indicate an object made of wood. The radical 魚 may also denote part of the body of a fish.

13. For the etymologies of *cai* 采, *wei* 薇, *ji* 擊, and *rang* 壤, see Chang Hsuan, *The Etymologies of 3000 Chinese Characters in Common Usage* (Hong Kong: Hong Kong Univ. Press, 1968), 340, 298, 347, 182. For their Archaic pronunciations, see Karlgren, *Grammata Serica,* 373 (no. 942a-c), 274 (no. 584f), 351 (no. 854 a-b), 314 (no. 730d).

14. The earliest known Chinese songs consist of only two characters per line, usually a verb and a noun. A five- to six-thousand-year-old song, *Tan ge* (Shooting song), cited in Chen Shengsheng, *Xiandai shixue* (Modern poetics) (Beijing: Shehui kexue wenxuan, 1998), 37, reads: "*Duan zhu, / xu zhu; / fei tu, / zhu rou*" ("Cut bamboo, / tie bamboo; / shoot clods, / chase game").

15. *Putonghua,* or common spoken Chinese, is based on the Beijing dialect. The

government of the People's Republic of China consistently backs its popularization. As a step of making the Chinese writing system less cumbersome, a simplification of characters was introduced in 1956. Some of the simplified characters are deprived of their phonetics, and others their significants. For example, the abridged version of the character 寶 (*bao,* "treasure"), is deprived of 缶 indicating its archaic sound, and the abridged version of the character 聲 (*sheng,* "sound") has lost 耳 depicting an ear. Pinyin as a romanization of the Chinese characters was introduced in 1958. While it is widely used for teaching and transcription purposes, the system has not been able to replace the characters.

16. While electronic Chinese texts are produced by digital means (the pinyin), shown on the screen are still characters. There are so many homophones in Chinese that the pinyin is not as readable as we imagine.

17. Pound defines *Phanopoeia* as "a casting of images upon the visual imagination." Complementing *Phanopoeia* are *Melopoeia,* "musical property," and *Logopoeia,* "the dance of the intellect among words." See *LE,* 25.

18. *Jiagu,* or bone and shell inscription, is of the Shang period, ca. sixteenth to eleventh centuries B.C. *Jinwen,* or bronze inscription, is of the Western Zhou period, ca. eleventh to sixth centuries B.C. *Zhuan* or seal script is of the Eastern Zhou and Qin periods, ca. sixth to second centuries B.C.

19. According to Liu Fei of *Renmin Ribao, Hanzi suyuan* ("Etymologizing Chinese") is based on Xie Guanghui et al., *The Composition of Common Chinese Characters: An Illustrated Account* (Beijing: Beijing Univ. Press, 1997). Other works on Chinese etymologies include Li Leyi, *Tracing the Roots of Chinese Characters: 500 Cases* (Beijing: Beijing Language and Culture Univ. Press, 1993); Shi Zhengyu, *Picture Within a Picture: An Illustrated Guide to the Origins of Chinese Characters* (Beijing: New World Press, 1997).

20. Kenner, *Pound Era,* 231.

21. The character preceding *xia shuijing lian* ("lower the crystal curtain") is *que,* meaning "and." The characters preceding *wang qiu yue* ("watch the autumn moon") are *ling long,* meaning "adeptly" or "clearly."

22. The late Xu Guozhang of Beijing Foreign Studies University introduced this term to a graduate seminar in 1980.

23. Giles, *History of Chinese Literature,* 52. Compare Hawkes, *Songs of the South,* 115.

24. Altieri, *Painterly Abstraction,* 236–47.

25. Bush, *Genesis of Ezra Pound's Cantos,* 10.

26. Ibid., 179. See also Pound, *Instigations,* with an essay on the Chinese written character by Ernest Fenollosa (New York: Boni and Liveright, 1920), 383n.

27. On Pound's 1916–18 study of Chinese poetry, see my *Orientalism and Modernism,* 89–104.

28. Quoted in ibid., 102.

29. Ibid., 109.

30. On Pound's use of the "cherry-rose-rust-flamingo" bit, see Christine Brooke-Rose, *A ZBC of Ezra Pound* (Berkeley and Los Angeles: Univ. of California Press, 1971), 109–10; Laszlo Gefin, *Ideogram: History of a Poetic Method* (Austin: Univ. of Texas Press, 1982), 29–31.

31. For Fenollosa's acknowledgment of "the mobility of sounds" in Chinese characters, see *Character,* 9.

32. "Chinese Poetry: Mori [E. P.'s notes for editions of lectures, 1935]," YCAL-PP, 99–4222.

33. Ibid.

34. Ibid.

35. Ibid.

36. "Chinese Poetry: Mori [E. P.'s notes for editions of lectures, 1958–59; in part reworked from 1935]," YCAL-PP, 99:4223.

37. Cheadle, *Pound's Confucian Translation,* 44–45.

38. For Pound's note in Italian, see Mary de Rachewiltz, trans., *Catai* (Milano: All'Insegna del Pesce d'Oro, 1959), 45. The given English version is Pound's found in his 1958–59 notes for editions of Mori's lectures, YCAL-PP, 99:4223.

39. Cheadle, *Pound's Confucian Translations,* 45. Not knowing that Pound's 1959 note in Italian is based on his unpublished notes in English (YCAL-PP, 99:4223), Cheadle in ibid. offers her translation from the Italian: "It is not true that it is possible to translate *gratis* what is naturally lost when turning something into another language."

TEN. Stevens as Art Collector

1. See Percival David, "The Exhibition of Chinese Art: A Preliminary Survey," *Burlington Magazine* 67.393 (December 1935): 239–51.

2. Binyon, intro., *Chinese Art* (London: Kegan Paul, Trench, Trubner & Co., 1935), ix. Stevens could have gone over David's survey in *Burlington Magazine* (December 1935), but more likely he was reading *Chinese Art* with "well-written descriptions."

3. MacLeod, *Stevens and Modern Art,* 11.

4. See Wallace Stevens to Elsie Stevens, 14 March 1918; Wallace Stevens to Harriet Monroe, 8 April 1918, in *L,* 205, 206.

5. Harriet Monroe, *A Poet's Life: Seventy Years in a Changing World* (New York: Macmillan, 1938), 233, 234.

6. HL-WAS, 33.

7. I wish to thank Peter and Gail Hanchak for their generosity in locating Stevens's Far Eastern treasures and inviting me to examine them. I thank also Emily Mitchell Wallace for introducing me to the Hanchaks.

8. For a list of Wallace Stevens's collection of paintings and prints, including those purchased through Anatole and Paule Vidal, see MacLeod, *Stevens and Modern Art,* 199–200.

9. Henri Lebasque's *Paysage avec femme* is now in the Montgomery Gallery, San Francisco. For a reproduction, see J. D. McClatchy, ed., *Poets on Painters: Essays on the Art of Painting by Twentieth-Century Poets* (Berkeley and Los Angeles: Univ. of California Press, 1988), 108.

10. Harriet Monroe sailed from Vancouver to the Far East in August 1934, spent over two months with her sister Lucy Monroe Calhoun in Beijing, and returned to Chicago by the end of January 1935. For accounts of her two trips to China, see Monroe, *Poet's Life,* 230–39, 444–47.

11. Monroe to Stevens, 11 March 1935, HL-WAS, 36.

12. James A. Powers, a business associate, had put Stevens in touch with Benjamin Kwok. See Stevens to Powers, 17 December 1935, in *L,* 301.

13. Stevens got the name and address of Leonard C. van Geyzel from Sophie Sigmans, sister of Anthony P. Sigmans, a business associate. Sophie Sigmans had met van Geyzel's friends in England. See *L,* 323.

14. In June 1938 Stevens would ask van Geyzel to look for "a seated Buddha and also a reclining Buddha that would go along with the one" he had received. See Stevens to van Geyzel, 6 June 1938, in *L,* 333.

15. Stevens's letter soon brought from Otaru, Japan, five packages, including two specimens of calligraphy in Japanese by Mary Alice Cary, several little dolls, and no peasant pottery. See Stevens to Mrs. Cary, 27 December 1935, in *L,* 304.

16. HL-WAS, 81.

17. For reproductions of official portraits of Chenghua, see Fang Zhiyuan, *Chenghua huangdi dazhuan* (A biography of Emperor Chenghua) (Shenyang: Liaoning jiaoyu, 1994).

18. Arthur Davison Ficke, *Chats on Japanese Prints* (1915; reprint, Tokyo and Rutland, Vt.: Tuttle, 1958), 379.

19. Fenollosa, *Epochs,* 2:204.

20. *Ghost Foxes,* ca. 1840, reproduced in Fenollosa, *Epochs,* 2:205.

21. *Exhibition of Japanese Prints, 1909: Illustrated Catalogue, with Notes and an Introduction by Arthur Morrison* (London: Fine Arts Society, 1909).

22. Wallace Stevens to Ferdinand Reyher, 23 November 1920, HL-WAS, 1558.

23. Five hundred copies of Alfred Salmony, ed., *An Exhibition of Chinese Sculpture* were printed by Morrill Press of Fulton in New York in June 1944, and two hundred more were printed in February 1945. Stevens's copy, held in the Huntington Library, is one of the additional two hundred.

24. The Fogge Annual Report, July 1944-June 1945, in the archives of the Harvard University Art Museums.

25. "Japanese Painting and Sculpture, Sponsored by the Government of Japan, 15 November-15 December 1953," listed in the MFA Annual Report for 1953.

26. The Fogge Annual Report, July 1953-June 1954, lists a Chinese show—Chinese Prints, 6 July-30 September 1953. Abigail Smith, Archivist, told me on 27 October 1999 that "Additional objects which might have been on display in the Asian galleries at the time could have been in an informed 'in house' display for which no documentation exists."

27. See Stevens to Monroe, 13 March 1935, 5 April 1935, 4 December 1935, in *L,* 278, 280, 299.

28. See Stevens, "The Whole Man: Perspectives, Horizons," *Yale Review* 44 (winter 1955): 196–201; reprinted in *OP,* 284–88.

29. Lee to me, 26 May 1998, 8 February 1999.

30. Ch'oe Sun-u, "Korean Painting," in *Traditional Korean Painting,* ed., Korean National Commission for UNESCO (Arch Cape, Or.: Pace International Research, Inc., 1983), 10.

31. Lee to me, 27 May 1998.

32. See chapter 11, note 19.

33. Peter H. Lee, ed. and trans., *Anthology of Korean Poetry: From the Earliest Era to*

the Present (New York: John Day, 1964). For references to Lee's translations, see *L*, 826, 840, 864, 871.

34. Lee to me, 28 May 1998. Peter Hanchak's repeated search through the art objects left by his mother, Holly Stevens, uncovers no trace of this painting.

ELEVEN. Moore and *The Tao of Painting*

1. The *Guide-Posts* presents twenty illustrations. Those cited by Moore represent three genres: landscapes, flower-and-bird studies, and human figures.

2. "The Tao of Painting" ("Tedium and Integrity"), RML-MMC, II: 06: 12. My thanks to Linda Leavell for drawing that typescript to my attention.

3. Leavell, *Moore and the Visual Arts,* 157n. Moore lost only three pages of her typescript, since the four surviving pages are numbered 4–7.

4. Moore received two other books from the Bollingen Foundation: Kenneth Clark, *The Nude: A Study in Ideal Form* (1956); C. G. Jung, *The Collected Works,* vol. 1, *Psychological Studies,* trans. R. F. C. Hull (1957).

5. Moore to Barrett, 22 January 1957, RML-MMC, MML 1485.

6. Moore to Barrett, 5 September 1957, RML-MMC, MML 1485.

7. David Playdell-Bouverie, second son of the Earl of Longworth, England, came to America in the 1940s. He hosted a literary party for the Sitwells in late 1948, where he and Moore first met. In the 1950s Playdell-Bouverie, an architect, bought a ranch in Glen Ellen, California, where he grew wine grapes. I am grateful, once again, to Patricia Willis for sharing her personal knowledge of Playdell-Bouverie. The set of *The Tao* going to Mrs. Kauffer was not for her but for "her two young employees." See Moore to Barrett, 5 September 1957, RML-MMC, MML 1485.

8. Moore to Barrett, 5 September 1957, RML-MMC, MML 1485.

9. Moore to Barrett, 22 January 1957, RML-MMC, MML 1485.

10. Mai-mai Sze, *The Tao of Painting: A Study of the Ritual Disposition of Chinese Painting with a Translation of the Chieh Tzŭ Yüan Hua Chuan or Mustard Seed Garden Manual of Painting 1679–1701,* 2 vols. (New York: Bollingen Foundation, 1956), 1:vii; hereafter *The Tao.*

11. Kenneth Rexroth, "The Mustard Seed Garden," *Nation* 184.422 (11 May 1957): 1050.

12. On Shi Shaoji (Sao-ke Alfred Sze), see Warren F. Kuehl, ed., *Biographical Dictionary of Internationalists* (Westport, Conn.: Greenwood, 1983), 669–70.

13. Records in Wellesley College Registrar's Office.

14. Sze to Moore, 11 December 1957, RML-MMC, V: 64: 41.

15. See sixteen letters and a card from Sze to Moore, 28 September 1957 to 18 December 1968; the carbon copies of two letters from Moore to Sze, 18 April 1959 and 20 November 1963, in RML-MMC, V: 64: 41.

16. Moore to Sze, 18 April 1959, RML-MMC, V: 64: 41.

17. Moore to Sze, 20 November 1963, RML-MMC, V: 64: 41.

18. In the upper right of the front endpaper of vol. 1 (RML-MMC, MML 1485) is Moore's penciled note: "A Breath of Spring [p.] 48 / apparently the only recorded / painting by this artist."

19. The clippings laid in Moore's set of *The Tao* include: "A Breath of Spring," *New York Times,* 20 January 1957; five illustrations for "Masterpieces of Chinese Art,"

Time, 6 May 1957: calligraphy by Mi Fu and paintings by Shen Zhou (*Sitting up at Night*), Lu Zhi (*Grass, Flowers, and Wild Birds*), Tang Yin (*Gentleman and Attendants*), and Qiu Ying (*Intellectual Conversation*); notice of *The Tao* by Sze, *New York Times Book Review,* 17 May 1957; "Jiang Kaishi states his case with his history and hopes," *New York Herald Tribune,* 23 June 1957; review of *Like a Bulwark, Listener,* 12 September 1957; William Willetts, "The Way of Chinese Art," *TLS,* 31 October 1958; "Last Curtain for the King of Actors," *Newsweek,* 21 August 1961. Along with *The Tao* is a copy of its abbreviated paperback version, *The Way of Chinese Painting* (New York: Random House, 1959), inscribed "For Marianne Moore this pocket version! Affectionately, Mai-mai Sze, November 24, 1959."

20. The book is mentioned as a gift from Elizabeth Mayer in Moore to Mayer, 30 April 1945, in *SLMM,* 458.

21. "Genesis" 1:26, in *The Guideposts Parallel Bible* (New York: Guideposts, 1973), 4.

22. See Moore's 1958 review of *The Selected Writings of Juan Ramon Jimenez* in *PrMM,* 497–99.

23. Wang Shouren, *Chuan xi lu* (Record of instruction), 154. For an English version, see Fung, *Chinese Philosophy,* 2:601–02.

24. C. Miller, *Marianne Moore,* 26.

25. Ibid., 49.

26. See Stamy, *Moore and China,* 29.

27. The phrase occurs in *Spring and All* 1, in *The Collected Poems of William Carlos Williams,* ed. A. Walton Litz and Christopher MacGowan (New York: New Directions, 1986), 1:183.

28. For early versions of "Poetry," see *BMM,* 72–73, 205–7.

TWELVE. Moore and *O to Be a Dragon*

1. Moore to Sze, 18 April 1959, RML-MMC, V: 64: 41.

2. Sze to Moore, 16 September 1959, RML-MMC, V: 64: 41.

3. Litz and MacGowan, eds., *Collected Poems of William Carlos Williams,* 1:173. On the poem's allusion to the love tragedy of the Tang emperor Xuanzong and Lady Yang Guifei, see my *Orientalism and Modernism,* 113–27.

4. The quotation from Guanzi (active seventh century B.C.) is taken from William F. Mayers, *Chinese Reader's Manual* (London: Trubner & Co., 1874), 142.

5. E. R. Hughes, *The Art of Letters: Lu Chi's "Wen Fu,"* A.D. *302* (New York: Pantheon, 1951), 123. In Moore's copy, held in the Rosenbach Museum and Library, the passage is marked out.

6. Sze's description is based on Li Shizhen, *Ben cao gang mu,* quoted in W. Perceval Yetts, *Symbolism in Chinese Art* (London: China Society, 1912), 22.

7. Wu Tung's statement in *Tales,* 197–98, is based on "the artist's poem and inscription written at the end of the painting."

8. Bonnie Costello, *Marianne Moore: Imaginary Possessions* (Cambridge: Harvard Univ. Press, 1981), 150.

9. C. Miller, *Marianne Moore,* 43.

10. "Progress," *Tipyn O'Bob* (Bryn Mawr) 6 (June 1909): 10; reprinted in *BMM,* 343.

11. "You Are Like the Realistic Product of an Idealistic Search for Gold at the

Foot of the Rainbow," *Egoist* 3 (1 May 1916): 71, reprinted in *BMM*, 170. "A Jelly-Fish," *The Lantern* (Bryn Mawr) 17 (spring 1909): 110; reprinted in *BMM*, 342. On Moore's preoccupations with "contextual codes," see George Bornstein, *Material Modernism: The Politics of the Page* (Cambridge: Cambridge Univ. Press, 2001), 93–99.

12. Moore to Sze, 18 April 1959 and Sze to Moore, 16 September 1959, RML-MMC, V: 64: 41.

13. Stapleton, *Marianne Moore*, 167. Leavell, *Moore and the Visual Arts*, 112. Grace Schulman, *Marianne Moore: The Poetry of Engagement* (Urbana and Chicago: Univ. of Illinois Press, 1986), 82, 107.

14. Costello, *Marianne Moore*, 151.

15. Stapleton, *Marianne Moore*, 167.

16. Leavell, *Moore and the Visual Arts*, 112.

17. Schulman, *Marianne Moore*, 82.

18. Ibid., 107, 82.

19. Ibid., 82.

20. Moore to Sze, 18 April 1959, RML-MMC, V: 64: 41.

21. Costello, *Marianne Moore*, 152.

22. For "A Jelly-Fish" (1909), see *BMM*, 342.

23. C. Miller, *Marianne Moore*, 28.

24. Leavell, *Moore and the Visual Arts*, 73–74.

25. C. Miller, *Marianne Moore*, 35.

26. Ibid., 34.

27. Leavell, *Moore and the Visual Arts*, 29–37, 73–76.

28. Li Zehou, *Path of Beauty*, 186–87, 187–88.

29. C. Miller, *Marianne Moore*, 45.

30. Li Zehou, *Path of Beauty*, 186.

31. C. Miller, *Marianne Moore*, 45, where she adds: "she [Moore] states in 'Armor's Undermining Modesty,' 'What is more precise than precision? Illusion' (*CP*, 151)."

32. Paintings Moore saw at the Metropolitan Museum in March and April 1923. See Moore to Bryher, 5 May 1923, in *SLMM*, 197.

33. Moore to Sze, 20 November 1963, RML-MMC, V: 64: 41.

34. For Moore's further references to this notion, see *PrMM*, 487, 569, 618, 649.

35. See Stapleton, *Marianne Moore*, 75.

36. Costello, *Marianne Moore*, 156.

37. Compare Binyon's reference to the energy and beauty produced by "the rhythmical movements of the body, as in games or in the dance," in *Flight*, 13.

THIRTEEN. Nothingness and Late Stevens

1. Harold Bloom, *Wallace Stevens*, 88.

2. Vendler, *On Extended Wings*, 75.

3. The submission of "Decorations" is mentioned in Stevens to Zabel, 6 December 1934, in *L*, 272. The series appeared in *Poetry* 45.5 (February 1935): 239–49.

4. Litz, *Introspective Voyager*, 183.

5. Monroe to Stevens, 11 March 1935, HL-WAS, 36.

6. See Wu Tung, *Tales*, 180.

7. Bloom, *Wallace Stevens*, 106.

8. Vendler, *On Extended Wings*, 71.

9. On "lofty dryness" and other characteristics of Chan art, see Hisamatsu, *Zen*, 30–36.

10. "The Latest Freed Man" and eleven other poems first appeared in *Southern Review* 4.2 (autumn 1938) under the group title "Canonica."

11. Josephy Carroll, *Wallace Stevens' Supreme Fiction: A New Romanticism* (Baton Rouge: Louisiana State Univ. Press, 1987), 131, 180.

12. B. J. Leggett, *Early Stevens: The Nietzschean Intertext* (Durham, N.C.: Duke Univ. Press, 1992), 244.

13. Stevens's copy of Irving Babbitt, trans., *The Dhammanpada* (New York: Oxford Univ. Press, 1936) is held in the Huntington Library.

14. MacLeod, *Stevens and Modern Art*, 87.

15. Ibid., 47: "The Dutch sense of the dwelling-place as a center of revivifying meditation and a source of spiritual strength appears . . . in such titles as 'The Hermitage at the Center' and 'The House Was Quiet and the World Was Calm.'"

16. Babbitt, *Dhammanpada*, 55, 16, 18.

17. Ibid., 73.

18. Ibid., 55.

19. See Bevis, *Mind of Winter*, 208.

20. Babbitt, *Dhammanpada*, 20–23.

21. Beal, *Buddhism in China*, 83.

22. On Roger Bezombes, see Mark Jones, "Bezombes, Roger," in *The Dictionary of Art*, ed. Jane Turner (New York: Grove, 1996), 3:902–03.

23. On Eugène Fromentin (1820–76), see James Thompson, "Fromentin, Eugène," in Turner, *Dictionary of Art*, 2:800–01. See also Said, *Orientalism*, 1.

24. Tompkins, "Stevens and Zen," 26, 35.

25. J. Hillis Miller, "Stevens' Rock and Criticism as Cure," in *Modern Critical Views: Wallace Stevens*, ed. Harold Bloom (New York: Chelsea, 1985), 27–49; here 31.

26. Bloom, *Wallace Stevens*, 354.

27. George S. Lensing, *Wallace Stevens and the Seasons* (Baton Rouge: Louisiana State Univ. Press, 2001), 144.

28. Suzuki, *Zen and Japanese Culture*, 36.

29. Arthur Waley, trans., *A Hundred and Seventy Chinese Poems* (New York: Knopf, 1919), 173.

30. Harold Henderson, *An Introduction to Haiku* (New York: Doubleday, 1958), 20.

31. For Stevens's acknowledgment of "influence by Chinese and Japanese lyrics," see Stevens to Ronald Lane Latimer, 5 November 1935, in *L*, 291. For his denial of haiku as an important influence, see Stevens to Earl Miner, 30 November 1950, in *L*, 291n.

32. Compare Mitchell's characterization of Velázquez's *Las Meninas* as "an encyclopedic labyrinth of pictorial self-reference" in *Picture Theory*, 58. In *Las Meninas* the painter is glancing from the model to his unfinished painting.

33. Quoted from Stevens's newspaper clipping enclosed in his 20 August 1911 letter to his wife (HL-WAS, 1926).

34. Daniel R. Schwarz, *Narrative and Representation in the Poetry of Wallace Stevens* (New York: St. Martin's Press, 1993), 217.

35. Litz, *Introspective Voyager*, 293.

36. Bevis, *Mind of Winter*, 151.

37. Ibid., 153.

FOURTEEN. The Chinese in *Rock-Drill* and *Thrones*

1. Wyndham Lewis, "The Rock Drill," *New Statesman and Nation,* 7 April 1951, 398.

2. Jacob Epstein's *Rock Drill,* a plaster and ready-made drill created in 1913–15, is dismantled. For a reproduction of a photograph, see Dasenbrock, *Literary Vorticism,* 119.

3. See Pound, "Imagisme and England," *T. P.'s Weekly,* 20 February 1915, 185; reprinted in *P&P,* 2:19.

4. On the making of Ur-Canto 4, 1918–19 and the "ideogrammic method," see my *Orientalism and Modernism,* 104–09.

5. William Cookson, *A Guide to the Cantos of Ezra Pound* (New York: Persea Books, 1985), 90.

6. Jerome J. McGann, *The Textual Condition* (Princeton, N.J.: Princeton Univ. Press, 1991), 145. On "bibliographic codes," see ibid., 56–62.

7. See Ronald Bush, "Confucius Erased: The Missing Ideograms in *The Pisan Cantos,*" in my *Ezra Pound and China.*

8. On characters drawn by Dorothy and Ezra Pound, see Cheadle, *Pound's Confucian Translations,* 223. For Pound's requests for standard characters for *Rock-Drill* and *Thrones,* see his letters of 1954 and 1957 to Willis Hawley, YCAL-PP, 21:947–49.

9. For exceptions, see the large character that precedes the China Cantos in *C,* 254, and the thirteen small characters in Canto 55, *C,* 290. Compare Fang's remark on the Stone-Classics of Wei produced between A.D. 240 and 249, in *Con,* 12: "The unique feature of the Wei stones is that they are inscribed with three styles of calligraphy."

10. Minor differences in stroke shapes indicate that *Rock-Drill's* and *Thrones's* small characters were not photoengraved from Couvreur's or Legge's bilingual editions. Fang states in "A Note on the Stone-Classics," *Con,* 12–13: "The Stone-Classics of the T'ang dynasty, from a rubbing of which the Chinese text of this book is derived, were begun in A.D. 833 and completed in 837. . . . Originally set up in the Imperial Academy in Ch'ang-an (present Hsi-an [Xi'an]), these stones have weathered fairly well." Minor differences in stroke shapes affirm that the large characters in *Rock-Drill* and in *Thrones* were not photoengraved from that text.

11. Heidegger, "The Origin of the Work of Art," 35. George Bornstein in *Material Modernism,* 6, argues that "for literary works original mechanical reproductions can create their own aura." By using special types of characters, Pound has really created an "aura" for his own text.

12. Massimo Bacigalupo, *The Forméd Trace: The Later Poetry of Ezra Pound* (New York: Columbia Univ. Press, 1980), 232.

13. Marjorie Perloff, *Radical Artifice: Writing Poetry in the Age of Media* (Chicago: Univ. of Chicago Press, 1991), 148.

14. The phrase is taken from David Lévi-Strauss, "Approaching *80 Flowers*," in *Code of Signals: Recent Writings in Poetics,* ed. Michael Palmer (Berkeley, Calif.: North Atlantic Books, 1983), 86.

15. McGann, *The Textual Condition,* 146.

16. Séraphin Couvreur, *Chou King: Les annales de la Chine* (Paris: Cathasia, 1950), 285: "les empereurs de notre maison de Tcheou (Wenn wang et Ou wang), à cause de leur grande bonté, furent chargés d'exécuter l'oeuvre du roi du ciel." Compare James Legge, *The Chinese Classics,* vol. 3, *The Shoo King or The Book of Historical Documents* (1894; reprint, Hong Kong: Hong Kong Univ. Press, 1960), 458: "the sovereigns of our Chow, from their great goodness were charged with the work of God."

17. See note 7 above.

18. Cheadle, *Pound's Confucian Translations,* 48–53.

19. R. H. Mathews, *Mathews' Chinese-English Dictionary* (Cambridge: Harvard Univ. Press, 1956).

20. Fang to Pound, 12 January 1951, YCAL-PP, 16:708; Pound to Fang, 20 October 1951, LL-PM, II.

21. Mathews, *Dictionary,* 395, no. 2671, gives two forms of the character for "virtue." Pound chooses the second. Compare Couvreur, *Chou King,* 300; Legge, *Shoo King,* 256.

22. For Fang's offer and Pound's decline, see *Ezra Pound and James Laughlin: Selected Letters,* ed., David Gordon (New York: W. W. Norton, 1994), 202.

23. Compare "The arrow has not two points" in *C,* 576, with Couvreur, *Chou King,* 285: "Notre entreprise n'a tendu qu'à un seul but"; Legge, *Shoo King,* 458: "In our affairs we have followed no double aims."

24. Compare "naught above just contribution" in *C,* 577 with Couvreur, *Chou King,* 294: "et n'exigeait des principautés que le tribut fixé par les lois"; Legge, *Shoo King,* 469: "received only the correct amount of contribution."

25. Compare "train the fit men" in *C,* 577, with Couvreur, *Chou King,* 306: "et former les hommes de talent"; Legge, *Shoo King,* 485: "bring to light our men of eminence."

26. Ira B. Nadel, "Visualizing History: Pound in the Chinese Cantos," in Rainey, *A Poem Containing History,* 164.

27. David Gordon, "Thought Built on Sagetrieb," *Paideuma* 3.2 (1973): 171. In a card to me of 6 September 1999, Gordon confirms that "EP wrote 教 on his table page in autumn 1954."

28. Among those who visited Pound in the mid-1950s were Achilles Fang, David Wang, Tze-chiang Chao, Carson Chang, and Veronica Sun. Their letters to Pound with references to the visits are kept in the Beinecke Library of Yale University.

29. I count two characters in "Iong Cheng" (*C,* 714), three in "Chu Wan Kung" (720), and none in "Confucians" (722).

30. Compare "Nor scrape iron off the point of a needle" in *C,* 716, with F. W. Baller, *The Sacred Edict* (1892; reprint, Shanghai: China Inland Mission, 1924), 56: "hoarding in a regular skin-flint fashion"; "scraping-iron-off-the-end-of-a-needle-fashion saving."

31. Compare "pu / k'o / hsin" in *C,* 721, with Baller, *Sacred Edict,* 85: "you must on no account believe them."

32. Compare "che yang ti jen" in *C,* 724, with Baller, *Sacred Edict,* 47: "fellows of this sort."

33. Compare "Kuang / Kuang / Ming / Ming / tien / t'ang^2 / hsin^1 / li$^{3-5}$" in *C,* 722, with Baller, *Sacred Edict,* 87: "the mind enlightened is heaven."

34. *Histoire* was translated from a Manchu version of the 1708 *Tongjian gangmu,* a revised and updated edition of the twelfth-century *Tongjian gangmu* (Comprehensive mirror) compiled under the auspices of Zhu Xi. See Nolde, *Blossoms from the East,* 25–26.

35. Nolde, *Blossoms from the East,* 26.

36. Quoted in Wu Tung, *Tales,* 19.

37. Spence, *Search for Modern China,* 75, 86.

38. Wang, following Yongzheng, makes it clear in his version, 99, that the quotation is from *Han ru* (Han Confucians), which Baller renders as "The scholars of the *Han* Dynasty."

39. Peter Makin, *Pound's Cantos* (1985; reprint, Baltimore: Johns Hopkins Univ. Press, 1992), 283.

40. In 1708 Kangxi removed the status of heir apparent from his son by his late empress, Yinreng. Until his last gasp he did not name a successor. See Spence, *Search for Modern China,* 70–71.

41. Cheadle, *Pound's Confucian Translations,* 234, 221.

42. Ibid., 222, 232–33, 240–41.

43. Quoted in ibid., 234.

44. Baller, *Sacred Edict,* iv.

45. Pound's doubt is manifest in a statement he made to Donald Hall in 1960: "I might have done better to put Agassiz on top instead of Confucius." See Hall, "Ezra Pound," 56.

Index